FOREIGN POLICIES OF THE FOUNDING FATHERS

Paul A. Varg attended the public schools of Worcester, Massachusetts and received his B.A. and M.A. degrees at Clark University and his Ph.D. at the University of Chicago. After serving with the Navy in World War II, he joined the Department of History at Ohio State University. In 1958 he became Professor of History at Michigan State University. His other teaching activities have included summer sessions at Colgate University and the University of Virginia, and a visiting professorship at the University of Oregon. In 1955-1956 he was a Fulbright professor at the University of Stockholm. His other works include *Open Door Diplomacy: The Life of William Woodville Rockhill* and *Missionaries, Chinese, and Diplomats: A Study of the Protestant Missionary Movement.*

FOREIGN POLICIES

of the

FOUNDING FATHERS

PAUL A. VARG

PENGUIN BOOKS INC.
BALTIMORE, MARYLAND

Penguin Books Inc.
7110 Ambassador Road
Baltimore, Maryland 21207

First published by Michigan State University Press 1963
Published in Pelican Books 1970
Copyright © Michigan State University Press, 1963

Printed in the United States of America by
Universal Litho., Inc.

To Barbara

Foreword

Every generation writes its own history. The period 1774-1812 takes on new meaning to those who study it from the vantage point of post World War II. The new nation confronted much the same problems as those which bedevil nations emancipated from colonial domination since World War II. For example, there were the same pressing needs for capital, and the same unhappy situation of a country engaged largely in producing raw materials to be consumed by other more advanced nations. And in a new nation where the government had not yet firmly established itself, just as in the new nations of today, domestic political questions were of such pressing importance, if for no other reason than that the leaders were conscious of establishing precedents, that domestic affairs had a greater than customary influence on the shaping of foreign policy. For these reasons alone the foreign policies of the founding fathers are of especial interest today.

But it is not only a matter of rewriting the history of the early national period from the vantage point of the mid-twentieth-century. Man's concepts of historical studies also change as new experiences give rise to new questions. Since the days of Leopold Van Ranke historians have striven to portray the past as it actually happened. Today we recognize that the bare facts of the past may be determined with accuracy, but the interpretation of those facts will vary according to the time and place of the interpreter. History, therefore, is always partly subjective.

This subjective element in history helps explain the varying nature of the questions that each generation seeks answers to as it turns to the past. The historians of the Progressive Era wanted to know why the democratic experiment had fallen upon evil days. Some, like Carl Becker, found the answer in the influence wielded by aristocratic merchants in the period of the Revolution. Charles Beard found an explanation in the restraints laid upon the nation in the Constitution he believed to be the creation of the conservative elements. The answers of Becker and Beard have been challenged by a later generation emancipated from the intellectual biases of the Progressive Era.

Today the intellectual world labors to find answers to the questions emerging from the chastening experience of two world wars, a sharply dehumanized technological society, and a world revolution of former colonial areas striving for the material advantages possessed by the older nations. If the study of history is to have any meaning for today's generation, it must deal with questions that today's generation asks. These questions are both social and personal. On the social side we are pressed for answers as to the nature of great historical movements, the causes of international conflict, and the nature of relations between advanced and less developed societies. On the personal level we feel the oppressions of the human predicament. The questions confronting the historian are both broader in that they emerge out of problems that engulf the world and more limited in that they arise out of a society in which the individual finds it ever more perplexing to discover his proper role.

In an age when sophisticated men have few simple answers

there is a growing awareness of the fortuitous element in history. The role of irrational elements in political decision making, the unforseen consequences of a political act, and the frightening limitations of man's capacities to cope with the problems confronting him are aspects of mid-twentieth-century life that impress themselves upon all sensitive human beings. The historian is no exception.

It is with these thoughts in mind that the author has studied the foreign relations of the United States in the period 1774-1812. He believes he understands the present better for having made the inquiry. Whether he has succeeded in conveying his findings to paper and has made his inquiry meaningful for others remains for them to judge.

During the time of the research and writing, I enjoyed the encouragement and frank criticism of my colleagues at Michigan State University. I benefited from the frank criticisms of Stuart Bruchey, Madison Kuhn, Gilman Ostrander, and Norman Rich who read portions of the manuscript. Three of my colleagues, Robert Brown, Charles Cumberland, and Richard Sullivan, have provided uncounted hours of stimulating discussion on historical problems and the nature of the discipline. My indebtedness to them is great. Professor James Rust of the Department of English made many helpful suggestions as to clarity and style.

Finally, I am indebted to my wife, whose typing of the manuscript and editorial criticism contributed so much that she might well lay claim to joint authorship.

Contents

The Economic and Ideological Framework of Foreign Relations

I

THE CLOSE RELATIONSHIP between domestic and foreign affairs, often asserted but seldom elucidated, is a major theme of this book. Preparatory to observing the intertwining of the two strands of domestic and foreign affairs, an overview of the American landscape in the early period will help to identify and clarify the elements that determined the profile that the United States presented to the outside world. Of major importance were the popular attitude toward the existing system of international relations, economic factors, and the prevailing mental image of Europe.

The attitudes intrinsic to a free society constituted the first major element in the formulation of foreign policy. A society is not likely to act one way at home and another way in foreign affairs. Americans conceived of themselves as establishing a nation based on the rule of reason. They distrusted power and particularly military power. The British heritage gave them a strong bias against standing armies. This conviction rested on political considerations, but it was buttressed by a full realization that the cost would make necessary direct taxes.

Abjuring the use of force in domestic affairs, John Quincy Adams once observed, Americans too readily dismissed the role that force plays in foreign relations. This was during the crisis in relations with France in 1798. Many years earlier, when the former colonies wrestled with the problem of establishing state governments, his father, John Adams, had advised that the new governments must have the confidence of the people and be in accord with their views. They must be governments based on the principle of agreement and consent. "Fear," he wrote, "is the foundation of most governments; but is so sordid and brutal a passion, and renders men, in whose breasts it predominates, so stupid and miserable, that Americans will not be likely to approve of any political institution which is founded on it."

Statesmanship, said John Adams, consisted in bringing man-made law into harmony with natural law. Natural law may strike the present day reader as an elusive idea that sometimes did no more than give expression to the dominant ambitions and desires of a group, but in theory it consisted of those observations that had been generally accepted as true after passing the test of critical discussion. The founding fathers, true sons of the Enlightenment, placed reason on a high pedestal. Reason must be left free to test the validity of all political policies, to set aside superstition, and to measure the artful contrivances of princes and courtiers. Only a political structure based on consent and agreement could leave reason free to correct the errors of the past and open the way for the bright new future.

A society committed to such ideas viewed with disdain the alliances, the cynical diplomacy, and the prestige of the military in Europe. These were evils from which the pure of heart must isolate themselves. America was a nation with a peculiar mission. The feeling was well expressed by Benjamin Franklin and Silas Deane in a note written in Paris in March 1777.

Tyranny is so generally established in the rest of the world, that the prospect of an asylum in America for those who love liberty, gives general joy, and our cause is esteemed the cause of all mankind. . . . We are fighting for the dignity and happiness of human nature. Glorious is it for the Americans to be called by Providence to this post of honor.

All Americans, regardless of section, believed that they stood for a new kind of society, one in which men were free to pursue their individual interests and where government was the servant rather than the master. From this conviction flowed their view of the existing system of international relations as inherently evil. Princes and ministers subordinated the welfare of their subjects to considerations of glory; foreign policy did not serve the people. The rivalries of the European courts explained the long history of wars. The people did not have anything at stake in these contests. Only if governments were free to pursue public interests, would rivalry and war give way to peace and cooperation. This faith had its basis in the views of the philosophers who had already exposed the evils of mercantilism and set forth the argument that if national economic systems were left free to follow the course dictated by nature all of mankind would be enriched. Americans proclaimed themselves the leaders of this new order. John Adams, piqued at the slowness of the European courts to establish commercial relations with the new nation, announced that it was this system of free exchange of goods between nations that constituted America's revolutionary message to the world. This system would enrich all, make nations so interdependent that they could not afford going to war, and bind them together as members of the human family.

The old order of diplomacy, where scheming ministers intrigued against other nations and where the court entered into binding alliances against third parties, was widely decried. John Jay, who represented the rebellious colonies in Madrid, warned against the illusion that any European nation would show a "disinterested regard for us." The absolute monarchies of Europe were to be guarded against because there "the prince, his ministers, his women, or his favorites," guided only by temporary views and fashions, dictated policy.

The first Americans involved in diplomacy paid little attention to the traditional forms and disregarded well established rules of diplomatic etiquette. This made good relations with foreign nations more difficult to achieve than would otherwise have been the case. The readiness to condemn traditional diplomacy contributed to a self-righteous and uncompromising spirit. The legitimate interests of other nations were often dismissed as evil.

In the years since World War II it has become fashionable to speak of a moralistic approach to foreign policy. The moralistic approach consists of making the ends and means of foreign policy consistent with a preconceived ideal. The predominance of the ideals associated with the Declaration of Independence led the founding fathers to conceive of a world of international relations radically different from the existing system. They believed that a nation, no less than the individual, had a set of rights that had their basis in the natural order. The determination to approach foreign relations in terms of the ideal rather than in terms of existing realities predominated during the Revolution, lost much of its hold during the Washington administrations, and regained prominence with the election of Thomas Jefferson.

Politics do not stop at the water's edge. Political parties are to a considerable degree the instruments of economic groups, and economic interests transcend national boundaries. Economic groups cannot be indifferent to the effect of the government's foreign policy on their overseas interests.

However, it is not only economic interest that reduces foreign policy to partisan politics. Whether one or another set of political ideals will win out depends in part on the foreign ties that a nation assumes. Liberals prefer close relations with nations that exemplify their own liberalism and are equally averse to close ties with those that symbolize reaction. Conservatives are no less sensitive to these considerations. It could not be otherwise for a diplomatic ally brings prestige to the political ideas it represents. In a new country, where political patterns are not yet set, this factor may become a major determinant of the foreign policy views of the political protagonists.

This was true during the early history of the United States. Party battles over foreign policy ensued because people sensed that issues close to home were at stake. At first glance the emergence of strong pro-French factions suggests that the question was whether the young republic should support one or the other of the two great European antagonists, but the primary question was whether the Federalists or the Anti-Federalists should rule at home. Both parties were intensely loyal to the nation, but each had a domestic program that would gain or lose depending upon whether the country drew closer to monarchical Great Britain or to republican France. The Federalists were obsessed with the fear that the rival party would align with France and that French ideas would completely triumph in the United States. The Republicans succumbed to an almost neurotic anxiety that the Federalist courting of the British would eventuate in the triumph of monarchical principles.

The feverish pursuit of party advantage almost obscured the fact that economic necessity narrowed the field of decision making. The United States was in one of the early stages of accelerated economic growth. The country was almost wholly a producer of raw materials and an importer of manufactures; it was desperately in need of foreign capital for the development of both its agriculture and industry; it was short of specie and threatened constantly with an unstable currency; any significant program of direct taxation was politically unpalatable; and its economic well being, due to the absence of a sizeable home market, depended upon the ability to dispose of its surpluses abroad on favorable terms.

Within these confines of fundamental economic interests existed much room for play of differences of opinion between mercantile and agrarian interests. These factions did not constitute hard and fast political entities. Shifts in alignments did take place, and each party sought to identify its own program with the national interest. Nevertheless, because the parties followed in a general way economic and sectional lines, the foreign policies of the two parties reflected the economic interests of various regions and economic groups.

The mercantile interest, centered in New England and spread out along the coast, concentrated its political efforts on achieving, partly through the central government, adequate credit and favorable trade treaties. Credit depended in large part upon access to British capital. Imports of manufactured goods could only take place upon advances of book credit to carry the merchant over until the money from the sale of the goods became available to him. The importance of credit is apparent when one recalls that the inability of the French to finance the transactions for the American merchant was the largest single factor in preventing the development of strong commercial ties between the two countries.

Next to credit in importance was legislative support that would enable the American ship owner to compete with his foreign rival who enjoyed the support of his own government. Before the Revolution American shipping enjoyed many advantages under the British mercantile system including free access to ports in the mother country, the protection of the British navy, and, of special importance, freedom to engage in the carrying trade with the British West Indies. American shippers exploited these advantages to the full and added to them by engaging in illegal trade with the foreign West Indies. As a result the merchant marine prospered, and when independence was achieved, they were ready and eager to have their own government support them with favorable legislation.

The mercantile interest incurred great risks in choosing to break with Great Britain. During and immediately after the

Revolution merchants realistically accepted close economic ties with the former mother country as inevitable, but they only learned by experience that the British would be none too gentle in laying down the conditions. The mercantile interest accepted the conditions and strongly opposed the agrarians who were unduly sensitive about British influence. The merchants had too much to lose in an economic tug of war and recognized, as the farmers did not, that the British possessed the means to win such a contest. It could only result in a sharp falling off of trade, consequently a decline in government revenue, and this in turn would endanger the financial order that Alexander Hamilton had constructed, a financial order that was the basis for the kind of economic stability necessary for the carrying on of highly speculative foreign trade.

The agricultural interest had no less at stake in relations with foreign nations than did the mercantile interest, but the foreign policy that suited agrarians clashed at several important points with the program desired by the merchants. In the colonial period the economy of the southern states was largely an appendage of the British economy. These states marketed their products through British merchants, purchased manufactured goods from the same source, and lived largely on British capital. By the time of the Revolution the planters of the South labored under a burden of debt. Unlike their northern compatriots they viewed credit as the road to servitude and not as the lifeblood of the economy. Consequently, lacking an appreciation of the role of capital, they felt less hesitation in indulging the resentment they felt toward the British.

The agrarians resented the British domination of their marketing facilities. They hoped to escape from the funneling of so great a percentage of their produce through England, and they wished to establish direct contact with the final consumer of this produce on the continent. To break the British hold, American shipping and the shipping of England's commercial rivals should be encouraged. To do this required favorable commercial treaties with the nations on the continent and legislation encouraging non-British shipping. Southern planters supported a legislative program aimed at promoting the carrying trade of the northern merchants, but they did so with the important reservation that northern shipowning interests must not be granted a monopoly for this would result in high freight rates. Aversion to such a monopoly gained strength beyond what reasonable economic considerations justified by virtue of deeply held rural prejudices against the avarice of merchants.

These economic interests made for division and sharp conflict at home. The reconciling of them and the formulation of a program embodying a national interest constituted the task of statesmen. If they should be successful, the United States would be able to present a united front.

Whereas economic interest worked as a divisive force, a latent hostility to Europe fostered a tentative unity. Vis-à-vis Europe, the United States stood for something new, a political order based on reason and emancipated from the hoary system of Europe where society continued to be in the grip of privileged orders desperately seeking to preserve the hold they had achieved under feudalism. This image of Europe as aristocratic, corrupt, and indifferent to the dictates of reason stood in sharp contrast to the virtue, reason, equality before the law, and representative government of the United States. This oversimplified image of themselves and of Europe provided the basis for a nascent nationalism. Where the conditions of life were more obviously different from Europe, in the South and the West, the lines of the image were bolder and a stronger system of national honor prevailed.

The two-worlds image varied according to time and place. Prior to the growing division between mother country and the colonies after 1763, England was viewed as sharply different from the rest of Europe. Rule by "King, Lords, and Commons," a phrase that expressed approval of the principle of balance of power in the British political system, was repeated a thousand times in colonial political writings. The rule of law, civil rights, the various checks on arbitrary rule, plus the fact that England was Protestant received general acclaim. It gave to the colonists a sense of belonging to a political unit that had its center in London. France, in direct contrast, was depicted as under the rule of unenlightened and superstitious Romanism buttressed by an arbitrary monarchical government. This image changed after 1763, but the transition was not only slow but the original did not wholly disappear even during the War for Independence.

After the war the old image came to the fore again in the Northeast where economic ties to England reinforced it. This bias helps explain why merchants after 1789 found it so easy to take a sympathetic view of British policy and actions. More and more frequently they reaffirmed their belief that British political institutions had a close affinity with republican principles. The violence of the French Revolution and the rise of Napoleon strengthened these feelings until by 1807 many New Englanders believed that they had more in common with Britishers than they did with the Jeffersonians.

The pro-British bias, especially in New England, was by no means wholly the product of economics. It is better explained in broad sociological terms. Fear induced by the rapid changes taking place in the country as a whole brought to the fore the ideal of a stable and well ordered society. The revival of orthodox religion under the leadership of Timothy Dwight and Nathaniel Taylor after 1798 is symptomatic of what was taking place. In this atmosphere the stability of the British order appeared more and more attractive. That all of this had its influence on foreign relations seems clear.

The image of the two worlds, one American and one European, passed through quite a different metamorphosis in the South and West. The fighting during the Revolution resulted in greater ravages in Virginia and southward than did the more limited campaigns in the North. The heavy indebtedness to the British merchants added to the hostility. The distrust of Great Britain was made permanent by the section's foreign economic interests which called for emancipation from the hold held by the British and the desire for closer economic ties with the continent. By the time of the Jay Treaty of 1795 the image in the South and West of a United States pitted against Great Britain had advanced to the stage where there was a deep suspicion of anything British, and the treaty evoked an emotional outburst that made impossible any realistic response to the world situation and ruled out any sober analysis of national self interest. The events after 1807 made resistance to British imperious rulings on the high seas a matter of national honor. Economic interests supported this position, but the image was in such ascendancy by the time that James Madison came to office that it was quite strong enough to dominate without the aid of economic forces.

This brings us to what is probably the most important clue for understanding the tumultuous political struggles of the period. Statesmen might well have succeeded in coming to some agreement on what was the national interest if the problem had been simply the economic difference between the maritime interests and the agrarian interests. Unfortunately, the problem was not that simple. Two other factors entered to put it into a realm of complexity where statesmen were left enmeshed. First, the rapid expansion of the South and West aroused fears that the Northeast was to be left stranded on a shoal where the main stream would inundate it. Secondly, the symbols of British and French societies took the place of realistic evaluations of the situation at home. Politicians of the sections used these symbols in attacking each other and conjured up fears that would have been impossible if these two foreign societies had not served to illustrate so well the dangers of which they warned. The symbols served to distort the realities of the sectional differences at home, differences of a much more modest order than the differences between Great Britain and France.

The Beginnings of
Foreign Policy

II

NECESSITY rather than preference dictated the Declaration of Independence and the alliance with France. The consequences which flowed from the decision to separate from Great Britain caused later generations to forget how very reluctant the colonists were to break with the mother country. To resist British imperious interference in colonial affairs was one thing; to break off from the mother country and sail forth on the uncharted sea of independence was quite another. That there were reefs in that sea the colonists well knew, and none seemed more dangerous than the probability that independence would to some degree make them suppliants of France. Other doubts also entered their minds. Their uncertainties added up to one of the most excruciating periods of indecision in American history.

The colonists gave themselves to two contradictory ideals, loyalty to the mother country and self-government at home. At the beginning there appeared to be no inconsistency between the two. The founding fathers admired the check and balance of the rule by "King, Lords, and Commons," glorious British liberties, and the vesting of the taxing power in the elected representatives, and cherished these advantages for themselves. Herein lay the difficulty. Loyalty to the Crown may very well have been stronger than the nascent feeling of

unity between the various colonies, but when the Stamp Act Congress of 1765 found that all could agree that the power of the purse must reside in their own elected assemblies, the Congress forged a bond of union and helped make possible the gradual emergence of a national feeling.

At the same time the strength of the imperial tie was matched by a pride in the colonies that was quick to resent any imputation of a less than equal status. No one was prouder of the British Empire than Benjamin Franklin, but no one was more contumacious in the face of any suggestion of a less than equal status. England needed America more than America needed England, Franklin observed in a conversation with Lord Kames in 1767.[1] And the British who lightly talked of their subjects in America prompted him to warn John Bull that his haughtiness "will, if not abated, procure you one day or other a handsome drubbing."[2] At the dedication of the Tree of Liberty in Providence, Rhode Island in 1768, a local Son of Liberty deplored the habit of every paltry British scribbler who wrote "in this lordly stile, *our colonies—our western dominions—our plantations—our subjects in America—our authority—our government* with many more of the like *imperious expressions.*" "Strange doctrine," he thought, "that we should be the subject of subjects, and liable to be controlled at their will."[3]

The two sets of loyalties might not have come into conflict had not the two parties become more rigid in their positions under the pressure of military hostilities and had not fighting in turn forced upon the colonists the need for foreign aid. During fourteen long months of bitter struggle, the colonists eschewed the question of independence. Only after they confronted the desperate situation of the spring of 1776 and the increasing evidence of the British determination not to yield any ground, did it become clear that they must either submit or make a complete break. The Declaration of Independence lay at the end of a tortuous process, an act strange to their long and firmly held intentions.

In the fall of 1774 only a few radicals viewed reconciliation as hopeless and were therefore prepared to insist on independ-

ence. They wisely avoided talking of independence for they knew that it would only frighten the majority into becoming unduly conciliatory. As long as the aim was not independence the debates in Congress did not touch on foreign affairs.

In September, 1774, a false report reached the Congress that fighting had commenced in Boston. The delegates, cautious up to this point, responded with vigor. By October 8 they had adopted the Suffolk Resolves calling for military preparations and, while the excitement prevailed, they agreed to a policy of nonimportation, nonexportation, and nonconsumption. They established the Continental Association, a network of local committees, to enforce these measures. The southern delegates, aware of the sacrifices involved in nonexportation, agreed only after rice was removed from the list and after the enforcement of nonimportation was postponed from December, 1774 to September, 1775.

Faith in the efficacy of commercial warfare led to predictions that England would be injured so severely that Parliament would gladly accede to their demands. England would be brought to the edge of bankruptcy; the West Indies would face ruin; and the Irish linen industry, dependent upon imports of American flaxseed, would be idled, leaving thousands unemployed. The colonists were so confident of the success of peaceful persuasion that they gave no thought to the difficulty of either retreating or advancing from this position if the policy failed.

When they adopted these measures, the delegates in Philadelphia did not foresee that the outbreak of military hostilities the following April would prevent British merchants from coming to their support. The expected dire consequences for the British, moreover, did not materialize because of a temporary boom in other channels of foreign trade. Indeed the policy boomeranged. It led to sharp economic distress in the colonies and made it even more difficult for them to procure adequate military supplies. Cut off from England, the colonists were forced to grant bounties to stimulate domestic manufactures and campaigns to encourage the wearing of homespun suddenly became popular. By the autumn of 1775 a committee of Congress recommended the wearing of leather waistcoats and breeches and urged the members of Congress to set the example.[4] More seriously, the army was desperately short of supplies. "Our want of powder is inconceivable," Washington noted on Christmas day, 1775. By the end of January there was not a pound of powder in his magazines.[5]

Necessity dictated a search for foreign supplies as early as the autumn of 1775. To do so would endanger the possibility of a reconciliation and force consideration of independence, but not to do so would in all probability end in submission. Concern over the possible domestic consequences of independence added to the reluctance to make a final separation. Many feared that independence would lead to an internecine war over the issue of western land claims. Some, like Edmund Rutledge, at first opposed independence because a purely American government would be subverted by the scheming New Englanders who favored democracy. "I dread their low Cunning," wrote Rutledge, "and those leveling Principles which Men without Character and without Fortune in general possess, which are so captivating to the lower class of Mankind, and which will occasion such a fluctuation of Property as to introduce the greatest disorder."[6]

However, the great deterrents to seeking foreign aid and thereby shutting the door to reconciliation lay in the popular attitudes toward Great Britain and France. John Adams ranked sentimental ties to Great Britain as the great obstacle.[7] The frightening prospect of having to turn to France probably played as great a role. For a hundred years that nation had been a determined enemy of both Great Britain and the colonies. In public addresses, sermons, and in writings, France appeared as the nation of despotism and intrigue, the citadel of Roman Catholicism, and the scheming encroacher on British territories in the new world. To cast oneself on the mercy of such a nation required a sense of desperation.

Committees in Congress were ready to seek French aid long before the people at large saw the necessity for it. In the autumn of 1775, the Committee on Trade arranged for the purchase of $200,000 worth of provisions to be sold to France for the purpose of establishing credit which could be used for the purchase of supplies. On November 29th, Congress established the Committee of Secret Correspondence, and in December the committee directed Arthur Lee, who was already in London, to inquire as to the disposition of foreign powers.

The following March the committee named Silas Deane to go to Paris as its agent. To avoid giving offense Deane was to pose as a merchant buying goods for the Indian trade. If Count Vergennes gave him any encouragement, he was to explain that the trade with the colonies which had made England wealthy was now open to France. "France," read the instructions, "had been pitched on for the first application, from an opinion that if we should, as there is a great appearance we shall, come to a total separation from Great Britain, France would be looked upon as the power whose friendship it would be fittest for us to obtain and cultivate."[8] Vergennes was to be sounded out on the question of diplomatic recognition and an alliance. The term "alliance" meant no more than a commercial treaty, but the committee had moved far out ahead of the people and the delegates in Congress.

Three weeks after Deane received the instructions, Congress voted down a resolution placing all blame on the king rather than the ministry because of fear that this would close the door to negotiation.[9] As late as March 23rd John Adams wrote to Horatio Gates that independence was a "Hobgoblin of so frightful Mien that it would throw a delicate Person into Fits to look it in the Face."[10] The fact is significant. Loyalty to England had survived eleven months of fighting and more than eleven years of bickering.

The colonists had yet to see that the contest had passed the halfway house of reconciliation, but the fact would soon become apparent. Thomas Paine's *Common Sense* had appeared in January, and its eager reception is a measure of the change taking place. British actions hastened the change. When news arrived that the mother country had reached agreements with some of the German states for the hiring of mercenaries to put down the colonists, it ended the colonists' confidence that they were capable of maintaining the war without outside aid. In

December, 1775 England had thrown cold water on hopes that she would reconsider by closing all American ports and ordering the seizure and confiscation of all American goods on the high seas.[11]

Pressures of the moment likewise led Congress to take steps that added up to independence even while the delegates denied the name. In April Congress declared all ports open to ships of all nations, authorized American warships to sail against the enemy, and sanctioned privateering.[12] These were acts of a sovereign power, but they were dictated by expediency rather than by principle. Opinion was changing and the delegates from Massachusetts and Virginia were taking the lead in arguing for independence, but strong opposition still remained.

The image of Great Britain as a nation in which wrongs were rectified by petition and where conflicts ended in compromise mutually satisfactory to the contending parties was affirmed and supported by pointing to the English revolutions of the seventeenth century. The image continued its hold upon the Whigs of Pennsylvania and New York after it had been eroded in the other colonies.

The reluctance of these two provinces to accept independence is a measure of the enduring quality of loyalty to Great Britain. By July of 1776 both provinces were controlled by opponents of the measures of the British ministry and the legislative bodies in each fairly represented popular opinion.

Pennsylvania was already a generally democratic state by June, 1776. Suffrage was based on property qualifications, but these could scarcely have prevented any significant percentage from voting. Farmers who owned fifty acres of land, ten of which were under cultivation, and residents of towns and cities owning personal property valued at £50 enjoyed the franchise. The counties in the north and west and of the city of Philadelphia had long been under represented, but in March, 1776 the assembly carried out a major reapportionment that made the legislative body truly representative.[13]

The new assembly held its first session in the middle of May and immediately faced the issue of independence. Congress had passed a resolution calling for the establishment of new governments "where no government sufficient to the exigencies of their affairs have been hitherto established." The Pennsylvania delegates did not object to this, but when a committee composed of John Adams, Edmund Rutledge, and Richard Henry Lee, introduced a preamble that called for replacing every government that had exercised authority under the Crown, the Pennsylvania delegates saw that those favoring independence sought to circumvent the opposition of the old Penn charter government by overthrowing it. James Wilson immediately protested that the Pennsylvania delegates could not vote for it without violating their instructions. He won a postponement by pleading that no action be taken until the new provincial assembly, scheduled to meet in a few days, could be asked for a decision. When the assembly met, a resolution in favor of new instructions was defeated by two votes.[14] Congress then adopted the preamble. Public meetings in Philadelphia passed resolutions favoring independence and called for the establishment of a new state government.[15] When Richard Henry Lee, on June 7th, introduced a resolution calling for independence, the Pennsylvania delegates pleaded that the middle colonies were not yet ready for such a drastic step and they voted against it. The provincial assembly, on June 8th, considered new instructions that would have opened the way for support of independence, but final action was never taken. Control was already passing to the Provincial Congress called to draft a new government. When the Continental Congress voted on the Declaration of Independence on July 2, only Benjamin Franklin, among the Pennsylvania delegates, approved of it although James Wilson voted for it. Two delegates, Willing and Humphrey, voted in the negative, and Dickinson and Morris absented themselves.[16]

The same conservatism on this issue made itself felt in New York. By 1776 the provincial assembly exercised little if any power, and government was largely in the hands of extralegal committees and the Provincial Congress. These were dominated by Whigs. The Mechanic's Union of New York City favored independence long before the Provincial Congress, but it had no success in getting its view adopted. The Third Provincial Congress, meeting in June, 1776, was asked by the delegates at Philadelphia for instructions as to how they should vote on the issue of independence. The Congress voted unanimously against new instructions and advised the delegates that it would be "imprudent to require the sentiments of the people relative to the question of Independence, lest it should create division and have an unhappy influence."[17] In accord with this instruction the New York delegates did not vote for the Declaration of Independence on July 2.

The necessity of securing foreign assistance had finally forced the hand of the reluctant rebels. Richard Henry Lee observed: *It is not choice then but necessity that calls for Independence, as the only means by which foreign Alliance can be obtained,* and a proper Confederation by which internal peace and union may be secured."[18] Progress on the question of independence and an alliance marched forward hand in hand. On the same day that Congress established a committee to draft a declaration of independence it also set up a committee to draw up a plan of treaties. The most noteworthy fact is that only after fourteen long months of hostilities had the colonists been able to bring themselves to accept a final separation. John Adams, who had impatiently attributed the delay to the proprietary interests of the middle colonies, admitted when the contest was over that it had been necessary to wait if the country was to achieve a general consensus of opinion. The tie to England had been almost too strong. Only after much debate and discussion were the people ready to accept independence. As John Adams put it, "The hopes of reconciliation which were fondly entertained by multitudes of honest and well-meaning, though weak and mistaken people, have been gradually, and at last totally extinguished. Time has been given for the whole people maturely to consider the great question of independence, and to ripen their judgement, dissipate their fears, and allure their hopes.

. . ."[19] If action had been taken earlier the result would in all probability have been disunion.

The issue of independence had delayed any consideration being given to the question of what type of foreign policy would serve the American best. The need for supplies had led to a discussion of trade with other nations as early as October, 1775 when Congress considered the employment of commercial measures to force Great Britain to come to terms, but not until the following February did Congress give any consideration to foreign relations and then only briefly and without coming to any decisions. How the first thinking on the subject was guided by the attitudes and beliefs that prevailed in domestic affairs is well illustrated in the case of John Adams who, in March, 1776, made two consecutive entries in his diary, one on the nature of man and one on the principles that ought to govern any plan of future relations with France. Adams observed:

Resentment is a Passion, implanted by Nature for the Preservation of the Individual. Injury is the Object which excites it. Injustice, Wrong, Injury excite the Feeling of Resentment, as naturally and necessarily as Frost and Ice excite the feeling of cold, as fire excites heat, and as both excite Pain. A Man may have the Faculty of concealing his Resentment, or suppressing it, but he must and ought to feel it. Nay he ought to indulge it, to cultivate it. It is a Duty. His Person, his Property, his Liberty, his Reputation are not safe without it. He ought, for his own Security and Honour, and for the public good to punish those who injure him, unless they repent, and then he should forgive, having Satisfaction and Compensation. Revenge is unlawfull.

It is the same with Communities. They ought to resent and to punish.[20]

The next entry is a set of notes on relations with France. Adams asked the question: "What Connection may We safely form with her?" His views on the nature of man and society extended to foreign relations. This is evident in the three rules he laid down for guidance. He wrote:

1st. No Political Connection. Submit to none of her Authority—receive no Governors, or officers from her.

2d. No military Connection. Receive no Troops from her.

3d. Only a Commercial Connection, i.e. make a Treaty, to receive her Ships into our Ports. Let her engage to receive our Ships into her Ports—furnish Us with Arms, Cannon, Salt Petre, Powder, Duck, Steel.[21]

The author of these principles was to play a leading role in the formulation of American foreign policy.

In June, 1776, Congress established a committee to draw up a plan for treaties. The committee, John Adams records in his *Autobiography,* debated the question of how far it would be necessary to go if the colonies were to secure French support. Adams argued that they should "avoid all Alliance, which might embarrass Us in after times and involve Us in future European Wars. . . ." A treaty of commerce, he maintained, would be ample compensation, for by it France would increase her commerce, encourage her manufactures and agriculture, stimulate the growth of her merchant marine, and "raise her from her present deep humiliation, distress and decay, and place her on a more equal footing with England, for the protection of her foreign Possessions, . . ."[22] The committee report, drafted by John Adams, embodied his ideas. It was submitted to Congress on July 18, but it was not debated by the committee of the whole until late August. Some delegates thought that a simple treaty of commerce would not be adequate to secure French support and they proposed additional provisions for an alliance, special trade privileges, and territorial guarantees.[23] Adams strongly warned that an alliance would reduce the new nation to a puppet danced on the wires of the cabinets of Europe. No significant changes were adopted. On September 17 the committee presented its final draft to Congress.

Congress had spent a large part of the preceding summer drafting the Articles of Confederation. The debates over the questions of western boundaries, representation, and finance led to heated argument. The government structure upon which they finally agreed was little more than a league of sovereign states. When the document was submitted to the states, it stirred up another debate over the western boundaries that delayed its ratification until 1781. Economic interests, together with a fear on the part of small states owning no western lands that they would be wholly dominated by the larger ones, stood in the way. The zeal with which factions pursued their own interests even in times of grave crisis and the deep distrust of vesting power anywhere where state political groups could not hope to exercise complete control endangered the American cause, but the historical importance of this development, in part, lies elsewhere.

In the Plan of Treaties is illustrated the length to which each economic and political faction would refuse to tie its hands by future commitments. The attitude of each was that no other should have at its disposal a political structure for imposing its will on other groups. This situation was a product of the long separate existence of each of the colonies, of the geography of the country, of the underlying philosophy of realism which inculcated a bias in favor of believing that all men were knaves until proved otherwise, and, perhaps most important, the fact that in each state was a group of political leaders jealous and proud of the positions that they had acquired for themselves by dint of arduous revolutionary activity in building extralegal organizations within their own provinces for the purpose of curbing the imperious British ministry.

Given this political atmosphere the Plan of Treaties inevitably avoided future commitments. It is difficult to see how any special commercial privileges to France, any territorial compensations, or any commitments to support France in some future international crisis could find a place in the foreign policy of a people who so jealously stood guard over local and factional interests in domestic affairs short of a truly desperate crisis. The Plan of Treaties would have bound the new nation to nothing in these respects, but it did bind France not to seek territory on the continent of North America and not to seek to extend the fishing rights she already enjoyed in the area of Newfoundland.

This reduced relations with any prospective ally to commerce, and in this sphere the Americans sought to initiate a revolution whereby commerce would no longer be made subservient to the immediate interests of the political state. It was to follow freely the course dictated by the profit motive of economic interests. No mercantile barriers were to be imposed. Even in time of war a state was to recognize that only what was clearly contraband could be seized. The Plan further provided for most favored nation treatment, free commerce with the West Indies, and would have protected the merchants of both nations who resided in the other from any interference during the first six months of any future conflict.

The instructions to the commissioners to Europe, issued in December, 1776, compromised the ideal only slightly.[24] France was offered assistance in the conquest of the British West Indies and diplomatic support for the retention of the islands if she conquered them. Spain was to be promised support in a campaign against the Floridas and the United States was to accede to her possession of them in return for support of the American cause and for Spain's acknowledging the Americans' right to free navigation of the Mississippi River and free entry into the harbor at Pensacola.

Further steps in the direction of an alliance involving political commitments became acceptable only as the rebellious colonists developed a fuller appreciation of the value of French participation in the war. France had already begun to furnish valuable supplies. It has been estimated that ninety percent of American war material came from France during the first year after the Declaration of Independence.

Even this was not enough to banish the danger of disaster. The British fleet created difficulties that only French participation in the war could alleviate. The British navy not only endangered the supply route but reduced American exports to France to a mere trickle. Thereby Americans were prevented from paying for what they needed except insofar as French government loans covered the cost. Consequently,

French merchants, trading with the Americans faced bankruptcy.

The freedom of the British fleet also gave the British army the great advantage of mobility. While American troops could only move slowly overland, British troops could be readily transported by sea from one point to another. To this was added the difficulties faced by American privateers. They proved themselves an important weapon, but their effectiveness depended upon access to French ports. British protests in the summer of 1777 forced France to close her ports.[25]

Only active participation in the war by the French fleet could alleviate these difficulties, and Americans grew highly impatient with the cautious course pursued by Vergennes. The American commissioners in Paris assured Congress that "the united bent of the nation" was in their favor and that "the true interest of France is to prevent our being annexed to Great Britain, that so the British power may be diminished, and the French commerce augmented."[26] Franklin, ever ready to find consolation in whatever situation he found himself, wrote to Congress:

And we have these advantages in their keeping out of the war, that they are better able to afford us private assistance; that by holding themselves in readiness to invade Britain, they keep more of her force at home; and that they leave to our armed vessels the whole harvest of prizes made upon her commerce, and of course the whole encouragement to increase our force in privateers, which will breed seamen for our Navy.[27]

These blithe observations did not remove the difficulties created by the British fleet.

News of the American victory at Saratoga caused Franklin to forget the advantages of France's non-belligerency. On receiving the report he worked far into the night preparing a broadside aimed at committing France to an alliance. To spur on the French he entered into negotiations with the British. Vergennes, in a spirit of "now or never," quickly changed course.

On February 8, 1778, Franklin and Vergennes signed a

treaty of commerce and a treaty of alliance. The first incorporated the principles set forth in the Plan of 1776. The second committed both countries not to make a separate peace, bound France to continue the struggle until the United States achieved independence, and provided that France would never seek to regain the territory she had held in North America prior to 1763 or Bermuda. Finally the United States undertook the solemn treaty obligation to uphold the present French possessions in the new world and any others that she might acquire at the close of the war. A radical departure had been made from felt preferences and established principles.

Congress was so delighted that it approved both treaties the day after receiving them. The Virginia delegates in Congress notified their governor, praising the king of France for his "principles of Magnanimity and true generosity" and they gratefully observed that he had not taken "advantage of our circumstance" and had acted "as if we were in the plenitude of power and in the greatest security."[28] A citizen of Charleston drew the contrast between the conduct of the French king and his British counterpart who had "done everything in his power to rent from his crown the most valuable jewel in it and has at length irreconcilably lost three millions of loyal subjects and a vast extent of soil, with every concomitant advantage attendant upon a lucrative trade, . . ."[29]

The French alliance offered one great advantage above all others. By this time the British fleet had so tightened its control that it was nothing short of foolhardy to attempt making any remittances to Europe. As soon as France entered the war her fleet could be expected to deprive England of her monopoly of the waters off the coast of North America. In this way the lanes would be opened to American exports and the credit for the purchase of military supplies abroad assured. Richard Henry Lee saw as the great advantage of the alliance the fact that France "will now give protection to their Commerce to and from America. . . ."[30]

Some Americans looked upon the French alliance with deep suspicion. No less a person than John Jay believed it a mistake. Jay viewed "a return to the domination of Britain with Horror" but thought that once independence had been achieved, he would prefer "a connexion with her to a league with any power on earth." He favored giving England "advantageous commercial terms" and confessed: "The destruction of Old England would hurt me; I wish it well: it afforded my ancestors an asylum from persecution."[31]

Jay's feelings were undoubtedly shared by many. The French alliance was a marriage of convenience. It enjoyed popularity for some years after the pressures of war had been removed, but it imposed commitments that were not in harmony with the basic long term aims. To have endured, it would have needed firmer foundations. Once the war was over American security no longer hinged on the alliance and thereby the obligations it imposed became a burden without any equivalent compensation. For a few short years its most firm supporters hoped to undergird it with close economic ties. They failed, and with their failure came a return to the unilateralism that was more in accord with the American view of politics.

NOTES

1. Benjamin Franklin to Lord Kames, April 11, 1767, *The Works of Benjamin Franklin*, ed. John Bigelow (New York: G. P. Putnam's Sons, 1904), Vol. IV, pp. 285-6.

2. [Benjamin Franklin] to the printer of the *Gazetteer*, January 15, 1766, *The Writings of Benjamin Franklin*, ed. Albert Henry Smyth (New York: The Macmillan Co., 1907), Vol. IV, p. 398.

3. *Discourse, Delivered in Providence, in the Colony of Rhode-Island, upon the 25th Day of July, 1768 at the Dedication of the Tree of Liberty, From the Summer House in the Tree by a Son of Liberty*. Providence, 1768.

4. *Journals of the Continental Congress 1774-1789*, ed. Washington Chauncey Ford (Washington: Government Printing Office, 1906), Vol. III, p. 269.

5. Orlando W. Stephenson, "The Supply of Gunpowder in 1776," *American Historical Review*, XXX (January, 1925), p. 274.

6. Edward Rutledge to John Jay, June 29, 1776, *Letters of the Members of the Continental Congress*, edited by Edmund C. Burnett (Washington, D.C.: Carnegie Institution, 1923), Vol. I, p. 518.

7. John Adams to Horatio Gates, March 23, 1776, Burnett, *Letters*, Vol. I, p. 406.

8. The Committee of Secret Correspondence to Silas Deane, March 3, 1776, Burnett, *Letters*, Vol. I, pp. 375-377.

9. Richard Smith, Diary, entry for March 22, 1776, Burnett, *Letters*, Vol. I, pp. 403-404.

10. John Adams to Horatio Gates, March 23, 1776, Burnett, *Letters*, Vol. I, p. 406.

11. Allen French, *The First Year of the American Revolution* (Boston: Houghton Mifflin, 1934), pp. 567-568.

12. *Ibid.*, p. 711.

13. The author is indebted to Robert Money who is engaged in a study of the politics of Pennsylvania in the period prior to the Revolution.

14. Charles Page Smith, *James Wilson, Founding Father 1742-1798* (Chapel Hill, N.C.: Published for the Institute of Early American History and Culture by the University of North Carolina Press, 1956), p. 83.

15. *Ibid.*, p. 84.

16. Charles J. Stillé, "Pennsylvania and the Declaration of Independence," *The Pennsylvania Magazine of History and Biography*, Vol. XIII, No. 4 (1889), pp. 385-449.

17. *History of the State of New York*, ed. Alexander C. Flick; Alexander C. Flick, "The Provincial Congress and the Declaration of Independence," Vol. III (New York: Columbia University Press, 1933), p. 280.

18. Richard Henry Lee to Landon Carter, June 2, 1776, Burnett, *Letters*, Vol. I, p. 469.

19. John Adams to Abigail Adams, July 3, 1776, *Familiar Letters of John Adams and his Wife Abigail Adams, during the Revolution*, ed. Charles Francis Adams (Boston: Houghton Mifflin, 1875), p. 193.

20. *Diary and Autobiography of John Adams*, ed. L. H. Butterfield (Cambridge: Harvard University Press, 1961), Vol. II, p. 236.

21. *Ibid.*

22. *Ibid.*, Vol. III, p. 337.

23. *Ibid.*, 338.

24. Fred Rippy and Angie Debo, "The Historical Background of the American Policy of Isolation," *Smith College Studies in History*, Vol. IX, p. 88.

25. Vergennes to Commissioners in Paris, July 16, 1777, *The Revolutionary Diplomatic Correspondence of the United States*, edited by Francis Wharton (Washington: Government Printing Office, 1906), Vol. II, p. 364.

26. Commissioners in Paris to Committee of Foreign Affairs, September 8, 1777, Wharton, *Diplomatic Correspondence*, Vol. II, p. 389.

27. Franklin and Deane to Committee of Foreign Affairs, March 12, 1777, Wharton, *Diplomatic Correspondence*, Vol. II, p. 286.

28. *The Letters of Richard Henry Lee*, ed. James Curtis Ballagh (New York: The Macmillan Co., 1911), Vol. I, p. 397.

29. *South Carolina and American General Gazette*, June 4, 1778.

30. *The Letters of Richard Henry Lee*, Vol. I, p. 406.

31. *The Correspondence and Public Papers of John Jay*, edited by Henry P. Johnston (New York: G. P. Putnam's Sons, 1890), Vol. I, p. 180.

Looking to the Future

III

THE PROMOTION of trade and expansion of territory entered into the making of foreign policy from the first debates in Congress in 1776. These aims greatly complicated diplomatic negotiations and forced the founding fathers to give careful thought to the nature of their interests. The ideas and attitudes that emerged out of the day-to-day discussions clarified their thinking, and by the close of the war the broad outlines of future foreign policy were not only clear but certain ways of thinking about foreign relations were already well established. These ways of thought and the wartime negotiations out of which they evolved constitute our immediate line of inquiry.

The hope of establishing commercial relations with as many nations as possible rested on the unwarranted expectation that European powers would defy Great Britain in order to secure the advantages of American trade. Because the effort was futile from the beginning and ended without any success outside of the case of France, historians have usually dismissed the effort as of no account, but if the commercial program is viewed as the first step toward a long term policy, rather than merely a futile wartime measure, then the effort to establish commercial relations deserves close attention. As we shall see, around this program developed a whole body of thought as to the proper orientation of the republic to the outside world.

No thought was given to setting up a mercantile system after the British model. The exigencies of war demanded that trade be opened up on the most generous terms. The promotion of trade on the freest possible basis shortly became permanent policy; indeed, it became a cardinal principle in the American revolutionary message to the world. The policy flowed intuitively from the geographical position of the republic and was further affirmed by its economy. Americans were producers of raw materials beyond their own needs and therefore needed foreign markets, and they produced few manufactures and must therefore rely on imports. In sanguine spirits they assumed that the European nations would eagerly grasp for the trade that had made England rich and powerful. And in their haste for profits and in the pleasure they would take in striking back at the overweening ambition of England, the continental powers would recognize the independence of the United States, sell to her the military supplies she so much needed, and provide loans.

Trade was the solution not only to present difficulties but the shield of the republic for the future. A writer for the *Pennsylvania Journal* optimistically explained:

Every nation which enjoyed a share of our trade would be guarantee for the peaceable behaviour and good conduct of its neighbours; and Great Britain herself would twenty years hence become a firm friend and ally. . . . It never will be the interest of any nation to disturb our trade, while we trade freely with it, and it will ever be our interest to trade freely with all nations.[1]

This delightfully simple picture reflected the American's acceptance of a world view popular during the Enlightenment. If reason were permitted to rule and dictates of nature followed, mankind would discover a harmony of interests. Each country could then concentrate on producing what natural advantages enabled it to produce best and cheapest, and every merchant would be free to buy and sell where he made the greatest profit. And the more nations came to depend on foreign trade the less they could afford to jeopardize that trade by going to war.

Arthur Lee, in the summer of 1776, read Adam Smith's recently published *Wealth of Nations*. Lee urged Silas Deane to make use of Smith's arguments to convince the French that the Americans were victims of a commercial monopoly. Lee particularly approved of Smith's classifying England's expenses in the colonies as a bounty she must expect to pay to support the monopoly. He quoted from Smith: "The monopoly of the colony trade, therefore, like all other mean and malignant expedients of the mercantile system, depresses the industry of all other countries, but chiefly that of the colonies." The *Wealth of Nations* embodied ideas that Americans had derived from experience, and although Americans did not accept Smith's arguments in favor of complete laissez-faire in the domestic sphere, they did approve of his argument against mercantilism in the field of foreign trade.[2]

The American commissioners in Paris, Benjamin Franklin, Silas Deane, and Arthur Lee, enthusiastically described the wealth to be gained by any nation entering into commercial relations with the United States and how England's loss of this trade would reduce her to a third rate power. Deane sent word to the Netherlands that the United States "only ask for what nature surely entitles all men to, a free and uninterrupted commerce and exchange of the superfluities of one country for those of another."[3] He hoped that the Dutch would recognize that "the first power in Europe which takes advantage of the present favorable occasion must exceed every other in commerce." Prussia, Tuscany, and Spain were approached with offers to trade phrased in the same grandiloquent terms.

Americans did not lack vision although they did lack experience. They reflected the unbounded faith of the age and above all the confidence which flowed from possession of a continent of riches waiting to be developed. It would be developed if the European markets for its agricultural products were not shut off by the artificial barriers of mercantilism and if the powers of Europe could be prevented from holding it in colonial status. Trade was requisite for the establishment of a new-modelled republic based on government by law, popular representation, and a society where advancement and privilege would be the rewards of ability and initiative. This vision was the heart of American nationalism.

At the close of 1776 every effort to open trade relations had failed except in the case of France. None of these caused greater disappointment than Spain's failure to grasp what Americans considered the great opportunity. Spain advanced one million *livres* in 1776 to the Hortalez Company for furnishing supplies to the rebellious colonists, but Spanish foreign policy took a sharp turn when Floridablanca came to power in February, 1777. A month later, when Arthur Lee arrived at the frontier town of Burgos he received word that his presence in Madrid would be embarrassing and that some court representatives would meet him in a small town where British eyes could not penetrate.

Lee argued that trade is what makes a nation rich, powerful, and secure. This all-embracing economic view of diplomacy held that national grandeur was to be achieved through commercial ties and not by means of political and miltary alliances. "And what object," he wrote, "can be more important than to deprive her of this great and growing source of her commerce and her wealth, her marine and her dominion?" Lee also explained the danger if Spain and France should reject the opportunity. "America," he said, "has been felt like Hercules in his cradle. Great Britain knit again to such growing strength would reign the irresistible though hated arbiter of Europe. This, then, is the moment in which Spain and France may clip her wings and pinion her forever."[4]

The Spanish-American negotiations fell asunder on the reef of conflicting interests in the Mississippi Valley. Lee returned to Paris empty handed.

Benjamin Franklin saw much to lose by too avid a pursuit of commercial treaties and therefore advised: "A virgin state should preserve the virgin character, and not go about suitoring for alliances, but wait with decent dignity for the application of others."[5] John Adams, on the other hand, favored approaching every court in Europe. The ever fearful Adams reasoned that the more lines to firm stakes the better the chance of the tent surviving some diplomatic twister.[6] A rejection, Adams felt, could only reflect on the court which chose to reject the virtuous advances. Congress accepted his advice.

The possibility of commercial relations with Frederick the Great of Prussia had intrigued Silas Deane as early as 1775, but the king had decided to continue a "tranquil spectator" and "await the *dénouement* of the scene with indifference."[7] He could never forgive England for letting him down in past crises, but neither could he afford a war with her. He must preserve his forces to deal with the aggressive and jittery Emperor Joseph whose ambitions posed a pressing danger.

Again in 1777 the Americans approached Frederick who gave a polite but firm negative. To Frederick's chagrin the Americans replied that they would send an accredited minister. The king impatiently observed that the Americans were "in too much of a hurry with their propositions for a formal negotiation."[8] Arthur Lee, who went to Berlin, explained that he would leave rather than cause uneasiness, but he was given permission to stay with the understanding that he would assume the role of a private citizen.[9]

Lee shortly became the center of a crisis. A servant of Hugh Elliot, the British minister in Berlin, committed the unpardonable by stealing Lee's correspondence from his hotel room. When the culprit was discovered and it appeared that he had acted on instructions from Elliot, Frederick wrote: "Oh! le digne écolier de Bute! Oh! l'homme incomparable que votre goddam Elliot! En vérité, les Anglais devraient rougir de honte d'envoyer de tels ministres aux cours étrangères."[10] But what might have become a cause for a break in diplomatic relations Frederick shrewdly used to assure England of his cordiality by not accepting England's offer to recall the offending diplomat. The incident, along with the polite rejection of American proposals, convinced Lee that he should return to Paris.

For a time Frederick hinted that if France recognized the United States, he would do likewise. But his real position was reflected in his instruction to his chief minister concerning the course to be followed with Lee: "Put him off with compliments."[11] Whatever possibility existed of Prussia extending a friendly hand was buried along with Max Joseph, elector of Bavaria, who died on December 30, 1777. With Austria ready to move in, Frederick faced a danger infinitely closer to his interests than any pleasure he might take in the breakup of the British Empire. He emerged from the short war with Austria in 1778 more determined than ever to remain the tranquil observer of events in America. Not until several months after England herself had recognized the independence of the colonies did the Prussian court grant the recognition that the Americans had pursued with such persistency.

In February, 1780, Catherine II of Russia issued a declaration of the rights of neutrals on the seas and invited the uncommitted maritime powers of northern Europe to join her in a League of Armed Neutrality. The appearance of a defender of the freedom of the seas led Congress to pass a resolution commending Catherine and offering to support her cause.[12] Francis Dana was commissioned to go to St. Petersburg to seek a treaty. Congress, not unaware of the risks involved, made Dana's departure from Paris and his instructions subject to the advice of Vergennes and Franklin.

These two gentlemen warned Dana that to go would be to invite embarrassment.[13] They feared that the British minister at St. Petersburg would protest and that Dana would be ordered to leave. Such an affront would weaken both France and the United States. Dana, desperately anxious to carry out his mission, finally won reluctant consent to go in the role of a private citizen. Stung by the negative attitude of Vergennes and Franklin, he went to the Netherlands to consult his old friend John Adams.

The foremost advocate of shirt-sleeve diplomacy believed that the United States could be proud of what it had to offer. Should the Russian court reject the overture, it would leave a mark of moral odium on Russia. The effect of a rejection on the Americans would be to put them on their own, lead them to adopt sound financial measures, and thereby encourage American capitalists to loan money to the government.[14]

Spurred on by the moral fervor of John Adams, who sent his son John Quincy along, Dana bought a carriage and set off. Dana and the younger Adams travelled night and day. Fifty-one days later, after a gruelling trip, they arrived in St. Petersburg, fifteen hundred miles to the north and east where the first crisp winds descending on the Russian capital heralded the coming of a long winter.

These first two citizens of the United States ever to visit Russia soon felt the chill that only the bearers of glad tidings can experience in a world that does not want them. Dana sought out the French minister who apprised him that Catherine had recently offered to mediate and that consequently she could not in any way risk offending the court in London. To soothe the impatient spirit of the American the French minister implied that the United States would be represented in the proposed conference, a suggestion unwarranted by the terms of Catherine's proposal.[15] Dana leaped at this, seeing in it, quite understandably, evidence of Catherine's readiness to acknowledge the independence of the United States.

He boldly questioned the French minister as to why, in the light of Catherine's proposal, he should not make himself known as the representative of Congress at once. Certainly a ruler with the penetration of Catherine, he wrote, must see the importance of the American Revolution, "at least to all the maritime powers of Europe." "Neither can I imagine," he protested, "that her Imperial majesty will now give herself much concern about any groundless complaints which the court of London may make against such a public mark of respect for my sovereign as any open reception in the character of its minister would be." Not to make a bid for recognition, wrote Dana "appears to me to be betraying the honor and dignity of the United States. . . ."[16] The French minister, Marquis De Verac, now stated the facts in full. The Russian court had not included the United States as one of the prospective participants in the conference. Dana had to accept the fact that Catherine was bent on winning glory as the grand arbitrator and that therefore she could not offend England by recognizing the United States.

He encountered other chilling opinions in the Russian capital. "Upon my arrival here," he wrote to Robert Livingston, the Secretary of Foreign Affairs, "I found a strong apprehension prevailing that we should rival this country in the other parts of Europe, especially in the important articles of iron and hemp."[17] He noted also that the British had emphasized that it was their country which bought the greater part of Russia's agricultural surpluses. Certainly Catherine recognized the vital importance of the British market for the goods produced on the landed estates of Russia's aristocracy, and Dana could not contravene this fact even to his own satisfaction. He prepared a statement for circulation contending that Russia had much to gain by establishing commercial connections with the United States. America, he argued, would provide a customer for Russian iron and hemp.[18] The colonies had found it necessary to import both. What little hemp was produced in the United States was produced only because of the inducement of the British bounty. As for iron, Sweden had exported iron to the colonies and Russia could take over this trade. The Americans, said Dana, would not develop any mining for years to come for no man could be induced to go down into the bowels of the earth and work for another man when he could acquire good land for little or nothing.[19]

Dana spent two gloomy years in St. Petersburg. From time to time he confessed to a feeling of futility. Not until after the peace treaty had been signed did Russia consent to recognition.

In the hope of opening commercial relations with the Dutch, Congress appointed Henry Laurens commissioner to the United Provinces in November, 1779. The ship on which he sailed was captured by the British, and Laurens was taken prisoner and confined in the Tower of London. In December, 1780, England declared war against the Dutch because of their failure to comply with her rulings concerning Dutch ships carrying badly needed naval stores to France.

John Adams first went to Amsterdam in 1780 and there established connections with many of the merchants who had led the movement in favor of asserting a broad interpretation of neutral rights. The Dutch, although at war with England, did not recognize the United States until April, 1782. Establishment of diplomatic relations opened the way for an all-important loan of 5,000,000 guilders. The success in the Netherlands came too late to help the Americans in the war, but Dutch loans carried them through the trying years of financial stringency after the war.

The American conjecture of European nations rushing to take advantage of the new commercial opportunities proved visionary. Congress commissioned Ralph Izard to represent them in Tuscany but that state refused him permission to enter. William Lee went to Vienna only to find himself wholly unwelcome.

American diplomacy failed in this respect because the immediate prospects for a profitable trade could not overcome the caution induced by England's ability to exact a high price of any nation that dared support a revolution within the empire. Failure to open new channels of trade, aside from the important commercial treaty negotiated with France, sharpened concern for the two interests that had contributed so much to the growth of commerce in the colonies, fishing rights and trade with the West Indies.

For Massachusetts and New Hampshire, the right to fish off the banks to their north and east was as important as was the right to move into new lands west of the mountains to the planters of the southern states. The overwhelming support of both interests by all areas was achieved in spite of the sectional distrust which led Congress to appoint a peace commissioner from each of the major sections.

In a letter to Franklin in January, 1782, Livingston summed up the reason why fishing rights constituted a *sine qua non* of any settlement. Fish was the chief commodity the people of these states could exchange for goods in foreign trade, and that trade furnished their chief means of livelihood. Livingston based the "right" on two grounds; first, the New Englanders had played a major role in the wars by which England gained control of the fisheries and, secondly, the law of nations permitted no one nation to usurp the high seas.[20]

Congress urged that the right to trade with the West Indies be included in the treaty of peace. Secretary of Foreign Affairs Robert Livingston wrote to Franklin, "Without a free admission of all kinds of provisions into the islands our agriculture will suffer extremely."[21] Livingston, very typically, argued that it was to the mutual advantage of the British and French on the one hand and the Americans on the other. If these islands were closed to American merchants, the resulting decline in agricultural prices would cause the Americans to take up manufacturing and this would curtail the American market for European manufactures. The people of the West Indies also had an important stake in this trade for it would enable them to buy what they needed more advantageously. Livingston believed that if France would open the islands to American trade, it would be easier to induce the British to do the same.

It was the field of foreign trade that evoked most pronouncements of economic dogma. Those who wrote justifications of independence after 1776 usually cited the burden of the British commercial monopoly. A regular contributor to the *Pennsylvania Gazette* wrote a public letter to the British commissioners who, in 1778, came to the United States with a plan of reconciliation. The writer had some observations on the British offer to "concur to extend every freedom of trade that our respective interests can require." "Unfortunately there is a little difference in these interests," he explained, "which you might not have found it very easy to reconcile, . . ." "The difference I allude to is," he shrewdly observed, "that it is your interest to monopolize our commerce, and it is our interest to trade with all the world."[22]

Dr. David Ramsey, of South Carolina, went further in his condemnation of British mercantilism. He depicted it as "a glaring monument of the all grasping nature of unlimited power" and told his hearers that rather than "enumerate all the ungenerous restrictions" he preferred to let time "unfold this mystery of iniquity."[23]

Americans conceived of themselves as the leaders of commercial revolution world wide in scope.[24] They would break down the barriers to trade. They prided themselves on helping to destroy the British monopoly, and they invited nations at large to join them in unrestricted trade. A part of this revolution would consist in safeguarding the rights of neutrals to trade in time of war. No longer were the British with their powerful fleet to be permitted to subvert the rights of smaller nations.

Many saw in this commercial revolution the solution to the two great problems of achieving economic well being and security. A free flow of commerce would enrich all. And once commerce had been allowed to develop, it would make nations so interdependent that they would never forego the profits of trade by going to war. This view gained such general favor that Alexander Hamilton devoted the very first of his Federalist papers to attacking it so that Americans might recognize that only a powerful state could give them security.

This set of mind made for impatience. Americans somewhat self-righteously congratulated themselves on asking only for what would benefit humanity at large. In the aims of others they saw only selfishness guided by the false assumption that their own welfare depended upon injuring their rivals. John Adams growled:

There are at this moment so many politicians piddling about peace, general and separate, that I am sick to death of it. Why is there not one soul in Europe capable of seeing the plainest thing in the world? Any one of the neutral powers saying to the rest, "America is one of us, and we will all share in her commerce. Let us all as one declare it." These words once pronounced, peace is made, or at least soon and easily made. Without it, all may nibble and piddle and dribble and fribble, waste a long time, immense treasures, and much human blood, and they must come to it at last.[25]

The roots of these anti-mercantilist and anti-balance of power views extended to the very depths of the American experience. In fact it seemed so natural that it was not then and has scarcely up to now been recognized as an ideology. It seemed like nothing more than common sense, or in the words of the Age of Enlightenment, the clear observations of reason emancipated from hoary superstition.

In these views lay in large part the force behind American diplomacy. To appreciate its full strength it is necessary to recognize that it was infinitely broader than a mere campaign to push profitable trade. To see it merely as that is to miss the fact that it was an integral part of a larger social and political philosophy, the philosophy of nineteenth-century liberalism.

The emphasis which the founding fathers gave to freedom to trade was part and parcel of their larger program. Their philosophy would have lacked relevance if it had not promised satisfaction of economic wants. The ideology likewise met the other requirements for success. It offered men the opportunity to become political participants and freedom to pursue their private interests. Private interests, they reasoned, would serve the public interest.

Territorial expansion, the other major aim, had an urgency about it that would brook neither compromise nor postponement. A victory short of acquisition of some considerable portion of the West would have been a hollow one. It was this ambition that greatly complicated the relations with France, for Spain, her ally, fully expected France to hold the Americans in check and prevent their drive in the direction of Spain's colonies.

From the beginning of the Revolution the Americans assumed that the new nation would include all of the territory that Great Britain held on the North American continent. To win not only independence but to gain additional territory far surpassing the original thirteen colonies in area constituted the goal.

In 1776 Congress wrote this expansionist dream into the draft of the proposed treaty. The king of France was to agree never to "invade, nor under any pretence attempt to possess himself of Labradore, New Britain, Nova Scotia, Acadia, Canada, Florida, nor any of the Countries, Cities, or Towns, on the Continent of North America, nor of the Islands of Newfoundland, Cape Breton, St. John's, Anticosti, nor of any other Island lying near to the said Continent, in the Seas, or in any Gulph, Bay, or River, it being the true Intent and meaning of this Treaty, that the said United States, shall have the sole, exclusive, undivided and perpetual Possession of the Countries, Cities, and Towns, on the said Continent, and of all Islands near to it, which now are, or lately were under the Jurisdiction of or Subject to the King or Crown of Great Britain, whenever they shall be united or confederated with the said United States."[26]

When the treaty of alliance was signed, it specified the United States was to have possession of any territory, formerly British, conquered on the continent of North America and also Bermuda, should that island be taken. Any other islands that might be taken during the course of the war would go to France. These treaty provisions represented promises rather than accomplished facts. The hard pressed American army could not hope to conquer and occupy these vast territories. They had to place their faith in diplomacy, and this gave them little comfort for they had great fear that the European belligerents would barter away what the Americans claimed but did not possess.

American ambitions clashed with those of Spain. Spain not

only rejected the French thesis that an independent America, by weakening England, would create a situation in Europe favorable to Spain as well as France, but she was convinced the new republic would threaten her territory. The Marquis de Castejon observed in February, 1777, that as regards America, Spain "should be the last country in all Europe to recognize *any* sovereign and independent state in North America." An independent America, he warned, would soon become powerful, was already ambitious, and being free to ignore considerations of balance of power politics in Europe would have a free hand to threaten Spain's empire.[27]

In September, 1779, Congress appointed John Jay minister to Spain. Jay's residence in Spain simply served to illuminate the gulf between American and Spanish interests. Jay's instructions did nothing to conceal the ambitions of the United States. The United States would guarantee Spain's possession of the Floridas if she captured them "provided always that the United States shall enjoy the free navigation of the river Mississippi into and from the Sea."[28] Jay was "particularly to endeavour to obtain some convenient port or ports below the 31st degree of north latitude on the river Mississippi free for all merchant vessels, goods, wares and merchandize, belonging to the inhabitants of these states."[29] Well aware that Spain feared the United States would expand to the south and west, Jay warned the secretary of his mission, William Carmichael:

> In speaking of American affairs, remember to do justice to Virginia, and the western country near the Mississippi. Recount their achievements against the savages, their growing numbers, extensive settlements, and aversion to Britain for attempting to involve them in the horrors of an Indian war. Let it appear also from your representations, that ages will be necessary to settle those extensive regions.[30]

In his first meeting with Jay, Floridablanca spoke of America's pretensions to the navigation of the Mississippi as the great obstacle.[31] Jay was first of the opinion that the United States could afford to sacrifice these interests for the time being in return for Spain's recognition of American independence, financial aid, and military assistance.[32] But when Spain went to war with England and not only disregarded the United States but "declared war for objects that did not include ours, and in a manner not very civil to our independence," Jay decided "that we ought not to cede to her any of our rights, and of course that we should retain and insist upon our right to the navigation of the Mississippi." Before Jay had been in Spain many months, he advised M. Gardoqui

that the Americans, almost to a man, believed that God Almighty had made that river a highway for the people of the upper country to go to the sea by; that this country was extensive and fertile; that the General, many officers, and others of distinction and influence in America, were deeply interested in it; that it would rapidly settle, and that the inhabitants would not readily be convinced of the justice of being obliged, either to live without foreign commodities, and lose the surplus of their productions, or be obliged to transport both over rugged mountains and through an immense wilderness to and from the sea, when daily they saw a fine river flowing before their doors and offering to save them all that trouble and expense, and that without injury to Spain.[33]

Congress had to weigh the possibility of gaining Spanish loans against Spain's insistence on full control of the Floridas and the Mississippi River. The Floridas presented no great obstacle. In 1778 Congress gave its approval to Spain's taking Florida and in 1779 promised assistance in the conquest, but the Mississippi question found Congress unyielding. The French ministers at Philadelphia repeatedly urged Congress to make the necessary concessions.[34] France, desperate for Spain's naval help, thought she could only get it if Spain got what she wanted in the new world.

Congress, desperate for funds to purchase supplies in Europe, persisted in seeking Spanish aid. Even if the territorial issue had not stood in the way, Spain's own financial difficulties after the declared war on England in June, 1779, militated against her extending loans. The British cut off the shipment of treasure from her colonies, and Spain was forced to borrow

from France. In spite of stringent finances the Spanish government did encourage Jay to expect that a loan was forthcoming. Jay reported this to Congress, and Congress took the
hazardous step of underwriting orders of supplies to be paid
for out of this prospective loan. Spain, in the meantime, made
available only a part of the funds agreed upon. Consequently,
Jay faced a critical situation in which merchants held bills
payable by him.[35] In July, 1780, Jay was told by a representative of Floridablanca not to accept any further bills until
Spain's agent at Philadelphia, Miralles, returned. The Spanish
government was waiting to see if Congress would come to an
agreement on the western boundary. When Jay had a conference with Gardoqui in September, he made clear that the
Americans could scarcely expect financial aid unless they
offered something in return, and he raised the question of the
Mississippi and Spain's needs for ship timber and vessels.

The following day Del Campo lectured Jay on the evil of
underwriting purchases for which he had no funds. He told
Jay "that the king must first take care of his own people before
he gave supplies to others; that Spain, instead of deriving advantage from America, heard of nothing but demands."[36]
America, Del Campo charged, was in a ruinous condition and
some of the states were secretly suing for peace. The brusque
talk of the Spaniard deeply offended Jay. Only Franklin
among the Americans avoided pique. He confided to Jay that
Spain owed the Americans nothing and that it would be best
to be patient and accept in a gracious spirit the minor advantages she might bestow.[37]

On February 15, 1781, Congress agreed to concede Spain's
control of the Mississippi if that would serve to make her an
effective ally.[38] Jay soon learned of this step from the French
ambassador and he concluded that Spain knew of his new
instructions. After mulling over his situation from every point
of view, Jay decided not to adhere to the decision of Congress.
He came to the conclusion that Spain would not commit herself to an alliance, and that she merely sought to pry offers
from the United States which could be used in some future

negotiation. Jay explained to Congress that he would have used the instruction as a trump card to prevent a separate peace between Spain and Britain but as the situation stood he could not justify using it. His reasoning had a ring of *realpolitik:* why, he asked, make concessions to secure an alliance when Spain, already at war with Great Britain, would not "render her exertions more vigorous or her aids to us much more liberal." Jay concluded: "The cession of this navigation will, in my opinion, render a future war with Spain unavoidable, and I shall look upon my subscribing to the one as fixing the certainty of the other."[39]

Spanish coolness stemmed not only from fear of a hardy race of American settlers pushing down on their own colonies, but from the more immediate danger of American commercial competition in the Gulf of Mexico. In 1781 the Spanish minister candidly explained that Spain must have an exclusive monopoly of the trade there.[40] To admit one nation would be as contrary to Spanish interests as admitting several, for she would not be able to compete. Here lay the great fear that guided Spanish policy.

On the eve of the peace negotiations the Reverend John Witherspoon, member of Congress, observed that the territorial ambitions of Americans had already made Europeans uneasy.[41] He was quite content to confine the United States to the territory whose rivers flowed into the Atlantic, but in this respect Witherspoon was unique. Congress agreed almost unanimously that the western boundary should be the Mississippi river. They held that under the English charters these lands belonged to the colonies, and therefore they were already rightfully theirs. Economic considerations strengthened this conviction. Fear of powerful neighbors likewise was a factor, and this gave rise to nightmarish protests in which the United States was portrayed as grimly hanging on to a narrow strip of coastal territory, its independence made subject to mockery.

By 1782 the hope of acquiring the territory to the north had yielded ground to the unpleasant fact that Canada was still in

British hands, but this did not prevent an effort being made at the peace negotiations to acquire it. Hopes of gaining the Floridas had died completely as far as immediate prospects were concerned. Yet, whatever the boundaries might be at the end of the war, Americans did not view them as necessarily permanent. Telfair, member of Congress from Georgia, thought that the claims beyond the Mississippi to the South Sea could be left to discretion, but his eyes clearly envisaged the Mississippi as only a temporary limit.[42]

NOTES

1. *South Carolina and American General Gazette,* March 27, 1776, quotation from *Pennsylvania Journal,* February 14, 1776.

2. *Ibid.,* p. 111.

3. *Journals of the Continental Congress 1774-1789,* ed. Washington Chauncey Ford (Washington: Government Printing Office, 1906), Vol. V, p. 128.

4. Wharton, *Diplomatic Correspondence,* II, p. 282.

5. *Ibid.,* II, p. 298.

6. *Ibid.,* IV, p. 430.

7. Frederick to Baron de Maltzan, June 29, 1775, in Adolphe de Circourt, *Histoire de l'Action Commune de la France et de l'Amerique pour l'Indépendance des Etats-Unis* (Paris, 1876) III, p. 173, quoted by P. L. Haworth, "Frederick the Great and the American Revolution," *American Historical Review,* IX (April, 1904), p. 463.

8. Circourt, III, 89, quoted by Haworth, p. 464.

9. *Ibid.,* p. 465.

10. Wharton, *Diplomatic Correspondence,* II, p. 358.

11. Haworth, *op. cit.,* p. 468.

12. Wharton, *Diplomatic Correspondence,* IV, pp. 80-81.

13. *Ibid.,* IV, p. 354.

14. *Ibid.,* pp. 368-370.

15. *Ibid.,* p. 684.

16. *Ibid.,* p. 698.

17. *Ibid.,* V, p. 781.

18. *Ibid.,* pp. 529-531.

19. *Ibid.,* p. 782.

20. *Ibid.,* pp. 90-92.

21. *Ibid.,* p. 697.

22. *Pennsylvania Gazette,* June 20, 1778.

23. *Ibid.,* January 20, 1779.

24. John Adams wrote to the President of Congress on May 20, 1780: "In the next place, it is not in fact the King of Prussia, but the United States of America, who have effected the revolution in the political sys-

tem and the variation in the balance of power. Thirdly, it is not because certain powers contemplate coldly the fall of England, but because they see England is unable to stand in the rank she once held, and that there is a new power arising in the west, in which they are all interested,* who will not only maintain her ground, but advance with a rapidity that has no example, and that it is the interest of all the powers that no one of them should have an exclusive monopoly of the commerce or political weight of this rising state that stimulate them to favor it." Wharton, *Diplomatic Correspondence*, III, pp. 693-694.

25. *Ibid.*, V, p. 415.

26. *Journals of the Continental Congress 1774-1789*, ed. Washington Chauncey Ford (Washington: Government Printing Office, 1906), Vol. V, p. 770.

27. Edward S. Corwin, *French Policy and the American Alliance* (Princeton: Princeton University Press, 1916), p. 109.

28. *The Correspondence and Public Papers of John Jay*, Vol. I, p. 249.

29. *Ibid.*, pp. 249-250.

30. *Ibid.*, pp. 266-267.

31. *Ibid.*, pp. 322-323.

32. *Ibid.*, p. 329.

33. *The Revolutionary Diplomatic Correspondence of the United States*, ed. Francis Wharton (Washington: Government Printing Office, 1889), Vol. IV, p. 135.

34. Corwin, *French Policy and the American Alliance*, pp. 197-198 and pp. 267-268. See also Wharton, *Diplomatic Correspondence*, Vol. III, pp. 488-490 for letter of Luzerne to committee of Congress, February 2, 1780.

35. John Jay to Count de Vergennes, September 22, 1780, Wharton, *Diplomatic Correspondence*, IV, p. 140.

36. *Ibid.*, IV, p. 64.

37. *The Correspondence and Public Papers of John Jay*, Vol. I, p. 433.

38. Wharton, *Diplomatic Correspondence*, Vol. IV, p. 743.

39. *Ibid.*

40. Jay reported: "The Count admitted this, and made several observations tending to show the importance of this object to Spain and its determination to adhere to it, saying with some degree of warmth that unless Spain could exclude all nations from the Gulf of Mexico they might as well admit all; that the king would never relinquish it; that the minister regarded it as the principal object to be obtained by the war, and *that obtained,* he should be perfectly easy whether or no Spain procured any other cession; that he considered it far more important than the acquisition of Gibraltar, . . ." *Ibid.*, IV, p. 146.

41. *Ibid.*, V, p. 649.

42. *Ibid.*, p. 650.

Foreign Affairs and the
Articles of Confederation

IV

FOREIGN AFFAIRS played a major role in undermining the Articles of Confederation and contributed in an important way to the movement that led to the Constitution of 1787. The most conspicuous failure of the Confederation was in meeting challenges from abroad. In the realm of domestic affairs Congress and the state governments performed reasonably well. The highly decentralized political structure of the Articles accorded with the combined preference for the retaining of control of the purse in local hands and the general distrust of political power. The major factors in overriding this preference were the dependence on profitable foreign commercial relations and the importance of security for the wave of settlers crossing the mountains into the lands that bordered on British and Spanish territory.

The sovereignty of the states under the Articles of Confederation accorded with lofty republican ideals, but the experiment rested on at least one fatal flaw. It assumed that even an impotent Congress could deal with foreign relations. Some leaders feared the worst even before the nominal union of thirteen sovereign republics faced the test of intense national rivalries. In February, 1783, Thomas Jefferson bemoaned the "pride of independence taking deep and dangerous hold on the hearts of individual states" and prophesied a civil war in which the contending parties would call on Great Britain and France to aid them.[1] John Adams, in London seeking to negotiate a trade treaty, criticized the individual states for not standing together and warned that they would become the "sport of transatlantic politicians of all denominations, who hate liberty in every shape, and every man who loves it, and every country that enjoys it."[2] As early as March, 1783, Alexander Hamilton confided to George Washington that only the establishment of a strong union could "prevent our being a ball in the hands of European powers, bandied against each other at their pleasure. . . ."[3] Less discerning eyes, more inclined to concentrate on the realization of republican ideals, tended to dismiss these warnings as the trumped up fears of conservatives who distrusted popular government and sought an excuse to tighten the reins at home.

The opponents of centralization held the upper hand until 1785. Four factors favored them. First, Americans gloried in republican principles, chief of which they held to be popular control of the purse. The purse strings must reside in the hands of the state legislators who, being closer at hand, could be subjected to closer control. As regulation of foreign commerce involved revenue this, too, must be reserved to the states. Secondly, state officeholders conditioned by long experience to defending the interests of their own states, provided the political leadership. As practical politicians they were not inclined to bold innovations. Only when more imaginative spirits among their constituency pushed them would they rise above their local orientation. Thirdly, the major factions distrusted each other. Land speculators and frontiersmen feared that under a strong central government the eastern states would exercise control and use it to profit themselves at the expense of the West. This western interest group did not forget that

Congress, during the Revolution, yielded to French pressure on the question of free navigation of the Mississippi. Southern planters suspected northern merchants of being ready to establish a monopoly of shipping that would impose high freight rates on the export of southern commodities. Northerners, in turn, distrusted the avaricious land speculators who impatiently pressed for western interests and likewise believed the South generally hostile to commercial interests.

If a deep distrust among those who favored centralization had not existed, they might have been able to provide effective leadership earlier than 1785. The fourth factor was the ill will that had its roots in the crisis of 1779 and 1780. A rapid decline in the value of the continental currency, a desperate financial plight, and military disaster in the South led to a demand for a more efficient husbanding of resources. In this situation Robert Morris rose to a position where he controlled foreign loans, purchase of supplies, and made his influence felt in diplomacy.[4] Few questioned his ability, but his bold tactics and alliance with the merchants of Philadelphia left deep sores. The two representatives of Massachusetts, Stephen Higginson and Samuel Osgood, were among the many determined opponents of Morris. Higginson appeared before the Massachusetts legislature in 1783 "and gave them a general view of matters touching upon the Designs of the Aristocratic Junto in Congress."[5] The Massachusetts legislature, as a result, refused to approve the five per cent impost duty recommended by Congress. Samuel Osgood traced the intrigue of the French minister and Morris in acrid terms and warned of the insidious influence of Philadelphia where there were plans underway that would sacrifice the lower classes and give rise to an aristocracy.[6]

A later generation has looked back on the period of the Articles as one of both disaster and general dissatisfaction. Such was not the case. Professor Merrill Jensen has pushed back the shadow that John Fiske cast upon the constructive aspects of what was essentially a period of post-war reconstruction.

The southern states made strides toward developing their

own merchant marine and increased the exports of major commodities. Locally owned ships soon carried one-fourth of South Carolina's exports, a sharp gain over prewar years.[7] Georgia greatly expanded its production and before long a third of her exports left her harbors in Georgia bottoms.[8] James Madison, in August, 1784, noted the recovery that had taken place in Virginia:

Notwithstanding the languor of our direct trade with Europe, this Country has indirectly tasted some of the fruits of Independence. The price of our last crop of Tobacco has been on James River from 36/ to 42/6 per Ct. and has brought more specie into the Country than it ever before contained at one time.[9]

North Carolina, by 1789, had doubled its exports over the prewar figure.[10]

Signs of progress in the northern states were not lacking. There, too, some economic indices moved upward. New York City, virtually without a ship owned by one of its own citizens at the close of the war, had a merchant marine by 1789 that may have totalled 100,000 tons.[11] New Hampshire experienced some recovery as her shipowners engaged in a lively trade in livestock and lumber with the French West Indies.[12] The port of Salem witnessed a coming and going of ships that contrasts sharply with the traditional picture of stagnation.[13]

By 1790 American tonnage on the high seas reached impressive proportions. Of the ships entering from Great Britain 30,168 tons were American owned and 95,828 tons entering from the French West Indies belonged to Americans.[14] To these general observations must be added the fact that by 1787 the postwar depression had lifted and there were signs of recovery in all areas.

These signs of growth lend weight to the description of the critical period as one of postwar reconstruction. Some historians have gone beyond this point of reinterpretation to hold that the Articles satisfied the great majority of people and that it was only a minority group of conservatives, fearful of popular government, who brought about the Constitutional Convention and the replacement of the Articles with a more conservative plan of government. There is, of course, much truth in the statement of this school of historians that the Articles were not responsible for the spotty economic conditions but that the spotty economic conditions were certainly responsible for the demise of the Articles.

But the venture in historical revisionism appears to be weak at three major points. First, the movement for a stronger central government was by no means wholly the work of conservatives. Secondly, while the Articles were not the cause of economic difficulties, they did make it impossible for Congress to meet the major economic problem as understood by contemporaries. Finally, the thesis fails to give due weight to the problems of foreign relations both as regards foreign economic policy and the difficulties presented by the British and Spanish in the West.

First, it should be recognized that the fear of popular government did play an important part. There was a rather widespread apprehension that all authority was breaking down and that a reign of licentiousness was beginning. This feeling was shared by men of quite different points of view and was not limited to the conservatives who took their lead from Alexander Hamilton. In February, 1787, James Madison observed: "Indeed the Present System neither has nor deserves advocates; and if some very strong props are not applied will quickly tumble to the ground." He was appalled by the "late turbulent scenes in Mass'ts and infamous ones in Rhode Island" and thought that they had done "inexpressible injury to the republican character."[15] The existing order, he noted, had so lost the public confidence that some spoke of establishing a monarchy and others were now openly and seriously contemplating regional confederations. What Madison deplored was not popular government but the seeming inability of the states to become effective agents within their own boundaries and cooperative partners in the Confederation for achieving the public good. He was concerned with factions that irresponsibly pursued their own ends to the public detriment.

Such fears were widespread, and they need not be interpreted as opposition to popular government.

Secondly, the history of the Critical Period centers around the widely held conviction that the existing system of commercial relations with the outside world, and particularly with Great Britain, deprived the country of the just fruits of its industry and natural wealth. A nationalistic spirit did underlay the struggle among local sovereignties. This nationalism gained its greatest strength from the common bond of republican principles which seemed to contemporaries to set the United States apart from the rest of the world. Next, it rested on the common dependence on foreign trade.

Virtually everyone had an interest in access to foreign manufactures and to foreign markets, in buying cheap and selling dear, in maintaining favorable trade balances that would increase the supply of specie and in lessening the weight of foreign debts that pressed heavily upon them. More important than the fact of a debtor class was the fact that the United States was a debtor nation. Herein lay the basis for the various states and the many interest groups in seeking a posture of strength that would enable them to counter the hostile measures of European mercantilism.

Americans in the postwar years labored under the conviction that the nations of Europe had contrived to lay down conditions for commercial relations that were inequitable. Great Britain played the role of the arch villain in this economic game. That nation had declined entering into a commercial treaty. Instead she laid down the rules of commercial relations in a series of orders from the Crown. These orders closed the West Indies to American ships and excluded American salt meat and fish from the islands. American ships were likewise excluded from the trade with the British provinces to the north. American built ships were no longer admitted to the British merchant marine; in fact, a ship that had been repaired by Americans thereby lost its right to sail under the British flag. American fish oil and whale products were likewise deprived of their former market in the British isles. These restrictions gained far more attention than did the fact that Great Britain permitted American ships to enter British ports in Europe on the same basis as British ships.

The British freedom to dictate terms without any fear of retaliation by the Americans was especially galling, because the greater part of American trade continued to be with the former mother country. The hoped for trade with the nations on the continent of Europe increased but failed to attain the proportions expected. It at first appeared that the French government would pursue a less monopolistic policy. By an *arrêt* of August 30, 1784, the French government opened seven ports in the West Indies to foreign ships and admitted American meat and fish free of discriminatory duties. In the next few years the granting of special bounties to French competitors limited the effect of this order, but trade with the French West Indies did become of first rate importance and most of it was carried in American ships.[16] Trade with France itself was encouraged and American ships admitted, but the inability of French merchants to extend credit and the limited variety of French manufactures handicapped the trade. Prussia, the Netherlands, Sweden, Portugal, and Morocco entered into commercial treaties, and Russia and Spain admitted American ships, but none of these new commercial connections nor all of them together greatly changed the former close commercial relations with Great Britain.

The growth of an American merchant marine gave but slight comfort as long as American harbors were dominated by British bottoms. In January, 1785, Pierse Long, a Portsmouth shipowner, while visiting in New York, wrote: "It is amazing to see the quantity of Vessels in this City from all parts of England now in this Harbour carrying goods to market. . . ." "I hope very soon," he wrote, "there will be an end put to so diabolical a trade."[17] This was a constant complaint. In 1785 it dominated the discussions in Congress. Whether this British domination resulting from the monopolistic orders of the Crown in 1783 was the basic cause of the postwar depression is less important than the fact that most

Americans thought it was. And there is no reason to question that the British did dominate the carrying trade. In the first year for which complete statistics are available, 1789-1790, more than 85,000 tons of British ships arrived from the British West Indies to none for the Americans, while in the direct trade with England the British tonnage was more than double that of the Americans.[18] Under these circumstances the growth of the American merchant fleet scarcely gave much consolation.

Depression stalked through the once prosperous state of Massachusetts where the former merchant fleet had dwindled to almost nothing by the close of the Revolution. During the last two years of the war the British tightened their blockade until insurance rates ran as high as forty per cent. A large part of the state's privateers fell into British hands.[19] The few ships still available at the close of the war were largely in disrepair. The new relationship between New England and old England required a readjustment of trade routes and the finding of new markets. True enough, Americans freely violated the prohibition against their ships entering the British West Indies, but the greater proportion of this trade was nevertheless carried in British bottoms.[20] In 1786 the exports of Massachusetts amounted to only one-fourth of the prewar total.[21] The fishing industry was particularly hard hit. At the close of hostilities only four or five boats survived of the prewar fishing fleet of more than two hundred. Recovery was slow in the face of the closing of the former markets in the British West Indies. The whaling industry suffered because the British market was closed to American whale oil. The shipbuilding industry, once of prime importance, recovered slowly as the former British demand no longer existed.

Stephen Higginson, a wealthy Boston merchant, in August, 1785, portrayed the far reaching effects of British measures closing both the northern maritime provinces and the West Indies to American ships. The difficulty centered about the problem of remittances. The Boston merchant deplored the disastrous effect on business at large. Many failures had already taken place and others would occur, for those in-debted to England would, in many cases, never be able to meet their obligations.[22] Higginson thought the economy would recover, but he did not portray a bright picture. At the close of 1785 he observed that a good beginning had been made in the manufacture of nails, shoes, and clothing, that exports of pork, butter, and cheese had greatly increased, and that Massachusetts now enjoyed a favorable balance of trade with Pennsylvania, Virginia, and Carolina. These indices did not add up to prosperity. He could only take comfort in the fact that necessity would bring an end to the importation of British luxuries and a return to frugality and high morals.[23]

In each of the northern states one of the most compelling arguments for a stronger central government was that such a government would be able to negotiate a commercial treaty with Great Britain that would give greater advantages than the unilaterally imposed conditions set forth in the orders of the Crown. In New York trade and Federalism "appeared hand in hand." E. Wilder Spaulding, in his study of that state during the critical period, states:

No other symptom of hard times had so marked an effect upon politics as had the depression of commerce. It was the stimulus most responsible for the organization of the Federalists by 1787 and their constant agitation for a Federal government strong enough to protect American commerce.[24]

The sharp commercial depression in New York in 1785 was due to broader causes than the impotence of Congress, but this does not negate the fact that merchants believed that a stronger Congress would be able to restore trade. In 1785 the New York Chamber of Commerce appealed to the state legislature to grant Congress the power to regulate commerce and attributed the decline of trade to the ineffectiveness of the central government.[25] The merchants of Boston had taken the initiative and appealed to the New York merchants to do so.[26] The fact that conditions of trade greatly improved before the Federal Convention met in Philadelphia did not prevent the merchants from continued use of the argument. In New Jersey, where geography and not the Articles was clearly responsible for the failure of efforts to promote foreign trade, the same argument was used. In October, 1787, Lambert Cadwallader wrote that one of the advantages offered by the Constitution was that it would give New Jersey "prodigious advantages from the Regulation of our Trade with foreign Powers who have taken the opportunity of our feeble State to turn everything to their own Benefit." He now looked forward to playing one nation against another and compelling them to show consideration to the United States.[27]

Rufus King, of Massachusetts, so long opposed to changing the Articles, noted the disadvantages imposed on American commerce by Great Britain and observed that these disadvantages now constituted the subject for general conversation. He thought the subject would again arouse the patriotic spirit, and

if once more it becomes vigilant, and can be made active by the pride of independence, the idea of national honor and glory, the present embarrassments of trade and the vain sophisms of Europeans relative thereto, will not only direct but drive America into a system more advantageous than treaties and alliances with all the world —a system which shall cause her to rely on her own ships and her own marines, and to exclude those of all other nations.[28]

Joshua Wentworth, long active in New Hampshire politics, warned that the Union could only be supported by commerce, "it is the spring and life of the Most respectable Nations, and beside the honor & dignity of America depend on her asserting the right of sovereignty, and not suffer any Nation on earth to Ligislate [sic] for her,—at present Great Brittain [sic] does."[29] Charles Pettit, of Pennsylvania, mourned over the fact that instead "of supporting the respectable Rank which we assumed among Nations, we have exposed our Follies to their View." He noted the result: "they treat us accordingly, they severally shut the Door of commercial

Hospitality against us, while ours being open they enter and partake with us at their Pleasure."[30]

In the southern states the dominance of the British in the carrying trade was only part of the larger picture of the complete economic subordination of the planters to the British merchants. In all of these states the British merchants or their factors regained the complete domination they had enjoyed during the colonial period. The planters needed supplies at the end of war and they bought these at high prices using the credit that the British merchant offered. As a result the prewar debts owed by Virginians to British merchants, amounting to an estimated £2 million soon rose far above this figure.[31] Virginia had an essentially one crop economy, namely tobacco. While prices after the war were high for a period of years, the freight costs were also higher and sometimes amounted to as much as 14 per cent of the sales price.[32] British goods sold at premium prices but no others were available. This left the typical Virginia planter struggling to make up the balance between the income from his tobacco and the goods he purchased on credit. The merchants were constantly engaged in trying to collect. In this they met the opposition of the Virginia legislature which passed laws holding all pre-Revolutionary debts liquidated by the war. Scores of planters moved to the West leaving their debts unpaid. The net effect of this mercantile-agrarian relationship was great bitterness. When the prospect of a new federal government loomed, many planters opposed it on the ground that it would render the debts owed to British merchants payable. Ratification of the new Constitution by the state convention caused a prominent Virginian to write to his stepsons:

You will have heard that the Constitution has been adopted in this State. That event, my dear children, affects your interest more nearly than that of many others. The recovery of British debts can no longer be postponed, and there now seems to be a moral certainty that your patrimony will all go to satisfy the unjust debt from your papa to the Hanburys. The consequence, my dear boys, must be obvious to you. Your sole dependence must be on your own personal abilities and exertions.[33]

Some Virginians might oppose the Constitution for this reason, but a majority saw the new government as offering the only escape from the British economic yoke.

The debtor relationship of planters throughout the southern states was much the same as in Virginia. The anonymous writer of a pamphlet in South Carolina, in 1786, stated that British ships filled the harbor at Charleston, and British merchants now ruled the state through their capital as effectively as before independence was achieved.[34] William Kilty, of Maryland, an astute and cautious observer, granted that there were many causes for the economic plight of Maryland, not least of them the effects of the war, but he concluded that it was the accumulation of these "with old British debts, now pressing on them with an interest nearly equal to the principal, and the addition of new ones which have been, through necessity, contracted, that has reduced them to their present state."[35]

Many believed that the answer to this economic problem lay in the encouragement of the American merchant marine so that their goods could be marketed more profitably not only in England but in the countries on the continent, which finally consumed a large proportion of them. Little attention was given to the fact that the merchants of other countries could not extend credit or that no other country could offer such a large variety of manufactured goods. The South bristled with a general resentment against the British who were made the scapegoat for all of the section's many problems. While proposals to grant Congress the power to regulate foreign trade invariably aroused fears in the southern states that the northern states would use such a power to achieve a monopoly of shipping, the opposition in the South gradually declined though it by no means disappeared.[36]

The assumption that a strong central government could quickly strike back with discriminatory legislation against those nations that continued to adhere to the monopolistic practices of mercantilism was an effective argument in favor of creating a stronger union. In the *Federalist Papers*, Hamilton, Madison and Jay gave great emphasis to the necessity of changing from a posture of "imbecility" before the outside world to one of strength. In view of the later conflict between Hamilton and Madison over the question of discriminatory trade laws, it should be noted that it was Hamilton who wrote:

Suppose, for instance, we had a government in America, capable of excluding Great Britain (with whom we have at present no treaty of commerce) from all our ports; which would be the probable operation of this step upon her politics? Would it not enable us to negotiate, with the fairest prospect of success, for commercial privileges of the most valuable and extensive kind, in the dominions of that kingdom?[37]

He predicted that discriminatory laws would lead Great Britain to relax her present system and cause her to admit the Americans to the West Indies "from which our trade would derive the most substantial benefits." The argument was certainly not new nor invented by Hamilton; it had been at the core of the many complaints that found themselves expressed in scores of writings ever since 1783. In the first session of the new Congress James Madison in his sponsorship of discriminatory legislation against Great Britain said that it had been generally understood that this was the first objective in establishing the new government.

That the question of foreign economic policy became the focal point in political and economic thinking has long run significance. The aims formulated during these years deeply influenced future administrations. Other considerations were to enter into later Federalist foreign policy, but the South and West continued to hold these aims as primary. The suspicion of Great Britain in those sections and their sensitivity to British interference with their trade on the high seas is best understood against the background of the merchant-planter relationship that caused such deep frustration in the 1780's.

British occupation of the American Old Northwest furnished an equally delicate problem. The peace treaty gave the territory north of the Ohio river and south of the Great Lakes and the 45th parallel to the United States.

The British refused to evacuate the forts of the Old Northwest for reasons of economics and out of a regard for the Indians inhabiting the territory. The string of British forts began at Lake Champlain, stretched along the St. Lawrence river and the southern shore of Lake Erie, and anchored at highly strategic Detroit, with a final outpost at Michilimackinac, eight forts all together. During the peace negotiations the British peace commissioners felt no pressure to hold on to this area, little recognizing either the potential importance of the area or its immediate value as the source of furs. Only after the treaty had been signed did the British government in London awaken to the fact that it had made a settlement so generous that it would be difficult to convince those immediately affected, the fur traders and Indians, to accept it as a final settlement.

Announcement of the treaty provisions shocked the fur traders into making vigorous pleas for postponing the evacuation. The Canadian fur trade, largely a monopoly of the Northwest Company, amounted to £200,000 annually. Most of the furs came from the Indians living in what was now legally American territory.[38] If England yielded its military forts, from which the Indians drew their daily sustenance as well as protection from the oncoming land hungry Americans, that valuable trade would collapse.

The Indians, faithful allies of the British during the War for Independence, held the London government guilty of acting in bad faith, and British military officers sympathized with them. To admit the Americans would be to deliver the Indians into the hands of their worst enemies. Americans would inevitably push the Indians out and divide the area into farms. Most British officers felt like General Maclean, commander at Niagara: "I do from my soul pity these poor people and should they commit outrages at giving up the posts it would not surprise me."[39]

Faced with the dilemma of living up to the treaty, thereby surrendering their economic interests and deserting their loyal Indian allies, or having to face angry protests from the United States, the British chose to procrastinate. This policy, it was thought, would permit the goods already on their way to the Indians to bring their return in furs within the next two years. Secondly, some arrangements might be worked out with the Indians so as to avoid probable Indian attacks on British garrisons which would almost inevitably follow an immediate withdrawal.

During the early months following the treaty the British thought only of postponing the inevitable but circumstances soon led them into a much less justifiable position. As months passed into a year the British realized that the American government was incapable of action and nothing was to be feared from delay in observance of the treaty. In fact intelligence reports from the United States spoke of the impending breakup of the Republic. If this should take place, the British could take permanent possession. The failure of the various states to abide by the treaty provisions dealing with the payment of British creditors furnished the government with a good excuse. England, said the foreign office, could not be expected to fulfill its obligations when the individual states, in defiance of Congress, passed legislation making impossible the collection of debts by British creditors, as provided by the treaty. Gradually, British policy evolved into a positive program for nullifying the treaty as concerns the Northwest. They continued their occupation of the forts and after 1785 encouraged the Indians to resist efforts of the Americans to work out a peaceful settlement.

In the late summer and fall of 1785, John Adams despaired of making any progress in London on either a commercial treaty or British evacuation of the forts. Adams argued that as long as the British held the forts the Indians would feel free to attack Americans. Nothing would so arouse the emotions of his countrymen as the inevitable atrocities in warfare with the Indians. This could lead to a more general war with grievous consequences for the remaining parts of the British empire in North America.[40] His pleas met with silence.

Adams' frustration caused him to recommend a navigation act closing American ports to British ships. Should that fail, the next step would be commercial treaties with other powers so favorable as to give their goods a clear advantage over the British in the American market. As a last resort Adams recommended entry into alliances with the other powers.

Added to the controversies over trade and the Northwest were the disputes over such matters as British failure to pay for the great numbers of Negro slaves taken during the war and the British willingness to work with Ethan Allen and his brothers in a move to detach Vermont from the new republic. On their side the Americans violated the treaty by refusing to pay debts owed to British merchants and by discrimination against Loyalists who returned to the country. The treaty provided that Congress recommend to the states that the Loyalists be indemnified for their losses. No state government chose to compensate them for few measures would have been more unpopular.

Relations with Spain posed difficulties that for a time threatened more serious consequences.[41] These involved the interests and ambitions of a politically powerful group of Americans in a direct way. In this case the failure of the government to protect American interests threatened to lead to a breakup of the Union.

Spanish and American interests first came into conflict in the Trans-Appalachian Southwest during the Revolution when the Spanish retrieved the Floridas from the British. The peace treaty of 1783 between England and Spain recognized the Spanish conquest. The frontier posts seized by the Spanish in the course of the war now became the peacetime centers for the exercise of Spanish control. The Spanish success represented more than the acquisition of valuable territory. From the shores of that territory British merchant ships had sailed into the ports of New Spain, undermining the whole

Spanish colonial system. It would be easier now to insulate the empire against British competition.

The Spanish had long recognized that the Americans posed no less a threat to the empire than the British and they had no intention to compromise on their recently acquired territory. But compromise they must, for Spain lacked the resources for transforming the southwestern wilderness into a strong colony capable of withstanding American pressure.

The prize in the impending struggle was nothing less than the Mississippi Valley. To the Spanish it was something more, the maintenance of monopoly control over the trade of their empire. Control of the Mississippi and the gulf coast increased its chances of perpetuating its traditional system. So it seemed, but economic forces were arrayed against it. The Spanish government, recognizing that it could not compete with rival powers, would have preferred to exclude all foreigners, but it could not escape the fact that it could neither supply the newly acquired American territory with the goods it needed nor could it absorb the products of this vast territory in its own markets. So if it were to hold that territory it must of necessity compromise with tradition and admit foreigners to the trade.

On taking over the forts in East Florida in 1784, the Spanish official faced a crowd of Indians expecting supplies. Having none at hand, he turned to the British Panton, Leslie and company for the goods needed by the Indians and agreed in return that the company should be permitted to continue its operations in the area for another year. What was at first a temporary expedient became a permanent policy for the Spanish were not prepared economically or by training to run the Indian trade. Consequently the British company soon took over the fur trade in the entire area. To have refused this concession to a foreign concern would have thrown the trade into the hands of the Americans and given them an opportunity to win over the Indians to their side. The Spanish followed up this action with a series of conferences with the Chickasaws, Creeks and Choctaws and negotiated treaties in which the savages acknowledged Spanish sovereignty.

During the same period that Spain was taking over control of the Floridas and Louisiana, the Americans marched across the mountains into what is now Kentucky, Tennessee and western Georgia. Free from the restrictive policies of both the British and the colonial governments, the poorer elements along the coast could satisfy their yearning for land only by leaving the plantation area where economic opportunity was limited. By the close of the Revolution some 75,000 settlers had located in the trans-mountain area. Many of these frontiersmen saw in the war for independence nothing more than a fight for what they considered to be the inalienable right to emigrate. They had no intention of permitting Spain to deprive them of this "natural right."[42]

Leading the frontiersmen were the land speculators, many of them governors, members of Congress and in most cases leaders in their communities. John Sevier, governor of the State of Franklin, acquired title to 70,000 acres when North Carolina opened up its western tracts. James Robertson and William Blount, two more political leaders, secured sizable tracts and Patrick Henry, of Virginia, likewise engaged in land speculation. Their fortunes depended upon the United States making good its claim to the territory north of the thirty-first parallel and compelling Spain to open the Mississippi.

The ambiguity of the treaties of 1783 invited both Spain and the United States to pursue their own conflicting interpretations. The Spanish could claim both Floridas. West Florida had no specific boundaries in the Anglo-Spanish treaties but the Spanish soon claimed the territory as far north as the mouth of the Tennessee River. The Anglo-American treaty set the boundary at the thirty-first parallel but a secret provision, unknown to the Spaniards, provided an alternative boundary at 32° 26′ if the territory should be returned to Great Britain. The American treaty provided that both the United States and Great Britain should have free access to the Mississippi; the Spanish treaty with Great Britain made no mention of navigation rights.

Spain's foreign minister, Floridablanca, responded to the American pressure by issuing orders for the closing of the Mississippi to foreign ships and by sending Diego de Gardoqui on a special diplomatic mission to the United States to negotiate a treaty. The United States was to be wooed with an offer of direct trade with Spain and the Canary Islands, some compromises on the line which Spain had drawn marking the boundary of West Florida, and an offer of a pact of military alliance and mutual guarantee of each other's territories. The instructions stipulated that there must be no concession to the United States on the question of navigation of the Mississippi River.

John Jay, Secretary for Foreign Affairs, made no headway on the issue of navigation of the Mississippi. A resolution passed by Congress in August, 1785 prevented Jay from agreeing to the closing of the river. Two considerations led him to venture a request from Congress for new instructions. As the American representative to Madrid during the war he had been instructed to agree to the closing of the river in return for a recognition of independence and a commercial treaty. The mercantile interests would be willing to make a similar agreement now. As yet the traffic on the Mississippi amounted to little. Jay reasoned that an agreement to close it would do little harm if the treaty provided that the question could be reopened after twenty-five years.

The Jay proposal became involved in internal politics at once. Virginia, North Carolina, and Georgia, the states with territory in the southwest, had long been of one mind on the question of the Mississippi. Even before Spain laid down any policy, James Madison, apprehensive that Spain would close the Mississippi, argued that such a course would be foolhardy and contrary to the laws of nature. In a letter to Lafayette he wrote:

If the United States were to become parties to the occlusion of the Mississippi they would be guilty of treason against the very laws under which they obtained and hold their national existence.[43]

He had a firm ally in James Monroe who took the lead in opposing Jay in Congress. These Virginians held that Congress was under obligation not to sacrifice the vital interest of one section for some minor convenience to another section. Madison and Monroe not only believed that the United States had a right to free navigation of the Mississippi, but they knew that a sacrifice of western interests at this time would do irreparable injury to the movement to increase the powers of Congress. In the early summer of 1786 they looked forward hopefully to the Annapolis convention. Approval of Jay's proposal by Congress would convince the south and west that they could not afford to entrust their interests to Congress.

Monroe's arguments before Congress failed to prevent the approval of Jay's proposal. Frustrated at the hands of Congress, Monroe joined with others in drafting a new proposal and sending it to Vergennes with a plea that he use his influence at the Spanish court. Monroe warned Vergennes that Spain was driving the westerners into the hands of Great Britain. That rival power, he added, would in all probability come to their aid, negotiate a trade of Gibraltar for West Florida, and then take over control of the interior of North America.[44]

Jay's victory in Congress was a hollow one for the seven to five vote showed that he could never get ratified a treaty closing the Mississippi. Open talk of disunion in the western settlements led him to drop the whole matter. From this time on Jay served as a symbol in the west of the unscrupulous and snobbish mercantile interests of the east.

In the spring of 1787 the convention for strengthening the Articles of Confederation was about to meet in Philadelphia. Jay had made no announcement of what course he would pursue in the Spanish negotiations but James Madison learned from Gardoqui that Jay had decided to surrender to the southerners. This was a victory but Madison feared that the consequences of what had taken place "are likely to be very serious. . . . Mr. [Patrick] Henry's disgust exceeds all measure, and I am not singular in ascribing his refusal to attend the Convention to the policy of keeping himself free to combat or espouse the result of it according to the result of the Mississippi business, among other circumstances."[45]

The new constitution was ratified by the people, but old habits of thought and sheer inertia manifested themselves in the relatively narrow margin by which the new structure won approval. The puzzling question is not so much why the opposition was so strong but, given the tradition in favor of local government and the deeply held view that any surrender over the power of the purse was tantamount to a sacrifice of sovereignty, that the change should have come so quickly. The change was undoubtedly hastened by such purely domestic factors as the financial problem, the fear inspired by the threatened breakdown of orderly government in Massachusetts and Rhode Island, the frustration of Connecticut and New Jersey in the face of the rise of New York, and the difficulties attending postwar reconstruction. However it is when we look at the close relation between domestic affairs and foreign relations that the abandoning of the Articles of Confederation after only six short years of experience appears less enigmatic. Economic interests with much at stake in the field of foreign affairs had solid reasons for supporting a change. And in advocating reform they could do so in the name of national honor. American nationalism was still in the nascent stage, but the most ardent of the states rights advocates was quick to resent injury at the hands of foreign powers.

NOTES

1. *The Papers of Thomas Jefferson*, ed. Julian P. Boyd (Princeton: Princeton University Press, 1954), Vol. VI, pp. 248-249.

2. *The Works of John Adams, Second President of the United States; with a Life of the Author*, ed. Charles Francis Adams (Boston: Little, Brown and Company, 1853), Vol. VIII, p. 82.

3. Gottfried Dietze, "Hamilton's Concept of Free Government," *New York History*, Vol. XXXVIII, October, 1957, p. 361.

4. E. James Ferguson, *The Power of the Purse: A History of American Public Finance, 1776-1790* (Williamsburg: Institute of Early American History, 1961), pp. 112-113, 119.

5. Stephen Higginson to Theodorick Bland, October 6, 1783, *Letters of Members of the Continental Congress*, ed. Edmund C. Burnett (Washington, D.C.: Carnegie Institution, 1936), Vol. VII, p. 323.

6. Samuel Osgood to John Adams, December 7, 1783, *ibid.*, pp. 378-380.

7. Forrest McDonald, *We The People: The Economic Origins of the Constitution* (Chicago: University of Chicago Press, 1958), pp. 213-214.

8. *Ibid.*, pp. 131-132.

9. James Madison to Thomas Jefferson, August 20, 1784, *The Papers of Thomas Jefferson*, ed. Boyd, Vol. VII, p. 402.

10. John Richard Alden, "The South in the Revolution, 1763-1789," Vol. III of *A History of the South*, ed. Wendell Stephenson (Baton Rouge: Louisiana State University Press, 1957), p. 369.

11. This figure is taken from an article by Samuel Duff McCoy, "The Port of New York (1783-1789): Lost Island of Sailing Ships," *New York History*, Vol. XVII, (January, 1936), p. 387. Whether the tonnage owned by New Yorkers was this great appears doubtful, but the growth during the 1780's was significant.

12. McDonald, *We the People*, pp. 38-39.

13. James Duncan Phillips, "Salem Ocean-Borne Commerce From the Close of the Revolution to the Establishment of the Constitution, 1783-1789," *The Essex Institute of Historical Collections*, Vol. LXXV (April, 1939), pp. 140-143.

14. *American State Papers: Documents, Legislative and Executive, of the Congress of the United States, From the First Session of the First to the Third Session of the Thirteenth Congress, Inclusive: Commencing March 3, 1789, and Ending March 3, 1815. Selected and Edited, Under the Authority of Congress*, By Walter Lowrie, Secretary of the Senate, and Matthew St. Clair Clarke, Clerk of the House of Representatives (Washington: Gales and Seaton, 1832), Vol. I, p. 45. Hereafter cited as *American State Papers*.

15. James Madison to Edmund Pendleton, February 24, 1787, Burnett, *Letters*, Vol. VIII, pp. 547-548.

16. Henri See, "Commerce between France and the United States, 1783-1784," *American Historical Review*, Vol. XXXI (July, 1926), pp. 735-36.

17. Pierse Long to John Langdon, January 31, 1785, Burnett, *Letters*, Vol. VIII, p. 18.

18. *American State Papers: Commerce*, Vol. I, p. 45.

19. Samuel Eliot Morison, *Maritime History of Massachusetts 1783-1860* (Boston: Houghton Mifflin Co., 1921), p. 30.

20. This conclusion rests on the many observations recorded in the letters of members of Congress and also on the statistics for the first year under the new Federal Constitution.

21. Morison, *op. cit.*, p. 31.

22. "Letters of Stephen Higginson," *Annual Report of the American*

Historical Association for the Year 1896, (Washington: Government Printing Office, 1897), I, p. 719.

23. *Ibid.*

24. E. Wilder Spaulding, *New York in the Critical Period 1783-1789* (New York: Columbia University Press, 1923), p. 9.

25. *Ibid.,* p. 137.

26. *Ibid.*

27. It should be made clear that the strong support in New Jersey for the Constitution rested on the difficulty of raising revenue by impost duties in a state with virtually no foreign commerce. As a result New Jersey had to resort to direct taxes. New York served as the port of entry for most foreign imports to New Jersey and was able to raise adequate revenue by duties on imports. Nevertheless New Jersey did make some effort to promote foreign trade, and to some extent the British regulations were blamed for the failure. For a valuable discussion of the situation in that state see Richard P. McCormick, *Experiment in Independence: New Jersey in the Critical Period,* New Brunswick, N.J.: Rutgers University Press, 1950.

28. Rufus King to John Adams, November 2, 1785, Burnett, *Letters,* Vol. VIII, pp. 247-248.

29. *The State of New Hampshire Miscellaneous Provincial and State Papers,* Vol. XVIII, pp. 772-773.

30. Charles Pettit to Jeremiah Wadsworth, May 27, 1786, Burnett, *Letters,* Vol. VIII, p. 370.

31. W. A. Low, "Merchant and Planter Relations in Post-Revolutionary Virginia, 1783-1789," *The Virginia Magazine of History and Biography,* Vol. LXI (July, 1953), p. 314.

32. W. A. Low states: "Whereas six percent of the total sale prices of tobacco went to pay freight expenses alone prior to the Revolution, the average after the war was higher—sometimes as high as fourteen percent. Duties on tobacco export also increased after the Revolution, consuming nearly four-fifths of the sale price." *Ibid.,* p. 313.

33. *Ibid.,* p. 317.

34. *A Few Salutary Hints, Pointing Out the Policy and Consequences of Admitting British Subjects to Engross Our Trade,* New York: Kollock, 1786.

35. William Kilty, *A History of the Session of the General Assembly,* Annapolis, 1786.

36. The question of regulating trade divided the northern commercial states and the southern staple states as did no other question. Richard Henry Lee freely predicted the avarice of the merchants would result in legislation ruinous to the South, a view he promoted with the greatest of vigor as President of Congress in 1786. But it is also interesting to note that when Nathan Dane went to Congress in 1786, he wrote to Governor Bowdoin of Massachusetts that "the disposition for vesting commercial powers in Congress appears to me to be more general particularly in the Southern States than I expected to find it." Burnett, *Letters,* Vol. VIII, p. 283.

The subject came up in the Constitutional Convention, and C. C.

Pinckney proposed that a two-thirds majority be required for any law regulating trade between the states and with foreign powers. The response of several southerners is significant. Thomas Pinckney of South Carolina immediately arose to oppose the proposal. James Madison expressed a willingness to accept the temporary disadvantage of high freight rates because the "Southern states would derive an essential advantage in the general security afforded by the increase of maritime strength." John Rutledge of South Carolina likewise opposed the motion. He wished the convention to remember the necessity "of securing the West India trade to this country." "That was the great object," he said, "and a navigation Act was necessary for obtaining it." Forrest McDonald points out that the shipping interests in the Southern port cities had suffered due to the closing of the British West Indies. Southern ships usually made a trip to Europe at harvest time and engaged in the West Indies trade during the remainder of the year. The merchants found the trade with the French West Indies much less advantageous than their trade with the British islands prior to the war. See Forrest McDonald, *We the People,* p. 213.

37. *The Federalist* (Washington, D.C.: National Home Library Foundation, 1937), Number 11, p. 63.

38. Samuel Flagg Bemis, *Jay's Treaty: A Study in Commerce and Diplomacy* (New York: The Macmillan Company, 1924), pp. 5-6.

39. *Ibid.,* p. 8, fn. 19.

40. *Works of John Adams,* Vol. VIII, p. 326.

41. The author highly recommends Arthur P. Whitaker's *The Spanish-American Frontier: 1783-1795: The Westward Movement and the Spanish Retreat in the Mississippi Valley* (Boston: Houghton Mifflin Co., 1927). This excellent analysis and narrative account of relations with Spain provided the basis for the author's own treatment of the subject.

42. Thomas Perkins Abernethy gives a very good account of land speculation in his *From Frontier to Plantation in Tennessee: A Study in Frontier Democracy* (Chapel Hill: University of North Carolina Press, 1932).

43. *The Writings of James Madison Comprising His Public Papers and His Private Correspondence, Including Numerous Letters and Documents for the First Time,* ed. Gaillard Hunt (New York: G. P. Putnam's Sons, 1901), Vol. II, p. 122. Hereafter cited as *Writings of Madison.*

44. *The Papers of Thomas Jefferson,* ed. Julian P. Boyd (Princeton: Princeton University Press, 1954), Vol. X. The editor presents a careful and detailed account of Monroe's maneuver on pages 277-279.

45. *Writings of Madison,* II, p. 329.

Credit Versus Markets:
The Origin of Party Conflict
Over Foreign Policy

V

FOREIGN POLICY QUESTIONS during the presidency of George Washington became the focal point of political debate and contributed in a major way to the rise of political parties. The Constitution did not envision parties, and George Washington was strongly averse to their becoming a part of the American political scene, but as Joseph Charles has shown in *The Origins of the American Party System,* the debate over foreign policy, culminating in the crisis over the question of ratification of the Jay Treaty, brought about the division of the people into two divergent groups.

It has usually been overlooked that the issues at stake in the debate over that treaty emerged in the first session of the first Congress. James Madison was then a leader in the House of Representatives, and he sought to carry out what he deeply believed had been the mandate of the public in establishing the new government, namely a change from the helpless posture in foreign affairs to a position of effective bargaining. His program centered on commercial relations and sought to extend commerce with nations other than Great Britain and thereby to free the republic from being a mere appendage of the British economy. He viewed British economic influence by means of close commercial ties as exceedingly dangerous to the cherished republican ideals. James Madison is usually associated with the states rights position in domestic history, but he was a highly sensitive nationalist whose patriotism rested on a deep commitment to the principles of the Revolution.

His opponent in the long controversy was Alexander Hamilton, another nationalist, with whom he had been a colleague in the Constitutional Convention and with whom he joined, along with John Jay, in writing the *Federalist Papers.* They were on cordial terms at the convention and the views they expressed in their written defense of the Constitution show a close harmony. The split between them arose over Madison's foreign commercial policy. Thereafter Madison became an ardent opponent of the views expressed by Hamilton in the famous reports he prepared as Secretary of the Treasury. Hamilton expressed surprise when he found Madison opposing him on the measures he recommended and he recalled that his opponent had expressed sympathy with similar proposals in 1787. There is evidence that Madison's essential disagreement with Hamilton was on foreign policy rather than the domestic measures. A recent writer, E. James Ferguson, raises questions concerning the genuineness of Madison's opposition to Hamilton's funding measures and suggests that political expediency rather than considerations of justice caused Madison to oppose Hamilton's proposal. This conclusion, of course, lends added weight to the view that the basic cause of the split between the two ardent nationalists was a difference in foreign policy.

Their differences on foreign policy are more than adequate to explain the struggle that developed. These differences went down to the very roots where every serious debate over foreign policy issues must inevitably find itself. Hamilton was above all a realist who fatalistically accepted the existing framework, and dedicated himself to obtaining the best bargain possible. He did not object to the *realpolitik* of balance of power diplomacy, chose to regard treaties as convenient arrangements binding on the parties until they no longer served the purposes of one or the other, accepted British dominance as a simple fact of life, and dismissed as dangerous embarking on goals that the limited power of the country could scarcely hope to achieve. His own limited aim in foreign relations was to guarantee access to what he considered the prime need of a nation that desperately needed capital for the development of its tremendous resources so that it might one day emerge as a major power.

James Madison exemplifies the idealist in foreign policy. He spoke often of the rights of the republic and of what was just in international affairs but never felt it necessary to balance goals with the power available. At the base of his nationalism was a moralistic view that the new republic would be false to its mission in the world if it compromised its ideals. To remain true to its mission the nation must free itself from British dominance over the carrying trade and from the marketing of its goods through the British mercantile houses because British influence through these channels would strengthen monarchical principles and jade the lustrous principles of republicanism.

When the administration of George Washington took office in March, 1789, the basic dilemma confronting the nation was not yet clear. The United States was allied to France not only by treaty but by sentiment; it was tied to Great Britain in terms of markets, sources of manufactures, and credit. The rivalry of these two nations, soon to break forth in war, imposed on the new nation issues that threatened to tear it apart. In these issues lies the thread of American diplomacy from 1789 to 1812.

In the first session of Congress Madison presented a program for a commercial system that would give the United

States economic independence. He explained that "the commerce between America and Great Britain exceeds what may be considered its natural boundary." British dominance, he said, was due to "the long possession of our trade, their commercial regulations calculated to retain it, their similarity of language and manners, their conformity of laws and other circumstances—all these concurring have made their commerce with us more extensive than their natural situation would require it to be."[1]

Madison's program called for discriminatory tonnage duties on British ships. France and other nations that had entered into commercial treaties were to be rewarded with preferential rates. The opposition quickly pointed out that the higher rates on non-British ships could only mean higher prices on the goods Americans bought. Madison replied that the patriotism of Americans would cause them to make the necessary sacrifice, and that Americans could be induced to build a merchant marine in a short time as American ships would have an advantage over all foreign ships. He admitted that he would much prefer to see a completely free system. "But," he said, "we have maritime dangers to guard against, and we can be secured from them no other way than by having a navy and seamen of our own; these can only be obtained by giving a preference." "I admit it is a tax," he continued, "and a tax upon our produce; but it is a tax we must pay for the national security."[2]

A nationalistic tone pervaded Madison's discourse on commerce. The economic advantages sought seemed at times less important than to command the respect of Great Britain. "We have now the power to avail ourselves of our natural superiority," he said, "and I am for beginning with some manifestation of that ability, that foreign nations may or might be taught to pay us that respect which they have neglected on account of our former imbecility."[3] It was all important to show that "we dare exert ourselves in defeating any measure which commercial policy shall offer hostile to the welfare of America."[4] He defended his program against the charge that it was a tax that the people would pay by asserting that his measures would "secure to us that respect and attention which we merit."[5] Great Britain, he charged, "has bound us in commercial manacles, and very nearly defeated the object of our independence."[6]

Madison's nationalism led him to place a high estimate on the strength of the new nation. He had no fear of British recriminations for "her interests can be wounded almost mortally, while ours are invulnerable." The British West Indies, he maintained, could not live without American foodstuffs, but Americans could easily do without British manufactures.[7] This same faith led him to the conclusion "that it is in our power, in a very short time, to supply all the tonnage necessary for our own commerce."[8]

Enamored with democratic ideals and absorbed with the need for markets for the ever richer flow of agricultural produce, James Madison set forth a foreign policy that would enable the new nation to carry on its experiment in republican principles and promote the economic well being of the farmers who constituted ninety per cent of the population. Like true agrarians they believed that the world lived by the produce of the farm; like true Americans they also believed that American farms were the most important in meeting the needs of the world's markets. Therein, they thought, lay the new nation's opportunity to influence world affairs.

Farmers had an eye for markets that would enter into competitive bidding for their ever expanding supplies. Dependence on Great Britain, they said, reduced them to a hostage of that country. British merchants took almost half of their exports and furnished three-fourths of the imports. Their patriotism rebelled at the sense of dependence that British economic connections fostered. How much better to trade with all the world. That others wanted their wheat, flour, and rice seemed self-evident. The other nations would gladly buy from them if only the dependence on British ships could be overcome. British ships funnelled everything through England's entrepôts, and then redistributed large amounts to other nations. How much better if a direct trade with consuming countries could be opened up. What a great advantage it would be if the United States could have its own merchant marine. That merchant marine would serve as a great nursery for seamen and would enable the nation to build a navy to protect the routes to markets. And what a sense of freedom would be imparted by the absence of the ubiquitous British creditor who stalked through the South collecting his debts. Virginians alone owed British merchants £2,300,000 (pounds sterling).

James Madison, and the new Secretary of State, Thomas Jefferson, who soon joined him, called for legislative measures to emancipate the country from economic bondage to Great Britain and the fostering of closer economic ties with other nations. France naturally attracted attention. Capable of absorbing large amounts of produce both at home and in her West Indies colonies, and also able to supply many of the needed manufactures, France seemed to offer the best counterpoise to England. Together the two nations could break the overwhelming British economic power that held Europe in its control.

The prospect took on a new glow when, in 1789, France embarked on revolution. Now it seemed that the two nations would complement each other politically as well as economically. Thomas Jefferson alone among foreign diplomats in Paris welcomed the event. "I have so much confidence in the good sense of man, and his qualifications for self-government," he wrote, "that I am never afraid of the issue where reason is left free to exert her force; and I will agree to be stoned as a false prophet if all does not end well in this country. Here is but the first chapter of the history of European liberty."[9] To Madison he observed that members of the French Assembly looked to America as their model and viewed American precedents as they would the authority of the Bible, "open to explanation but not to question."[10]

The kinship between the two nations received symbolic expression in Jefferson's assistance in the drafting of the

Declaration of the Rights of Man.[11] And in the last days of August, 1789, the leaders of the new government met in Jefferson's apartment to settle their differences on the degree of power to be exercised by the king.[12] Four years later the French Jacobins made James Madison an honorary citizen of France. Madison gloried in the thought that France ignored the traditional national fences that had divided humanity into hostile camps.

On August 28, two days after the French presented to the world the Declaration of the Rights of Man, Jefferson wrote to Madison expressing the hope that the United States would take steps to assist France and not be content to place the French "on a mere footing with the English."

> When of two nations, the one has engaged herself in a ruinous war for us, has spent her blood and money to save us, has opened her bosom to us in peace, and received us almost on the footing of her own citizens, while the other has moved heaven, earth, and hell to exterminate us in war, has insulted us in all her councils in peace, shut her doors to us in every port where her interests would admit it, libelled us in foreign nations, endeavored to poison them against the reception of our most precious commodities, to place these two nations on a footing, is to give a great deal more to one than to the other if the maxim be true that to make unequal quantities equal you must add more to the one of them than the other.[13]

At first all classes and parts of the country hailed the Revolution. George Washington, after learning of the developments in France in the summer of 1789, expressed fear that it "is of too great a magnitude to be effected in so short a space" but what had taken place struck him as "of so wonderful a nature, that the mind can hardly realize the fact." If it should end as recent events indicated "that nation will be the most powerful and happy in Europe."[14] Gouverneur Morris, who was in Paris, found it difficult "to guess whereabouts the flock will settle, when it flies so wild," but he too approved of the overthrow of the old order. He advised Washington: "I say, that we have an *interest* in the liberty of France. The leaders here are our friends. Many of them have imbibed their principles in America, and all have been fired by our example. Their opponents are by no means rejoiced at the success of our revolution, and many of them are disposed to form connexions of the strictest kind, with Great Britain."[15]

The revolution in France merely strengthened convictions that Jefferson and Madison had held since 1783. As minister to France since 1785 Jefferson had worked industriously to promote commerce between the two countries. And when the new government took office in 1789 Madison earnestly believed that a leading motive in its establishment had been to achieve a degree of reciprocity with England and to extend the trade with other countries.[16]

Congress did establish discriminatory duties on foreign ships, but it rejected Madison's proposal for further discrimination against ships of nations that had failed to enter into a commercial treaty. Those involved in trade saw no great hope of developing a trade with France, a nation they considered as staunch an adherent of the old exclusive mercantile system as the British. Madison would make his proposals another day when the country faced a dangerous foreign situation. By then he faced the hard fact that Alexander Hamilton had committed the nation to a foreign and domestic policy that ran directly counter to the most cherished ideals of the agrarians and tied the United States to England.

Hamilton boldly asserted that foreign policy must serve the ends set forth by national economic policy. Foreign capital constituted the great economic need of the United States, and, true to his principles, Hamilton fought desperately to make foreign policy an instrument for meeting that need. Concerning the value of foreign capital, he wrote that it ought to be "considered as a most valuable auxiliary, conducing to put in motion a greater quantity of productive labor, and a greater portion of useful enterprise, than could exist without it." In an underdeveloped country like the United States, "with an infinite fund of resources yet to be unfolded, every farthing of foreign capital" invested in internal improvements and in industry, "is a precious acquisition."[17]

The value he placed upon it appeared in more eloquent

fashion in the measures he put through. Capital would be available if the new nation demonstrated that it was friendly to capitalists and not ready to bend to the whims of an ignorant public guided by passion and by hostility to privileged classes. His program as the Secretary of the Treasury met all the requirements. Foreign, national domestic debts, and state debts were met with an alacrity that invited the fullest confidence of the creditor class. The funding system provided an opportunity for profitable investment guaranteeing to creditors an attractive rate of interest over a long period of time. The United States Bank added to the circulating media and thereby promoted business, but it had the added advantage of providing capitalists with a good investment opportunity. And Hamilton's leadership in the Washington administration approximated that of a British prime minister who steered Congress at will and reduced popular distempers to harmless frustration.

Hamilton's financial system necessitated a policy of friendship toward Great Britain. Only British capital could guarantee the economic leap that the Secretary of Treasury envisioned. Only duties on imports would meet the financial obligations the new government assumed, and three-fourths of the imports came from Great Britain. Any interruption of that trade would deprive the new government of its major source of revenue. National interest, then, dictated good relations with Great Britain.

The great danger facing Hamilton's financial structure lay in the anti-British feelings of the people and their readiness to accept revolutionary France as a sister nation fighting for the rights of man. Of these two hazards, the feeling of kinship for the French revolutionary leaders posed the greatest threat. Hamilton viewed with alarm the French messianic rhetoric and a mass psychological outburst in the name of liberty, equality and fraternity that suggested the immediate emancipation of mankind from the thralldom of the past. The French leaders startled the world with appeals to people everywhere to revolt against their masters. The powerful and deeply ingrained democratic sentiments of Americans provided a fertile soil for such appeals, and Hamilton lived in mortal dread of the excited multitude driving their representatives into a pro-French policy that would alienate the British and perhaps even pull the nation into partnership with France against Great Britain in war.

The fiscal party, as Jefferson dubbed Hamilton and his followers, worked zealously to portray revolutionary France as an international ogre. In this the indefatigable and brilliant Hamilton led the way. His first opportunity came in 1790 at the time of the Nootka Sound Affair. This international incident portended war between Great Britain and Spain and led Colonel Beckwith, the British representative in the United States, to sound out Hamilton as to what American policy might be in such a contingency. George Washington, fearing that a British request for the right to march troops from Canada across to New Orleans was in the offing, anxiously asked Hamilton, John Adams, and Thomas Jefferson to give their opinions as to how such a request should be met.

The Secretary of Treasury seized the opportunity to prepare a lengthy and thoughtful memorandum on every aspect of foreign relations. A war between Great Britain and Spain would in all probability soon involve France, and this raised the question of the responsibilities of the United States under the treaty of 1778 with France. Hamilton's anxiety for the national interest, as he understood it, led him to shrug off the obligations to that country with the greatest of ease. Americans did not, he said, owe the French gratitude. The motive of France had been to injure England and help herself, not to benefit the Americans. He considered France "entitled . . . to our esteem and good-will." "These dispositions towards her," he said, "ought to be cherished and cultivated; but they are very distinct from a spirit of romantic gratitude, calling for sacrifices of our substantial interests, preferences inconsistent with sound policy, or complaisances incompatible with our safety."[18]

Early in 1791 Jefferson proposed that some privilege be granted to France in return for a recent favor. Hamilton replied that such favors would prove temporary and would be interpreted by Great Britain as a manifestation of hostility toward her. This was only one of many such suggestions by Jefferson and Madison, and Hamilton accused them of "a womanish attachment to France and a womanish resentment against Great Britain."[19]

In 1792 Hamilton's fiscal measures stirred up a political storm. In the name of the country's good faith Hamilton pushed through his plan for paying the debts. At first he met no opposition, for the agrarians did not entertain any thought of repudiating the honest debts of the government. James Madison took a highly moralistic view of such obligations. During the first session of Congress a long debate took place on the need for discouraging the use of spirits by placing a high import duty on them. Some said such a duty would lead to smuggling and corruption. Madison considered both evils as lesser ones when compared to the evil of not meeting the government's financial obligations. "Have we not seen the turpitude of such conduct, and the consequent contamination of morals?" he warned. "Examine both sides, and say which of those evils is most to be deprecated."[20]

The issue between the merchants led by Hamilton and the agrarians led by Madison did not arise out of any difference over the necessity of paying the debts. The issue centered on other questions. Should the original holders of certificates, the soldiers who had sacrificed to win the war, be compensated or should the government be content to pay the present holders who had purchased the certificates in a speculative venture? Should the state debts be assumed by the national government or should those states which had not yet paid be left to meet their obligations as the others had already done? Should the debts be paid off as soon as the state of the revenue permitted or should the government establish a funding system?

Hamilton viewed these questions in the light of the nation's need of capital for rapid economic development. James Madison approached the same questions simply in terms of a moral obligation. Therefore his answers called for making some compensation to the original holders of certificates to whom the nation owed its existence. The state debts could be met by the states as his native Virginia had done.

In 1787 Madison accepted the principle of a funding system, but he had since been tutored by Jefferson on the evils of a long term debt. While in Paris Jefferson wrote at length to Madison on the general question "Whether one generation of men has a right to bind another." Jefferson explained that he accepted as self-evident the proposition *that the earth belongs in usufruct to the living.* From this he concluded that "no generation can contract debts greater than may be paid during the course of it's [sic] own existence." He urged Madison to present this question of debts "with that perspecuity and cogent logic so peculiarly yours." Jefferson thought a strict limitation on debts "would furnish matter for a fine preamble" to the first revenue law. It would, he said, "exclude at the threshold of our new government the contagious and ruinous errors of this quarter of the globe, which have armed despots with means, not sanctioned by nature, for binding in chains their fellow men."[21] Aside from this objection there was also the very practical matter that the loan certificates were held largely by creditors in the northern states.

The funding system became a central issue at once. Correspondents of Madison asked why the debt should not be paid off as soon as possible, and Madison favored internal taxes so that the burden of debt might be lifted. For years to come the agrarians pointed to the funding system as the source of all evils. William Giles of Virginia, in a speech before the House of Representatives, charged that the first object of its originators "was to divide the people of the United States into two classes, debtors and creditors." "Let us," said Giles, "have the privilege of honestly paying this Debt." The funding system, he said, was the great sore "and it is no wonder if the patient sometimes winces under it."[22] The creditors could cite the fact that Hamilton had been able to refinance the debt at a lower interest rate and that the system provided an orderly system of finance by which the government had put its house in order, but popular hostility toward the system mounted even higher when it became generally known that many of the holders of government bonds were Britishers.

The violent eruption of feelings owed much to Hamilton's overriding political methods. Jefferson and Madison saw in his bold and determined manner a trend away from the equal and separate station allotted to the executive by the constitution. The dominance of the executive branch violated a central maxim of Jefferson's political thought. No government could be kept true to its purpose unless each of the three branches held its own and checked the lust for power in the others. Madison shared this view. In later years as president, both men, but particularly Jefferson, exercised bold leadership, but in the early 1790's they took a different view of the proper relationship of the executive and legislative branches.

Hamilton made short shrift of the separation of powers. He managed a majority in Congress by brilliance, energy, and boldness of argument. When these did not assure him control, he sought to win over public opinion by writing in the newspapers or by the use of patronage. He had a talent for lining up support and exhausting those who stood in the way. Jefferson, after retiring as Secretary of State, noted: "I cannot wish to see the scenes of '93 revived as to myself, & to descend daily into the arena like a gladiator to suffer martyrdom in every conflict."[23]

The agrarians adopted the name Republican. They struck out at their opponents with the epithet "monocrat." The term did not express fear of a plot to set up an hereditary monarchy so much as it gave vent to their dislike of a system in which the executive held the upper hand. Hamilton appeared to be changing the Congressional system into a parliamentary one, and the parliamentary system of the eighteenth century meant rule by nothing much larger than a *junta*.

Most of the advocates of Hamilton's measures sincerely laid claim to being men of republican principles. Theodore Sedgwick, of Massachusetts, considered the attempt to fasten the aristocratic label on the representatives of the eastern states as a cheap political trick, and understandably so, for he took quite as much pride as anyone in the uniqueness of the American experiment and fondly boasted of the absence of an hereditary aristocracy and the blessings of economic equality, free public education, and the extensive participation of common citizens in all kinds of public corporations.[24] He dismissed the complaints against the funding system as so much nonsense that all Republicans who could read did not really believe themselves.

But the agrarians, from Jefferson down to the most remote frontiersman, did believe the charges. Sedgwick found that impossible because the Hamiltonian measures appeared to him as the application of sound business principles. The political implications of these measures escaped him as they did most representatives of the merchant class. But the Jeffersonians thought in political terms rather than economic terms; they did not view credit as of any great importance. Credit was that dangerous device by which southern planters had been reduced to bondage under the British merchants.

What had been a rift became a deep cleavage in 1793. Two developments sharpened the differences. In February of that year Great Britain and France went to war and forced the United States to give careful thought to its obligations under the French alliance. The Washington administration no sooner came to grips with that issue than Citizen Genêt arrived with a proposal for a new commercial treaty and instructions to promote the use of American manpower, port facilities, and produce. The merchant group made shrewd use of both to strengthen their political hold.

In April Washington's cabinet debated the question of the relationship of the United States to the two belligerents. The issue was not neutrality as much as it was the kind of neutrality. Hamilton contended that the treaty with France was no longer binding. He argued that the justice of Louis' execution appeared doubtful, that it remained to be seen whether the new government would prove stable, that it was guilty of taking extreme measures and of being the aggressor in the war, that it had violated all rights in seeking to promote revolutions abroad, and that it was undertaking military and naval operations involving risks never contemplated at the time the treaty was negotiated. Hamilton, the advocate of *realpolitik,* held that a nation's first duty was to uphold its own interests and that treaty obligations must always be subordinate to that duty. Jefferson expressed disgust at the expediency of the Secretary of the Treasury. "Would you suppose it possible," he wrote to Madison, "that it should have been seriously proposed to declare our treaties with France void on the authority of an ill-understood scrap in Vattel and that it should be necessary to discuss it?"[25]

Jefferson refused to throw off the treaty, but this did not prevent him from firmly resolving on a policy of neutrality. It must be a "manly neutrality" as opposed to Hamilton's "abject principles" and willingness to offer "our breech to every kick which Great Britain may choose to give."[26] He was equally determined to stand firm against any French violations of American neutrality. "I wish," he wrote to James Monroe, "we may be able to repress the spirit of the people within the limits of a fair neutrality."[27] A "fair neutrality" would yield no more privileges to France than to England. Jefferson gave the treaty with France a strict interpretation and narrowed the rights of that country to a minimum. He confided to Madison, "I fear that a fair neutrality will prove a disagreeable pill to our friends, tho' necessary to keep us out of the calamities of a war."[28]

Jefferson's "fair neutrality" gained the support of President Washington. He issued a proclamation warning citizens against unneutral acts. The tone of the proclamation disturbed the incorruptible Madison whose sense of moral obligation winced at the sacrifice of principle to what appeared to be national self interest. He disliked the use of the term "impartial" in the President's proclamation. "Peace," wrote

Madison, "is no doubt to be preserved at any price that honor and good faith will permit." "In examining our own engagements under the Treaty with France," he wrote, "it would be honorable as well as just to adhere to the sense that would at the time have been put on them."[29] "The attempt to shuffle off the Treaty altogether by quibblings on Vattel is equally contemptible." The difference between Hamilton's approach to a treaty and the approach of Jefferson and Madison was symbolic of the wide gulf that separated their broader concept of foreign relations.

The Secretary of State soon complained that his colleagues in the administration leaned toward England. "We are going on here in the same spirit still," he wrote. "The Anglomania has seized violently on three members of our council," said the Secretary of State. Jefferson saw that the "natural aristocrats" of the larger towns, the merchants trading in British capital, the "paper men," and all the "old tories" supported the English side on every question. The farmers, tradesmen, mechanics, and merchants trading on their own capital took the other side.[30] The same groups who supported Hamilton's fiscal policy followed him on the question of foreign affairs. Not all discerned the intimate relation between the recently adopted financial program and the question of what attitude to take toward Great Britain, but the connection by no means escaped such leaders in Congress as William Smith of South Carolina and Fisher Ames and Theodore Sedgwick of Massachusetts. Nor did the fact that domestic policy and foreign policy were essentially one and the same escape Jefferson and Madison. The latter saw in the "errors" of the administration a wound to national honor, a disregard of the obligations to France, and an injury to public feeling "by a seeming indifference to the cause of liberty."[31] But it was not the cause of liberty in Europe alone but in the United States as well that both Jefferson and Madison had in mind. What they did not understand was that Hamilton put national interest above all other considerations.

Jefferson and Madison had no inkling of the damage that

Genêt was to do their cause when he arrived at Charleston, South Carolina, in April, 1793. This revolutionary hotspur had recently been recalled from Russia where his untamed spirit had created deep embarrassment for his government. Late in April Jefferson welcomed Genêt's arrival in the country for it "would furnish occasion for the *people* to testify their affections without respect to the cold caution of their government."[32] Nor did he change his mind when he heard Genêt's account of what the government in Paris wanted. To Jefferson's relief that government did not want the United States to enter the war. He boasted that the government of France asked for nothing but the good of the United States. Most pleasing of all, Genêt brought proposals for a liberal commercial treaty. Perhaps the time had finally arrived for the carrying out of the commercial policy that he and Madison had set forth as the one way to achieve independence of Great Britain.

Genêt might convey the happy message that France did not desire military participation by the United States, but he exercised powers that violated the sovereignty of the United States. He commissioned Americans as officers and gave them authority to enlist their fellow citizens in military service, issued commissions to Americans to engage in privateering against British commerce, and instructed French consuls that they were to conduct prize courts on American soil. He finally appealed to the people to oppose their President.

"Never, in my opinion, was as calamitous an appointment made, as that of the present minister of F. here," Jefferson testified after a few weeks of trying to deal with this incorrigible.[33] Genêt acted as an agent of a revolutionary government who assumed too easily that the two republics were as one in fighting a common cause. Jefferson, too much of a nationalist to accept any such assumption, insisted on treating Genêt as a diplomat who must conform to treaty arrangements and customary diplomatic usage. He promptly called Genêt to task for issuing commissions and insisted that French privateers using American ports must not go beyond the strict letter of the treaty. They must not arm, they must not use these ports as bases for attacking British shipping, and they must not set up courts to dispose of the prizes they had captured. Genêt contended that the treaty bestowed the right to arm French privateers in the ports of the United States. Jefferson gave him a reply couched in legal language that revealed fully to the astonished Frenchman that the Secretary of State was an American first and pro-French secondly.[34] By August Jefferson gladly asked for Genêt's recall.

The Hamiltonian party understandably saw in the French minister's action a determination to involve the United States in war. No one who wished to preserve the nation's self-respect could have viewed Genêt's actions with equanimity. Under the very nose of the heads of government at Philadelphia and against their protests, he fitted out the brigantine *The Little Sarah*. When questioned as to whether arms for the ship had been procured from citizens of the United States, Genêt testified that they had been transferred from another French vessel. After he promised that *The Little Sarah* would not leave before President Washington returned to the city and could make a decision, the ship still put out to sea. At Boston a French ship, previously armed at that port, brought in a British prize. The federal marshal, under court order, placed the ship under arrest. Thereupon the French consul, accompanied by an armed force from a French warship, seized the prize. Numerous other instances of French ships arming in ports of the United States and then capturing British ships off the coast threatened to make the United States an associate in arms and open to attack by Great Britain.

In view of Hamilton's extensive campaign to marshal public opinion against these acts and to convert public opinion to the view that the United States had no obligations toward France, it is of prime importance to note that Jefferson firmly opposed the actions of Genêt before Hamilton dashed into print. As already indicated, before Genêt arrived in Philadelphia Jefferson told Madison that he expected that France would not like his rulings. He had already decided that the treaty with France did not obligate the United States to permit the arming of privateers nor to look on idly when French privateers captured British ships off the coast of the United States and then brought them into the ports of the United States.

On June 2, well before Hamilton began his newspaper attacks, Jefferson again wrote to Madison that France should not be permitted to arm privateers or enlist American citizens while in ports in the United States. Nor had he failed to act officially. On May 15, in a note to Ternant, who was still serving as the French minister in Philadelphia, he had firmly stipulated that the United States would not countenance French consuls condemning ships as prize in American ports, would not allow citizens to enlist in a foreign force to fight against a nation with which the United States was at peace, and would not permit French ships to seize ships within the jurisdiction of the United States and bring them into a United States port.[35] In June and July Jefferson maintained the same vigilance, and in August he demanded of Genêt that ships seized contrary to the rules laid down must be turned over to the United States so that restitution might be made to Great Britain.[36] Indeed, the diplomatic correspondence of Jefferson establishes that he firmly resisted every act of Genêt that would have compromised the neutrality of the United States.

Jefferson and Hamilton did not differ on the importance of maintaining neutrality, but they did differ sharply on the broader question of future relations with France. Whereas Hamilton welcomed an opportunity to alienate France, Jefferson hoped desperately that the actions of Genêt could be handled without opening a permanent breach with that nation. He continued to have faith in France. He lamented the "internal combustion" accompanying the revolution but excused it as the inevitable accompaniment of a great transformation taking place in a short space of time. Only a few months before Genêt's arrival he reprimanded William Short, commissioner to Spain, for his criticisms of France and excused the Jacobins' extreme measures, including the execution of

Louis XVI. "The liberty of the whole earth," wrote Jefferson, "was depending on the issue of the contest, and was ever such a prize won with so little innocent blood? . . . rather than it should have failed I would have seen half the earth desolated. Were there but an Adam and an Eve left in every country, and left free, it would be better than as it now is."[37]

To what degree Jefferson expressed such sentiments within the councils of the administration is not known, but there is no reason to think that either he or Madison kept their enthusiasms a secret. The Hamiltonians took great alarm when Jefferson's followers denounced the President's proclamation of neutrality as a violation of the treaty with France. Jefferson occasioned further concern when he sought to limit actions against Genêt to forms that would be less likely to offend the authorities at home. The instance of *The Little Sarah* occasioned a cabinet debate, and Jefferson argued that it would be best to remonstrate with Genêt and avoid the use of force. Hamilton and Secretary of War Knox proposed sending the militia to take her. Defeated on that score they won Washington over to the stationing of troops on Mud Island to prevent her departure.[38] Jefferson wished to avoid any military incident that would alienate France.

He had weighty reasons for his course. Genêt had arrived with a proposal for a liberal commercial treaty.[39] The good intentions of the French government had been demonstrated to Jefferson's satisfaction when she exempted American ships from a general decree ordering the seizure of all ships bound for enemy ports. Reports from William Short, who had interviewed various French officials on the subject, strengthened his conviction that a commercial agreement could be reached with France. Consequently, Jefferson, in the summer of 1793, rebuffed Genêt's actions with firmness but with due care because he was once again turning over in his mind the old project for a new commercial arrangement with France that would free the United States from economic dependence on Great Britain.

Hamilton had aims that went beyond the immediate question of restraining the actions of Genêt. What Genêt did and the degree of sympathy he apparently enjoyed among a few extremist French partisans provided Hamilton with an occasion for erecting a permanent barrier against any future realignment with France.

On June 29 the first of a series of articles on relations with France appeared in the *National Gazette* under the pen name Pacificus. No one would deny that the articles were closely reasoned and convincing. Hamilton set out to show that the President's proclamation was a proper measure, that the alliance with France was defensive in intent and that as France had been the aggressor in the present war the United States was not obligated to come to her aid, that a war would hazard the very existence of the United States, that France had defied the law of nations in calling for revolution in other countries, that Louis XVI had been executed for reasons of political expediency, and that the United States owed no debt of gratitude toward France.[40] In another series in the *Daily Advertizer* Hamilton outlined the actions of Genêt and showed that they were inconsistent with the sovereignty of the United States.[41] He made great capital out of Genêt's appeal to the people over the head of the President and exploited the President's popularity to stir up hatred against all those who showed any sympathy with France.

The effectiveness of Hamilton's appeals alarmed the leaders of the opposition. Jefferson begged Madison to combat his rival in the cabinet: "For god's sake, my dear Sir, take up your pen, select the most startling heresies and cut him to pieces in the face of the public."[42] Jefferson saw that Genêt had provided the fiscal party with a grand political opportunity. Genêt had "given room for the enemies of liberty & of France to come forward in a state of acrimony against that nation which they never would have dared to have done."[43] Madison too saw that the friends of France had been made to suffer a grievous political wound. The Anglican party, said Madison, was busy in making the worst of everything and in turning the public feelings against France.[44] He noted that loyalty to Washington reinforced the feelings against France.

How to counteract the severe blow posed the question.

Jefferson, disgusted by the turn of events and his isolated position in the Washington administration, contemplated resigning, but Madison urged that this would only open the way for the appointment of an Anglican. To resign, thought Madison, would make war with France much more likely.[45] Jefferson reconsidered and decided to postpone his withdrawal.

Madison's old formula of discriminatory duties on British ships now took on new life. By the end of August Jefferson received a newspaper report that Great Britain had issued orders for the seizure of neutral ships headed for French ports or ports controlled by France. He now planned to lay the whole business before Congress. The legislature would not disapprove of the way France had been treated, but "it will be in their power to soothe them by strong commercial retaliations against the hostile one." "Pinching their commerce," wrote the Secretary of State, "will be just against themselves, advantageous to us, and conciliatory towards our friends." In a postscript to the letter to Madison he noted that while market prices had advanced from fifty to one hundred percent in the cities, "the produce of the farmer, say the wheat, rice, tobacco has not risen a copper." "The redundancy of paper then in the cities is palpably a tax on the distant farmer," he concluded.[46]

He was already at work on a report on commerce. It should be presented, he thought, before Congress became bogged down in other business and before the "culprits" could develop a plan for defeating it. The report, he wryly commented, "might as well be thrown into a church yard, as come out now."

NOTES

1. *Annals of Congress, First Congress, First Session*, p. 182.
2. *Ibid.*, p. 237. Madison emphasized time and again the need for a merchant marine and a navy. At one point in the debate he said: "I consider that an acquisition of maritime strength is essential to this country; if ever we are so unfortunate as to be engaged in war, what but this can

defend our towns and cities upon the sea-coast? Or what but this can enable us to repel an invading enemy?" *Ibid.*, p. 189.

3. *Annals of Congress, First Congress, First Session*, pp. 201-202.

4. *Ibid.*, p. 202.

5. *Ibid.*, p. 237.

6. *Ibid.*, p. 238.

7. *Ibid.*, p. 239.

8. *Ibid.*, p. 258.

9. *The Papers of Thomas Jefferson*, ed. Julian P. Boyd (Princeton: Princeton University Press, 1958), Vol. XV, p. 326.

10. *Ibid.*, p. 366.

11. For Jefferson's correspondence with Marquis Lafayette and a discussion of his role in the drafting of the *Declaration of the Rights of Man* see *The Papers of Thomas Jefferson*, Vol. XV, fn. pp. 231-233.

12. *Ibid.*, p. 355.

13. *Ibid.*, pp. 366-367.

14. *American State Papers: Documents, Legislative and Executive, of the Congress of the United States, From the First Session of the First to the Third Session of the Thirteenth Congress, Inclusive: Commencing March 3, 1789, and Ending March 3, 1815. Selected and Edited, Under the Authority of Congress*, by Walter Lowrie, Secretary of the Senate, and Matthew St. Clair Clarke, Clerk of the House of Representatives (Washington: Gales and Seaton, 1832), Vol. I, p. 381.

15. *Ibid.*, p. 379.

16. Madison argued to this effect before the House of Representatives in 1789 and again in 1794. See *Annals of Congress, First Congress, First Session*, p. 202 and *Annals of Congress, Third Congress, First Session*, pp. 220-222.

17. *The Works of Alexander Hamilton*, ed. Henry Cabot Lodge (New York: G. P. Putnam's Sons, 1904), Vol. IV, p. 116.

18. *Ibid.*, p. 323.

19. *Ibid.*, Vol. IX, p. 527. Hamilton unburdened himself in a letter written to Colonel Edward Carrington. He claimed that Madison and he had fully discussed the funding program in 1787 and that they were then in complete agreement. He also charged that Jefferson and Madison "would draw us into the closest embrace of the former [France], and involve us in all the consequences of her politics; and they would risk the peace of the country in their endeavors to keep us at the greatest possible distance from the latter." In the same letter he said that his greatest fears were the threat of the states imposing on the Union and the rise of demagogues.

20. *Annals of Congress, First Congress, First Session*, p. 199. James Madison took a highly moralistic view of all public questions and insisted that the state must observe the same high moral code as an individual. Thomas Jefferson, in a letter to Madison, written on August 28, 1789, took the same position. Jefferson wrote: "To say in excuse that gratitude is never to enter into the motives of national conduct, is to revive a principle which has been buried for centuries with it's kindred principles of the lawfulness of assassination, poison, perjury &c. . . . I know

but one code of morality for man whether acting singly or collectively. He who says I will be a rogue when I act in company with a hundred others but an honest man when I act alone, will be believed in the former assertion, but not in the latter. . . . If the morality of one man produces a just line of conduct in him, acting individually, why should not the morality of 100 men produce a just line of conduct in them acting together?" *The Papers of Thomas Jefferson*, Vol. XV, p. 367.

Alexander Hamilton took a diametrically opposite position. In considering the treaty with France he argued that a nation has "the duty of making its own welfare the guide of its action." See *Works of Alexander Hamilton*, Vol. IV, p. 166.

This difference in an abstract matter tells a great deal about the complete lack of understanding between these leaders. It also calls attention to a major characteristic of almost all arguments presented by Jefferson and Madison. They emphasized justice, believed it was attainable, and dismissed their opponents too often as wicked men who stood in the way of justice because of ambition or petty self-interest.

21. *The Papers of Thomas Jefferson*, Vol. XV, pp. 392-397.

22. *Annals of Congress, Third Congress, Second Session*, p. 919. That the Funding System had become the great issue was readily admitted by its defenders. Fisher Ames, of Massachusetts, said: "The funding of the Debt has unhappily proved an occasion of division and jealousy in the country, and of acrimonious recriminations in public assemblies. The Debt was not augmented, it was diminished by funding, and almost none of the first Congress declared themselves opposed to funding the Debt. They resisted the assumption and some of the clauses of the bill. The sin and odium, therefore, of the Funding System, as a measure abstracted from the irredeemable quality, and the State debts, ought to have been shared among all the offenders, the Southern as well as the Northern members. Yet it has answered party purposes to represent the Eastern members as the patrons of a system of paper influence, of Treasury corruption, of certificate nobility; that they have attempted and succeeded to pervert and stretch the Constitution, to organize and uphold systems of concealed aristocracy; that they deem the Debt, as it promotes these vile purposes, a blessing. . . ." *Annals of Congress, Third Congress, Second Session*, pp. 1106-1107.

23. Thomas Jefferson to James Madison, January 22, 1797, James Madison Papers, Library of Congress.

24. *Annals of Congress, Third Congress, Second Session*, pp. 1005-1009.

25. Thomas Jefferson to James Madison, April 28, 1793, James Madison Papers.

26. Thomas Jefferson to James Madison, May 12, 1793, James Madison Papers.

27. *The Writings of Thomas Jefferson*, ed. Paul Leicester Ford (New York: G. P. Putnam's Sons, 1895), Vol. VI, p. 238.

28. Thomas Jefferson to James Madison, April 28, 1793, James Madison Papers.

29. James Madison to Thomas Jefferson, May 8, 1793, James Madison Papers.

30. Thomas Jefferson to James Madison, May 12, 1793, James Madison Papers.

31. James Madison to Thomas Jefferson, June 10, 1793, James Madison Papers.

32. Thomas Jefferson to James Madison, April 28, 1793, James Madison Papers.

33. *Ibid.*, June 2, 1793, James Madison Papers.

34. Jefferson transferred his protests to Paris early in August. See his letter to Gouverneur Morris of August 7 for a full statement of his complaints. *American State Papers*, Vol. I, pp. 167-171.

35. Thomas Jefferson to M. Ternant, May 15, 1793, *American State Papers*, Vol. I, pp. 147-148.

36. Thomas Jefferson to Citizen Genêt, August 7, 1793, *American State Papers*, Vol. I, p. 167.

37. Thomas Jefferson to William Short, January 3, 1793, *Writings of Jefferson*, Vol. VI, p. 154.

38. See *Reasons for the Opinion of the Secretary of the Treasury, and the Secretary of War, respecting the Brigantine "Sarah," The Works of Alexander Hamilton*, Vol. V, pp. 5-12.

39. By a decree of March 20, 1793, France freely opened her colonies in the West Indies to the United States. Six days later the Convention issued a decree proposing a liberal commercial arrangement with the United States. On May 9 the Convention ordered the seizure of neutral ships bound for British ports but by a decree issued on May 23 exempted American ships. In September Genêt renewed the proposal for a new commercial treaty. See Citizen Genêt to Thomas Jefferson, September 30, 1793, *American State Papers*, Vol. I, pp. 244-245.

French seizures of American ships continued in spite of decrees. Ninety-two American vessels that entered Bordeaux were seized and held. See Gouverneur Morris to Thomas Jefferson, November 26, 1793, *American State Papers*, Vol. I, p. 400.

40. The series of articles are reprinted in Vol. IV of *The Works of Alexander Hamilton*.

41. Hamilton entitled these articles "No Jacobin." They are reprinted in *The Works of Alexander Hamilton*, Vol. V.

42. Thomas Jefferson to James Madison, July 7, 1793, James Madison Papers.

43. *Ibid.*, September 1, 1793, James Madison Papers.

44. James Madison to Thomas Jefferson, September 2, 1793, James Madison Papers.

45. *Ibid.*

46. Thomas Jefferson to James Madison, September 1, 1793, James Madison Papers.

The Jay Treaty:
Foreign Policy and Domestic
Politics

VI

THE DEBATE OVER relations with Great Britain became inextricably involved with the question of which of the two emerging parties was to control the federal government for the next four years. The Jay Treaty was a reasonable give-and-take compromise of the issues between the two countries. What rendered it so assailable was not the compromise spelled out between the two nations but the fact that it was not a compromise between the two political parties at home. Embodying the views of the Federalists, the treaty repudiated the foreign policy of the opposing party. The Anti-Federalists saw in their party's foreign policy a set of principles of fundamental importance not only in relation to the outside world but also basic to the very nature of the kind of society they were seeking to establish at home. They were likewise intent on taking control of the government in the approaching election. Tied to the question of the ratification of the treaty was the question of the future prospects of the two camps of political leaders.

The British expected their rivals to fight. If they didn't, observed Henry Adams, they looked upon them as cowardly or mean. Alexander Hamilton's determination not to offend

Great Britain invited a high handed and callous disregard that nettled the American agrarians. The United States had turned its breeches to receive British kicks. So it seemed to Jefferson.

The list of grievances against Great Britain included retention of the military posts in the Northwest, at least indirect encouragement to the Indians who had launched a costly and troublesome war, the carrying away of several thousand Negro slaves at the close of the Revolution without making compensation, and a policy of extorting the most out of American trade without offering reciprocal advantages. For two years Jefferson invited negotiation of the issues without gaining any response. To this frustrating experience George Hammond, the British minister, added a tone of conversation that convinced Jefferson and Madison that the British planned to make war. A speech by Lord Dorchester, Governor General of Canada, encouraging the Indians to make war, and the building of a new fort at Maumee by Governor Simcoe, strengthened this view.

The British game poorly prepared the way for American acceptance of British rulings as to commerce on the high seas upon the outbreak of hostilities between Great Britain and France in February, 1793. On June 8 Lord Grenville issued orders to naval commanders to seize all ships carrying corn, flour, or meal bound for a port in France or any port controlled by the armies of France. Hammond, the British minister, defended the order with the dubious assertion that the law of nations sanctioned the treatment of all provisions as contraband and subject to confiscation "where the depriving an enemy of these supplies, is one of the means intended to be employed for reducing him to reasonable terms of peace."[1] Jefferson jumped upon the British contention with the eagerness of one who believed that the prospective enemy had overreached himself. In an instruction to Thomas Pinckney, American minister in London, Jefferson damned the measure as "so manifestly contrary to the law of nations, that nothing more would seem necessary, than to observe that it is so."[2]

Jefferson carefully outlined the dangerous implications of

the British contention for the United States. "We see, then, a practice begun, to which no time, no circumstances, prescribe any limits, and which strikes at the root of our agriculture, that branch of industry which gives food, clothing and comfort, to the great mass of inhabitants of these States," he stated. "If any nation whatever has a right," he said, "to shut up, to our produce, all the ports of the earth, except her own, and those of her friends, she may shut up these also, and confine us within our limits." "No nation," he proclaimed, "can subscribe to such pretensions; no nation can agree, at the mere will or interest of another, to have its peaceable industry suspended, and its citizens reduced to idleness and want."[3]

The question likewise involved, said Jefferson, the right of the American government to defend itself against involuntary involvement in war. To put the United States into a position in which it furnished supplies to one belligerent and not to the other could only be deemed a cause for war by the latter. There was no difference, he explained, in the United States restraining commerce with France and her suffering Great Britain to prohibit it. France would consider the latter a mere pretext. To permit Great Britain to bar commerce with France would impose on the United States a neutral duty to likewise withhold supplies from Great Britain. "This is a dilemma," he said, "which Great Britain has no right to force upon us, and for which no pretext can be found in any part of our conduct."[4]

Jefferson's firm posture contrasted with the note of supplication that so characterized Hamilton's every intrusion into foreign affairs when these involved Great Britain. Jefferson and Madison meant to demand respect. Privately, Jefferson confessed to Madison that he had no hope of Great Britain revoking her measures.[5] These two architects of the republic aimed at impressing the British with the fact that they could not deal with the United States with impunity.

Jefferson's efforts to counteract the appeasement policy of Hamilton gained strength when the British, in September, 1794, negotiated a truce between Portugal and the Algerines without the express consent of Portugal and on terms unsatisfactory to the Portuguese. Immediately the Algerines sailed into the Atlantic and began to attack American shipping, a result that Edward Church, American consul at Lisbon, described as the primary aim of the British in negotiating the truce. Church wrote to the Secretary of State that the truce furnished further evidence that British "envy, jealousy, and hatred, will never be appeased, and that they will leave nothing unattempted to effect our ruin."[6] In the next few months Americans denounced the British move as a deliberate act of hostility.

The rising feeling against Great Britain furnished the backdrop for Jefferson's report in December to the House of Representatives on the condition of American commerce. The Secretary of State again assumed a posture of forthrightness. Three facts in the report, duly emphasized, called for legislative measures. First, while imports from Great Britain totalled $15,285,428 compared to $2,068,348 from France, American vessels carried 116,410 tons from France and only 43,580 tons from Great Britain.[7] Secondly, a greater part of the exports to Great Britain were re-exported "under the useless charges of an intermediate deposite, and double voyage." One-third of the indigo, four-fifths of the tobacco and rice, and, when prices were normal, all of the grain, were re-exported.[8] Thirdly, Jefferson pointed to the exclusion of American ships from the British West Indies and the prohibition against both vessels and produce in the British continental colonies and Newfoundland.[9] Jefferson called for remedies. "Free commerce and navigation," he said, "are not to be given in exchange for restrictions and vexations, nor are they likely to produce a relaxation of them."[10]

The evil could not be measured solely in economic terms. Jefferson warned: "But it is as a resource of defense, that our navigation will admit neither neglect nor forbearance."[11] On their seaboard, he observed, Americans are open to injury and have a commerce to be protected. This security could only be achieved "by possessing a respectable body of citizen-seamen, and of artists and establishments in readiness for ship-building." To rectify the grievances, argued Jefferson, the United States should introduce discriminations against the offending nation.

On January 3, 1794 the House of Representatives took up the report and James Madison introduced a set of resolutions for carrying out Jefferson's program. One of the most crucial debates in the entire history of American foreign policy ensued. Madison explained euphemistically that what "we receive from other nations are but luxuries to us, which, if we choose to throw aside, we could deprive part of the manufacturers of those luxuries, of even bread, if we are forced to the contest of self-denial."[12] Great Britain must be forced into a more equitable relationship. "She refuses not only our manufactures," he stressed, "but the articles we wish most to send her—our wheat and flour, our fish, and our salted provisions. These constitute our best staples for exportation, as her manufactures constitute hers."[13]

Madison expanded on the evils from Great Britain's great predominance. A sudden derangement of commerce could be brought about by the caprice of the British sovereigns.[14] The situation subjected the United States to the danger of suffering a serious shock should bankruptcy overtake England.[15] England's numerous wars meant that dependence on her would result in serious embarrassments.[16] Finally, Madison spoke of the influence "that may be conveyed in public councils by a nation directing the course of our trade by her capital, and holding so great a share in our pecuniary institutions, and the effect that may finally ensue in our taste, our manners, and our form of Government itself."[17]

Two Virginia representatives bore the brunt of the burden of defending Madison's program. John Nicholas affirmed that the nation's interest demanded a larger share of the carrying trade. He made light of British credit. It only served, he said, to lead farmers into debt. As to the danger of a decline in revenue from import duties if Great Britain retaliated, Nicholas contended that the revenue could be made up by other taxes.[18]

William B. Giles appealed to patriotism. He wished to

know why there was not the same willingness to oppose Britain as at the time of the Revolution. To those who counselled patience, Giles replied that "patience is an admirable beast of burden." "Instead, therefore, of patience and forbearance," Giles explained, "wisdom, caution herself, would prescribe boldness, enterprise, energy, firmness."[19]

"Madison's wild system" struck terror in the hearts of the stolid representatives of business. Why imperil the nation's growth and prosperity? William Smith of South Carolina, armed with a speech prepared by Hamilton, argued that England pursued at least as generous a policy as other nations. He saw no reason to grieve over the predominance of British imports. That dominance flowed from natural causes, the availability of British credit, the influence of long habit, and the advantage of trading in the British market that offered such a great variety of goods.[20] He stressed the need for foreign capital: "There is no country in the world in a situation to benefit so much by the aid of foreign capital, as the United States." "This arises," said this spokesman for Hamilton, "not only from the inadequateness, compared with the objects of employment of our own capital, but from the condition in which we are, with numerous resources unexplored and undeveloped."[21]

Fisher Ames charged Madison with wishing to substitute an improbable theory for an actual prosperity. And the outcome of that theory, if applied, would drive Great Britain into a system of retaliation. Great Britain, he warned, could only consider discrimination at the present critical juncture of world affairs as an unneutral act.[22]

Ames knew that the present state of hostility toward Great Britain brought support to Madison's measures on patriotic grounds. He sought to undermine their patriotic appeal with the assertion that if "our trade is already on a profitable footing, it is on a respectable one." "While they will smoke our tobacco, and eat our provisions," said Ames, "it is very immaterial, both to the consumer and the producer, what are the politics of the two countries, excepting so far as their quarrels may disturb the benefits of their mutual intercourse."[23]

The debate came to a close one month after it had begun. On February 5 the House voted to delay action until the first Monday in March. Madison agreed to the postponement because he found it awkward to do otherwise.

The renewal of the debate in March took place in a setting where the most ardent of British friends deplored her policies. On November 6, 1793, the British Crown ordered the seizure of all ships laden with goods, the produce of any colony belonging to France, or carrying provisions or other supplies for the use of French colonies. By early March the British held 250 American vessels in their possession in the West Indies alone and American captains found that numerous obstacles in the form of legal procedures barred the way to the British promise of compensation.[24] Even Theodore Sedgwick, long a supporter of appeasement of the British, confided:

Such indeed are the injuries which we have received from Great Britain that I believe I should not hesitate on going to war, but that we must in that case be allied to France, which would be an alliance with principles which would prostitute liberty & destroy every species of security.[25]

The central issue now changed from that of Madison's resolutions to the best way of gaining immediate relief. Madison's measures had been framed as a long term program for bringing a better balance into foreign relations. Now the situation had become so critical that Madison acknowledged that commercial measures were "not the precise remedy to be pressed in first order; but they are in every view & argument proper to make part of our standing laws till the principles of reciprocity be established by mutual arrangements."[26] The real question now centered on what measures would be most likely to promote a successful negotiation.

Theodore Sedgwick took the lead in calling for a program of defense that included a standing army. He soon discovered that the advocates of Madison's proposals opposed every such defense measure. He wrote to his friend Ephraim Williams: "Is it not strange that at the moment these madmen are doing every thing in their power to irritate G.B. they are opposing every attempt to put our country in a posture of defense."[27] The grounds of opposition to Sedgwick's defense measures lay in fear of a standing army that would be at the beck and call of the executive for purposes other than defense against foreign aggression. Madison suspected that the emphasis on defense had its origin in part in an effort to sidetrack his commercial proposals but that the main aim lay elsewhere. He wrote to Jefferson: "you understand the game behind the curtain too well not to perceive the old trick of turning every contingency into a resource for accumulating force in the government."[28]

The agrarians preferred resolutions and economic weapons, but Madison's resolutions soon fell by the wayside as more extreme measures came forward. On March 26 the House, sitting as a committee of the whole, passed a resolution in favor of granting the President the power to lay an embargo for thirty days. A month later Congress laid an embargo on all foreign shipping for one month. Congress renewed the measure for another thirty days in April.

"Such madness, my friend, such madness! and yet many good men voted for it. . . ," wrote Sedgwick.[29] A few weeks earlier Sedgwick had called for the defeat of "Madison's wild system" so that the country could prepare for defense. Such measures, argued the followers of Hamilton, would improve the position of the United States in negotiating. The opponents' proposals, Sedgwick believed, would "enlist her pride and insolence against us."[30]

Late in March Jonathan Dayton, of New Jersey, introduced a resolution calling for the sequestration of all debts due from the citizens of the United States to subjects of Great Britain. William Giles supported the measure with the contention that only if the British people were brought to fear for their own interests would they exert pressure on their government to negotiate.[31] Dayton's resolution failed to pass.

In April the battle raged on another front. President Washington appointed John Jay special envoy to Great Britain. No appointment would have proved popular with the Republicans who much preferred to take economic measures before entering upon negotiations. The naming of Jay convinced them that further appeasement was to be expected. Jay had been ready to agree to the closing of the Mississippi in 1786 in return for a commercial treaty with Spain. His critics predicted that he would yield to the merchants again and negotiate a treaty that sacrificed the true national interest. The Republican societies engaged at once in a campaign of vilification of the envoy. This did not deter the Senate, always on the side of the executive branch, from confirming the appointment.

The instructions carefully spelled out the grievances, spoliations, violations of the peace treaty, and the restrictions on trade.[32] No commercial treaty should be negotiated unless American ships gained the right to enter the British West Indies.[33] But the firm tone of the instructions did not obscure the fact that the governing group at home desperately needed some kind of a treaty that would put an end to the dangerous tendency to take hostile measures toward England. Jay thought as did Hamilton and the merchants, and one paragraph of his instructions undoubtedly carried a special significance to him. That paragraph read: "You will mention, with due stress, the general irritation of the United States at the vexations, spoliations, captures, &c. And being on the field of negotiation you will be more able to judge, than can be prescribed now, how far you may state the difficulty which may occur in restraining the violence of some of our exasperated citizens."[34] And besides his formal instructions Jay carried with him the letters from Hamilton urging a settlement and outlining its nature.

Jay found Lord Grenville congenial and the British population amiable. His reports made clear at once that Great Britain desired peace. The triumphs of France at the time made any thought of engaging a new enemy most unpalatable. The British offered no resistance to an agreement to evacuate the posts in the Northwest. They yielded to Jay's interpretation of the peace treaty on the two major boundary disputes and agreed to have them settled by commission.

Jay looked to Hamilton rather than to Secretary of State Edmund Randolph. Hamilton fathered the negotiations, arranged the appointment of Jay, and watched over the whole proceeding with a paternal eye. The Madison proposals, the Dayton motion for the sequestration of debts, and the Non-Importation Act portended war and Hamilton saw in a new treaty with Great Britain the one way to put out the fire that the agrarians were kindling. He wrote to Jay, "We are both impressed equally strongly with the great importance of a right adjustment of all matters of past controversy and future good understanding with Great Britain."[35] But he recognized with perspicacity that any surrender of legitimate interests or too great a bending to British wishes would invite a revulsion among the American people that would make amicable relations impossible. Hamilton warned, "it will be better to do nothing, than to do any thing that will not stand the test of the severest scrutiny—and especially, which may be construed into the relinquishment of a substantial right or interest."[36]

Hamilton's letters penetrated more deeply into the problems of the negotiation than did the formal instructions. He foresaw that the most troublesome point in the discussions would be that of the seizures of American ships. It would be difficult and in fact impossible for Great Britain to accept the American interpretation of what constituted contraband or to yield the policy of seizing produce on its way to French ports. The Americans would find an agreement to accede to British practice equally unsavory. Hamilton did not hesitate to describe the British order of November 6 as atrocious.

Hamilton's approach to this delicate problem lay in placing the unpalatable British measures between two layers of extremely pleasing concessions. He wrote to Jay: "If you can effect solid arrangements with regard to the points unexecuted of the treaty of peace, the question of indemnification may be managed with less rigor, and may be still more laxly dealt with, if a truly beneficial treaty of commerce, embracing privileges in the West India Islands, can be established."[37]

Hamilton wished to push the British as far as possible on indemnification; it would serve no purpose to "make any arrangement on the *mere appearance* of indemnification."[38] If the British would not agree to a firm guarantee, thought Hamilton, then it would be best to leave the United States free to act in whatever manner might be deemed proper.[39]

In July Lord Grenville gave to Jay a draft of the proposed treaty altering somewhat the one submitted by Jay a few days earlier. Grenville's project probably reached Philadelphia in late August. Hamilton examined it and found two major weaknesses. He took strong exception to placing British vessels in American ports on the same basis as American vessels. He objected to Article XII dealing with the right of American vessels to enter the ports of the West Indies because the privilege was limited to two years and because it would have prohibited Americans from transporting produce of any of the West Indies to any other part of the world than the United States.[40]

Edmund Randolph, Jefferson's successor as Secretary of State, scrutinized Grenville's draft with an equally critical eye. The refusal of the British to make compensation for the slaves taken at the close of the Revolution disturbed him more than any other aspect. He too considered Article XII unsatisfactory. He likewise objected to postponing British evacuation of the Northwest posts until June, 1796.[41]

The criticisms of Hamilton and Randolph did not reach Jay until the treaty had been signed. Jay held that the treaty represented the utmost that could be expected in dealing with a nation so proud and so powerful. The fact that Article XII contained a two year limitation and prohibited the United States from engaging in the all important carrying trade from the West Indies struck Jay as less important than the fact that a wedge had been driven into the British barrier against American vessels.[42]

The essence of Jay's defense of the treaty lay in his explanation to Edmund Randolph. "Perhaps it is not very much to be regretted that all our differences are merged in this treaty, without having been decided; disagreeable imputations are thereby avoided, and the door of conciliation is fairly and widely opened, by the *essential* justice done, and the conveniences granted to each other by the parties," he reflected.[43] The treaty removed the most serious apprehensions concerning British intentions in the West. The two boundary disputes in the Northwest and the Northeast were to be settled by commissions. A *modus vivendi* assuring Americans of compensation for the losses on the high seas removed some of the ignitive quality from the controversy over neutral rights. The Hamiltonians, anxious about what war would do to the fiscal system and dreading a war in which they would inevitably become the allies of France considered these two as the great gains of the treaty.

The final treaty arrived in Philadelphia on March 7, 1795. Washington and Randolph decided at once not to make it public. The Senate received it in June and approved the treaty but without a vote to spare and subject to the removal of Article XII.[44] The President delayed ratification, finding serious objections to the document that Jay had signed. During the anxious months of indecision he weighed two notably thoughtful papers prepared by Alexander Hamilton and Edmund Randolph. Both recommended favorable action, but Randolph made his approval subject to the British withdrawal of a recently issued order for the seizure of all corn, grain and flour destined for France. Washington agreed to the condition laid down by his Secretary of State.

Hamilton's paper for the President, *Remarks on the treaty of amity, commerce, and navigation, made between the United States and Great Britain,* placed the treaty under a microscope. With a tough mindedness that deserves notice Hamilton dealt with the objections that had been put forward against the treaty with as much honesty as he did with the advantages. Concerning the first ten articles, the only permanent ones, he concluded: "They close the various matters of controversy with Great Britain, and, upon the whole, they close them reasonably."[45] Article XII was objectionable.[46] Article XVIII left something to be desired, a stricter list of contraband. It likewise suffered from the failure to define clearly by what special circumstances noncontraband might become contraband.[47] This lack of precision, due to a failure to reach agreement, could become "the pretext of abuses on the side of Great Britain, and of complaint on that of France. . . ." "On the whole," wrote Hamilton, "I think this article the worst in the treaty, except the 12th, though not defective enough to be an objection to its adoption."[48]

Hamilton then hammered home the major argument for ratification of the treaty. The "truly important side of this treaty" as he saw it, lay in the fact that it closed the "controverted points between the two countries."[49]

Jefferson contended for the ideal of "free ships make free goods" that had been incorporated in previous treaties of the United States. Both he and Madison held that the ideal was a part of the "law of nations." Hamilton rejected this. A majority of treaties did not incorporate this principle. No nation had gone to war in defense of it. The United States, yet weak, could scarcely find it advisable to contend for it at the price of war entailing economic ruin and probable loss of territory.[50]

Washington also received a carefully prepared analysis of the treaty from Edmund Randolph, the non-partisan Secretary of State. He found more to criticize than did Hamilton, and his paper partook of the nature of a brief outlining of the gains and losses. Almost as an afterthought he warned that the British order for seizing provisions so recently issued, if tolerated, "while France is understood to labour under a famine, the torrent of invective from France and our own countrymen will be immense."[51] This, of course, merely recorded the outburst against the treaty that had already occurred.

Randolph recommended ratification. This conclusion did not rest on the gains outweighing the losses in the treaty but on the larger consideration of preserving the peace. That this dominated Randolph's thinking is apparent from his reiteration of this in his letter to the President. "All our differences are closed," he noted. "This is a most valuable quality; altho' we have made some sacrifices," he wrote.[52] Again, weighing the advantages and disadvantages, Randolph said: "Old bickerings settled; except as to impressments and provisions."[53]

In July Hamilton began his series of articles in the *Argus* under the name Camillus. His analysis of the treaty itself left no point uncovered, but the historical importance of these articles lay in Hamilton's exposition of the reasons on which his policy rested and why he disagreed with Jefferson and Madison. "Few nations," he wrote, "can have stronger inducements than the United States to cultivate peace." War would be a calamity for a nation still in its infancy, still in want of a navy, and dependent upon commerce for its prosperity and government revenue. "Our trade, navigation, and mercantile capital would be essentially destroyed," he warned.[54]

The American prime minister knew that his opponents swelled with an extreme nationalism. The opposition, he observed, "seems to consider the United States as among the first-rate powers of the world in point of strength and resources," and advocated a policy "predicated upon that condition."[55]

Then he summoned the overly sensitive patriots to observe that only a "very powerful state" might "frequently hazard a high and haughty tone." A weak state, he warned, could "scarcely ever do it without imprudence." And, he continued, the "last is yet our character." The wise policy for the United States, he asserted, would be "to measure each step with the utmost caution; to hazard as little as possible, in the cases in which we are injured; to blend moderation with firmness; and to brandish the weapons of hostility only when it is apparent that the use of them is unavoidable."[56]

"True honor is a rational thing," Hamilton told the nationalistic Americans, and he went on to argue that the self-restraint the United States had shown would do more to win the respect of European nations than would the rash measures advocated by the opposition.[57]

Jefferson, upon reading these articles, wrote to Madison: "Hamilton is really a colossus to the antirepublican party. Without numbers he is an host within himself."[58] Jefferson urged Madison to refute the leader of the political enemy, but Madison chose to fight in the House of Representatives rather than in the public press after the President ratified the treaty.

Historians have sometimes said that the troubled situation in Europe would have restrained the British from provoking war. The Hamiltonians did not fear that the British would deliberately make war, but they did fear that the American government would be pushed into more and more extreme measures until the British would feel that they had no alternative.[59] The Jay Treaty outlawed some of the extreme measures contemplated by the agrarians and also deprived the agrarians of much of their ammunition. The Northwest posts would no longer serve to stimulate anti-British feelings and compensation for losses on the high seas would take the sting out of British seizures. The Hamiltonians believed that the treaty would prevent war because it made the British connection more nearly palatable.

After the President ratified the treaty, the opposition determined to carry on the fight in the House of Representatives. A resolution introduced early in March, 1796 called on the President to submit to the House the papers relating to the treaty. Immediately a debate, destined to last more than a month, ensued. Supporters of the treaty maintained that the lower branch had no power to act on treaties. The opponents sought to prove the contrary by two lines of argument. First, they contended that if they lacked the power, it meant that the Executive and the Senate acting in cooperation with a foreign power could make laws for the United States by means of treaties. Secondly, they argued that since Congress had the power to regulate commerce, any treaty containing commercial provisions must be subject to the approval of both branches of the legislature. James Madison granted that the Constitution gave the President the power, with the advice and consent of the Senate, to make treaties. This did not deprive the House, he said, of the power to consider the treaty when voting provisions for carrying it into effect. On March 24 the House voted 62 to 37 in favor of the resolution calling on the President to lay the papers of the negotiation before the House. Five days later the President notified the House that he could not do so.

Thereupon the House voted 57 to 36 in favor of the resolution maintaining its power to pass on any treaty that required laws to put it into effect. A debate on the treaty itself then ensued. James Madison found objections to almost every article. Great Britain should have been made to pay for the losses incurred from her continued occupation of the military posts. The treaty yielded the American claim for compensation due for the slaves taken away. The treaty provisions permitting free entry of goods for the Indians from Canada guaranteed British control of the fur trade and an influence over the Indians. The treaty ignominiously surrendered the principle of "free ships make free goods." The article prohibiting sequestration of debts deprived the United States of a defensive weapon. The right to add to the tonnage duties on British ships had been given up and thereby the power to stimulate the growth of an American merchant marine surrendered.[60]

Hamilton had made the danger of war a chief argument for approval, but Madison found this danger "too visionary and incredible to be admitted into the question." Great Britain could find no just grounds for war in a decision to decline a treaty because it failed to provide for American interests. And why would Great Britain, beset by powerful enemies, add to the list the best customer for her manufactured products? To believe England capable of such action was, thought Madison, to accuse her of madness.[61]

The anti-treaty leaders ridiculed the idea of war. Much of their argument rested on the troubled situation in Europe, but they also counted heavily on the strength of the United States as a deterrent to the British. The British West Indies were dependent on supplies from the United States. The British would also have to reckon with the fact that the

United States was England's best customer. Wilson C. Nicholas of Virginia said "it is not to be believed that she would embark in a new war, with the sacrifice of her best trade; more especially, as she has shown an intention of making her remaining efforts against France, in the neighborhood of the United States, where their supplies will be essentially necessary to her success."[62] William Giles found Great Britain too embarrassed by her situation in Europe to contemplate war against the United States. Americans, said Giles, would not "tremble at the sound of war from a nation thus circumstanced." He thought that Great Britain also placed greater value on trade with the United States than some would admit.[63]

The argument against the treaty rode high on nationalistic passions. The agrarians paid scant attention to British arguments on the issues involved. They viewed each point from the vantage of America and rejected every compromise. Only a British surrender on almost all points could have satisfied the agrarians. Their ethnocentric view made it easy to find nothing but evils in the treaty. Yet, their antagonism did not rise out of purely nationalistic considerations.

The Jay Treaty pinched the Jeffersonians at three points. It committed the United States not to establish discriminatory duties against the British. Thereby it forced the agrarians to lay aside their whole foreign policy program and to accept that of the opposition.

Secondly, the treaty offended the nationalistic and democratic sentiments of the agrarians. Jefferson lamented: "The rights, the interest, the honor and faith of our nation are so grossly sacrificed. . . ." He wrote to Madison: "Where a faction has entered into a conspiracy with the enemies of their country to chain down the legislature at the feet of both; where the whole mass of our constituents have condemned this work in unequivocal manner, and are looking to you as their last hope to save them from the effects of the avarice and corruption of the first agent. . . ."[64] Both Jefferson and Madison believed that a majority of the people opposed the treaty and that the popular will had been denied. When it became clear that the House of Representatives would appropriate the funds for putting the treaty into effect, Madison attributed it to the pressure of business interests.[65]

Jefferson's and Madison's denunciations of the treaty are also better understood if one takes into account that in their eyes the treaty surrendered a major principle in the "Law of Nations." That term—"Law of Nations"—had all the aura of the Age of Enlightenment. It had no well defined meaning and certainly few generally accepted points, but to Jefferson and Madison it connoted justice and reason. They never doubted that their own broad interpretation of neutral rights accorded with the "Law of Nations" and the welfare of mankind.

This approach, one of the central threads of their foreign policy from 1789 to 1812, owed something to the fact that American interests would have benefitted tremendously by a universal acceptance of their interpretation of neutral rights. It owed quite as much to an idealistic view of what would benefit mankind. They desperately wanted a world order in which the innocent by-stander nations would not be made to suffer because a few major powers engaged in the folly of war. Jefferson and Madison overlooked the fact that Great Britain could not accept such an ideal without granting victory to its enemies.

In the situation confronting the United States in the spring of 1796 the surrender of the ideal had an additional and more grievous meaning for Jefferson's followers. To yield to British dictates on control of the seas meant that France would be denied access to American supplies. The United States would provide Great Britain with supplies at a time when the traditional friend, France, was struggling for liberty.

In September, 1796, George Washington delivered his Farewell Address. The President, finding himself amid the dissensions of heated party strife, had striven manfully to avoid falling into the hands of either faction. In 1793 he had, to a great degree, followed Jefferson's advice in meeting the dangers brought on by the war between Great Britain and France. Throughout the heated debates he had retained a sense of gratitude toward France and a sincere desire to deal with her justly. In the summer of 1795, he had resisted the pressure of Hamilton to ratify the Jay Treaty at once and had deliberated long before making his decision to ratify it. To be sure he could not participate in the feelings experienced by Jefferson and Madison because he did not share their philosophical outlook and their intense concern for their particular political ideals. On the other hand, he found it more difficult than Hamilton to make the concessions necessary to preserve harmony with Great Britain. The President found himself in an isolated position.

When the time came to deliver a farewell address, he called on Hamilton to draft it, and the message warned against party spirit and against a passionate attachment to one nation. To the more extreme elements in the more extreme Republican societies the counsel was applicable, but it scarcely applied to Jefferson and Madison whose pro-French feelings were rigorously subordinated to American nationalism.

Their nationalism posed a danger for they confused their American view of the world with their proclaimed universal view of justice and right reason. Their strong desire to make their republic an example of what could be achieved by noble aspiration set free to apply reason made them impatient and particularly so concerning Great Britain's financial influence and arbitrary dicta as to how far the seas were to be open to a free exchange of goods. That they were misunderstood, that their views were dubbed theoretical, is not surprising. Idealists in the realm of foreign affairs trying to establish a program that would reconcile national interests and idealistic considerations were to find themselves in a difficult position many times in the future.

In the heated controversy over the Jay Treaty a set of symbols emerged that transferred the argument from the realm of the rational to the irrational. Followers of Hamilton were quickly denounced as monocrats; followers of Jefferson and Madison were identified as the dangerous disciples of the French school of reason. In the pamphlet warfare parties became images of the British or French systems. It was not only that Jefferson and Madison differed from Hamilton in the measures to be pursued but that the opponents read into them steps in the direction of a society patterned after popular conceptions of France and England. The differences between the foreign policies of the Federalists and Republicans had little relationship to the stereotypes of partisan political rhetoric. These widened the gulf beyond that warranted by a rather undramatic difference over practical measures.

A difference in basic attitudes also contributed to the political warfare. Thomas Jefferson and James Madison had no fear of society falling victim to instability, of individuals and factions irresponsibly following the whim of the moment, or of the social fabric being torn apart by the passions of men. Their confidence in the good sense of the body politic made a significant difference. When they encountered human foibles or systems that appeared to favor one group in society or one nation they boldly presumed that it was their duty to enlighten the misled and to change the system.

The Federalists certainly benefitted more directly from the measures of Hamilton and the close association with Great Britain, but that alone does not explain their stand on the Jay Treaty. They saw the social fabric as a frail gauze in constant danger of being torn apart. The British structure was their model because it gave stability to society and an orderly financial system that emphasized contracts, law and order. They saw no reason to risk present advantages for an untried experiment in reordering the nation's economic relations with the outside world, especially when to do so would align the nation with France. Hamilton's arguments in favor of the Jay Treaty rested on an acceptance of the world as it was and not on a vague concept of the world as it ought to be. Madison judged the Jay Treaty in terms of American rights and interests without making any concessions to the hard and fast economic realities. Hamilton succeeded in putting the problem of relations with Great Britain on the shelf. His whole argument centered on prudence; Madison's argument centered on what he believed to be just American claims.

NOTES

1. *American State Papers*, Vol. I, p. 240.
2. *Ibid.*, p. 239.
3. *Ibid.*
4. *Ibid.*
5. Thomas Jefferson to James Madison, September 1, 1793, Madison Papers.
6. *American State Papers*, Vol. I, p. 296.
7. *Ibid.*, p. 301.
8. *Ibid.*, p. 302.
9. *Ibid.*
10. *Ibid.*, p. 303.
11. *Ibid.*
12. *Annals of Congress, Third Congress, First Session*, p. 157.
13. *Ibid.*, p. 213.
14. *Ibid.*, p. 214.
15. *Ibid.*
16. *Ibid.*, p. 215.
17. *Ibid.*
18. *Ibid.*, p. 241-242.
19. *Ibid.*, p. 290.
20. *Ibid.*, p. 189.
21. *Ibid.*, p. 190.
22. *Ibid.*, p. 347.
23. *Ibid.*, p. 329.
24. *American State Papers*, Vol. I, p. 429.
25. Theodore Sedgwick to Ephraim Williams, March 3, 1794, Sedgwick Papers.
26. James Madison to Thomas Jefferson, March 12, 1794, Madison Papers.
27. Theodore Sedgwick to Ephraim Williams, March 29, 1794, Sedgwick Papers.
28. James Madison to Thomas Jefferson, March 14, 1794, Madison Papers.
29. Theodore Sedgwick to Ephraim Williams, April 22, 1794, Sedgwick Papers.
30. *Annals of Congress, Third Congress, First Session*, p. 567.
31. *Ibid.*, p. 568.
32. *American State Papers*, Vol. I, pp. 472-474.
33. *Ibid.*, p. 473.
34. *Ibid.*, p. 472.
35. *The Works of Alexander Hamilton*, ed. Henry Cabot Lodge, Vol. V, p. 124. Dice Robins Anderson, "Edmund Randolph," *American Secretaries of State*, ed. Samuel Flagg Bemis (New York: Pageant Book Company, 1958) provides an excellent treatment of Randolph's role and his resignation from office.
36. *Ibid.*

37. *Ibid.*, pp. 124-125.

38. *Ibid.*, p. 124.

39. *Ibid.*

40. *Ibid.*, pp. 136-137.

41. Edmund Randolph's letter to the President was published in the documents section of the *American Historical Review*, Vol. XII (April, 1907), pp. 587-599.

42. *American State Papers*, Vol. I, p. 503 and p. 520.

43. *Ibid.*, p. 503.

44. "Documents," *American Historical Review*, Vol. XII (April, 1907), p. 587.

45. *The Works of Alexander Hamilton*, Vol. V, p. 162.

46. *Ibid.*, pp. 162-163.

47. *Ibid.*, pp. 168-171.

48. *Ibid.*, p. 171.

49. *Ibid.*, p. 176.

50. *Ibid.*, VI, pp. 106-107.

51. Secretary of State Edmund Randolph to President George Washington, July 12, 1795, "Documents," *American Historical Review*, Vol. XII (April, 1907), p. 599.

52. *Ibid.*, p. 595.

53. *Ibid.*

54. *The Works of Alexander Hamilton*, Vol. V, pp. 201-202.

55. *Ibid.*, pp. 205-206.

56. *Ibid.*, p. 206.

57. *Ibid.*, p. 236.

58. Thomas Jefferson to James Madison, September 21, 1795, Madison Papers.

59. Alexander Hamilton made this abundantly clear in his letter to George Washington, April 14, 1794, *The Works of Alexander Hamilton*, Vol. V, pp. 97-115.

60. *Annals of Congress, Fourth Congress, First Session*, pp. 977-987.

61. *Ibid.*, pp. 986-987.

62. *Ibid.*, p. 1005.

63. *Ibid.*, pp. 1048-1049.

64. Thomas Jefferson to James Madison, March 27, 1796, Madison Papers. In a letter to Madison, September 21, 1795, Jefferson expressed his views along this same line: "Thus it is that Hamilton, Jay, etc., in the boldest act they ever ventured on to undermine the constitution have the address to screen themselves & direct the hue & cry against those who wished to drag them into light. A bolder party stroke was never struck. For it certainly is an attempt of a party which finds they have lost their majority in one branch of the legislature to make [?] by the aid of the other branch & of the executive, under color of a treaty, which shall bind up the hands of the adverse branch from ever restraining the commerce of their patron-nation." Madison Papers.

65. James Madison to Thomas Jefferson, April 23, 1796, Madison Papers.

Economic Ties to Great Britain and the French Alliance

VII

But they wish to interrupt or suspend our commerce with Great Britain; and are they ignorant that this would be impossible, even if they could produce a war between the two nations? Can France purchase of us, and pay for the articles which we sell to Britain? Certainly not.

JOHN QUINCY ADAMS *to* JOSEPH PITCAIRN,
January 31, 1797

I N NOVEMBER, 1796 Charles Cotesworth Pinckney, the newly appointed American minister, and his family landed at Bordeaux. James Monroe, shockingly indiscreet even in the eyes of James Madison, had been recalled and the South Carolinian had been appointed to take his place. From the first ill fate dogged Pinckney's mission. Bad weather delayed the unloading of his baggage for three days. Before he left Bordeaux his carriage had to have alterations to fit it for the horrible roads to Paris. The trip to the capital consumed ten days. Three carriage wheels had to be replaced during the journey. And while en route he heard rumors that the French government would not receive him.[1]

Indeed, the French political terrain proved infinitely more tortuous than the roads from Bordeaux to Paris. The revolution had come to an end in June, 1794 with the execution of Robespierre and the calling of a halt to the Reign of Terror. The Directory now sat at the top of a shaky political structure. It wholly lacked a broad basis of popular support. Reactionary royalists and constitutional monarchists hoped to turn back the wheel of political fortune and put it at rest over a more conservative order. An emerging proletariat led by Babeuf wished to spin the wheel again until the revolution had been completed.

The revolution let loose a holocaust of war in the name of liberty, equality, and fraternity. A nation in arms rose to the occasion and turned back the foreign enemies of the revolution. The great armies remained. The Directory preferred to have them available for imposing peace on discordant elements at home, but the army as a tool soon gave way before the army as the final residuum of power. After the Directory called on Napoleon to suppress the dissidents at home, he rapidly achieved fame as the conqueror of the Austrians in the northern Italian states. By the time Pinckney arrived in Paris French arms had achieved glory enough to obscure the real weaknesses at home, bankruptcy and political instability. The armies of Napoleon lived off the lands they conquered. At home those who held the political reins and made up the bureaucracy waited in vain for back payments of their salaries.

The financial plight of France explains in part the grievances of Americans that Pinckney had come to present. Merchants and government officials joined hands in making neutral shipping their prey. Privateers owned by merchants cruised against all neutral shipping.[2] Only Prussian vessels enjoyed immunity. The French did not wish to push Prussia into an alliance with Austria. But other neutrals did not escape. Swedish, Danish, and American vessels suffered capture and then confiscation.[3] French tribunals, presided over by the same merchants who owned the privateers, sat in the judges' seats.

The need for funds explains only in part why the French government authorized attacks on American commerce. Eventually the curbing of American commerce with Great Britain became a matter of policy. This policy rested on the belief that England, if deprived of the American market, would be compelled to make peace. The gradual weakening of the alliance preceded these attacks. Once war broke out in 1793 between Great Britain and France the United States had to face the unpleasant dilemma of choosing between its political obligations under the French alliance and its economic interest in maintaining friendly relations with Great Britain. Alexander Hamilton's foreign policy torpedoed the alliance with France but preserved the benefits of peace with England.

The difficulties attending the choice arose from the fact that, taking the long view, both the United States and France had a common interest in breaking British hegemony on the high seas. France saw British commercial supremacy as the great bar to economic growth and prosperity for herself and for all other nations. She had signed a commercial treaty with the United States underwriting the principle of *free ships make free goods*. The Americans, during their war for independence, appealed to the nations of Europe to emancipate themselves from British commercial manacles by opening a free trade. Indeed, the maxim of freedom of the seas had been the sum and substance of American foreign policy. France, after her own revolution of 1789, called for the same principle.[4] As late as 1798 John Quincy Adams, in spite of his frenzied feelings against France, admitted that France had never ceased to pay homage to that principle although she had done violence to it in practice. It would be unwise, he said, to surrender the principle now for sometime in the future France might again support it.[5] Then progress might be made in limiting British domination on the high seas.

But the long term aim of freedom of the seas could not bind together what more immediate considerations pulled asunder. The economic tie between the two countries failed to become closer. England, not France, offered the credit and the manufactures to which Americans had become accustomed. Consequently, the alliance with France lacked the economic undergirding to give it strength.

The outbreak of war in February 1793 put the alliance under a strain it could not withstand. France did not call on the United States to assist in the defense of the West Indies because she knew the new nation, having only a weak navy, could render little aid. She also saw that if the United States remained neutral and thereby retained the freedom to send desperately needed produce to the beleaguered colonies and to France herself, the United States could give invaluable assistance. The United States could also open her ports to French privateers thereby giving them an opportunity to deal heavy blows at British shipping.

The question of privateers put the first serious strain on relations. France held that the treaty not only barred other countries from using American ports but granted the right to France. The United States held otherwise. French privateers could enter American ports but could not receive arms there and could not have their captures judged by French consular courts in the port cities.[6] France, anxious to protect the advantage she believed her treaty with the United States granted, deeply resented the American ruling.

The Jay Treaty reduced the alliance to nullity. Technically no treaty provision violated any part of the agreement with France, and, in fact, the Jay Treaty specifically stated that no part was to be so interpreted as to conflict with previous treaty obligations. Americans could argue that all French rights had been reserved. This argument not only failed to convince many Frenchmen but left many Americans, perhaps a majority, believing that the pro-British Federalists had been guilty of bad faith. The commercial treaty with France provided for the application of the principle of *free ships make free goods.* France held that this imposed the duty on the United States of upholding that principle against Great Britain. The Federalist controlled executive branch held that the United States could not possibly impose the rule on England and was under no treaty obligation to do so.

The French, quite understandably, viewed the surrender of the central principle of her treaty arrangements with the United States to the rulings of her mortal enemy as a barefaced betrayal.[7] Republicans in the United States described it in just such terms. The Republicans had logic and the spirit of faithful treaty observance on their side.

France responded to the final ratification of the Jay Treaty with a forthright announcement to James Monroe that the alliance with the United States was no longer in effect.[8] The French foreign minister, Delacroix, said he would send a special envoy to the United States to deliver the message. The Directory favored a declaration of war. James Monroe mustered the best arguments he could to delay hostilities. A declaration of war, he warned, would push the United States directly into the arms of England. France, he urged, should take into account the fact that she had a host of friends in the United States. In desperation he held out the hope that the coming presidential election might bring a member of the pro-French party into office. Monroe believed that his arguments saved his nation from an immediate opening of hostilities.

The complete turnabout in relations with France left the Republicans stranded on the shoals of defending a foreign nation with whom the United States was on the brink of war. They could now be accused of being the party of treason, the party that supported France even while that nation exacted a heavy toll of American shipping and threatened war.

Ironically, the very exuberance of their nationalism had led them into this uncomfortable position. Since 1789 they had underestimated the value of good relations with England and had resisted every concession to the former mother country. They did not see the importance of credit and they followed Madison in considering imports from England as luxuries and their own produce as England's necessity. They permitted their nationalism and limited understanding of economics to convince them that the United States could look John Bull straight in the eye and defy his vaunted power with immunity.

They did not miss the remarkable similarity between Hamilton's economic measures and British financial institutions nor the Federalists' admiration for British political institutions. Consequently, when the Federalists bent American neutrality to suit British policy, they readily concluded that the bending was unnecessary and resulted only from Federalist desires to link the United States to England and thereby make it easier for strong executive leadership backed by the rich and well born to exercise the real power and make the elected legislative bodies its tools.

To prevent such a perversion of the ideals of the American Revolution, the Republicans believed it necessary to resist close association with England and to yield no more to her dictates than those of other nations. France must be kept as a healthy counterpoise to British seduction. Arthur Campbell best summed up the Republican attitude after the election of 1800 when he wrote to James Madison that the United States could have an alliance with any country except England. An alliance with England, "or over intimate connection with the *Mother Country,* with the Queen of the Isles, and Mistress of the Ocean," he wrote, "might raise longings and discontent that neither Moses nor Aaron nor Jefferson the *Restorer* could satisfy." "Let us then," he continued, "embrace the present opportunity to claim the rights of the Neutral Flag; to have an injurious Treaty amended, to be moderate and just to individuals, but proud and united as a people, who know their equal rights, and can assert them."[9]

In their determination to free themselves of British ties and British commercial "manacles" the Republicans had too fondly embraced France, but they remained a proud people and they would resent French intrusions on their sovereignty.

Economic Ties to Great Britain and the French Alliance

On the eve of John Adams' taking office as President, Jefferson wrote to Madison:

> I do not believe Mr. A wishes war with France, nor do I believe he will truckle to England as servilly as has been done. If he assumes this front at once and shews that he means to attend to self respect & national dignity with both the nations, perhaps the depredations of both on our commerce may be amicably arrested.[10]

But Jefferson also believed that the new President should "begin first with those who first began with us, and by an example on them acquire a right to redemand the respect from which the other party has departed."

The Federalists knew the importance of the British credit facilities and British manufactures. They found less to criticize about British politics than they did the equalitarian and anti-clerical note of French political rhetoric. The Republican denunciations of the National Bank and the funding system and the Republicans' persistence in insisting on discriminatory duties against England frightened the Federalists. They bent American neutrality in favor of England because they believed that their economy dictated peace at almost any cost. Just as the Republicans feared that an alliance with England would undermine their own principles, so did the Federalists believe that a war with England would open the door to an alliance with France and French political heresies.

French ministers to the United States took no notice of the underlying economic forces that tied the new republic to Great Britain. They ascribed Federalist foreign policy to British intrigue and to the pro-British sympathies of Federalist leaders. Convinced that France was being betrayed by a small group of American leaders, they became increasingly bitter and their recommendations more desperate. In February, 1795, on gaining the first bits of information on the contents of the Jay Treaty, Jean Fauchet advised that the only solution would be to annex Louisiana and frighten the Americans into amity.[11] Fauchet attached great importance to the good relations with the United States and was quite willing to resort to hazardous methods. The building of a French empire continued to win his support, but he also recommended French support of Republicans in the election of 1796.[12]

Fauchet's successor, Pierre Adet, acted on the recommendations of Fauchet. In March 1796 he commissioned General Victor Collot to make a survey of the states west of the Alleghenies to determine the nature of the terrain from a military point of view. Collot started his survey at Pittsburgh, passed down the Ohio River, inspected the situation in Kentucky, and went up the Mississippi River. The Federalists learned of Collot's mission and sent an agent to watch him. They soon learned of Collot's boasts that the French would make reprisals for the Jay Treaty. Collot had warned that France might soon have a colony in the west, control the Mississippi River, and thereby hold the key to the door to the world market of the western states.[13] Such boasts were at the moment quite empty, for France could scarcely carry out such a venture in the face of the British fleet, but the Federalists, eager to discredit both France and the Republicans, made the most of the French talk of a new empire in Louisiana.

France, anxious to undermine the British cause everywhere, fell to the temptation of intervening in the internal politics of the United States. When Adet was appointed minister, he had been instructed to avoid meddling in American politics and to concentrate on winning the United States over to admitting French privateers and permitting the sale of prizes. Adet shortly became a rabid partisan who denounced the Hamiltonians and described President Washington as a mere tool of the British party.[14] His dispatches conveyed to his government a picture of a deeply divided nation. He watched the struggle over the Jay Treaty and advised his government that British money had led to its approval. The treaty, he said, would never have been ratified if France had publicly protested. In September 1796, on a visit to Boston, he urged the Republicans to support Jefferson, and in the final days of October, in an effort to influence the election in Pennsylvania, he made public a French decree ordering that neutral ships be treated in the same manner "as they shall suffer the English to treat them."[15] By this time both Adet and his government had concluded that the United States was to be influenced only by threats. Adet became bitter and denounced the Americans for their lack of gratitude. When he learned of Pinckney's appointment, he warned the French government that the United States could never be trusted. If they should propose certain treaties, Adet warned, "you will recall that they are like Greeks and beware of their presence." The Americans, he said, "know of no other virtues than love of money," "do not understand the prize of liberty, of honor, of glory" and "are prepared to traffic the interests of their allies like the vilest merchandize."[16]

This was the state of United States relations with France when Charles Cotesworth Pinckney arrived in Paris in December, 1796. James Monroe, dealt with harshly by the Federalists, greeted him cordially and introduced him to Foreign Minister Delacroix. Two days after the interview the Directory notified Pinckney that they would not receive a minister from the United States. Another few days passed and an agent of the Directory came to tell him of a decree that made it necessary for him to obtain the permission of the police to remain in the country. In a spirited fashion Pinckney claimed diplomatic immunity and announced that he would not leave until ordered to do so by the French foreign office.[17]

In the meantime he had an enlightening conference with Major J. C. Mountflorence who explained that France was bankrupt, that her campaign against neutral vessels was motivated by a desire for funds, and that, although much was made of the Jay Treaty, other neutral nations fared no better.[18] By the time Pinckney's letters reached Philadelphia conveying this information John Adams was getting ready to take over the presidency.

John Adams surveyed the domestic and international scene from his Olympian perch and saw the forces of civilization arrayed against the system of profligacy that threatened "to deluge the globe in blood and lay prostrate every public institution and every moral sentiment which renders human life in civilized society agreeable or even tolerable."[19] To him the rhetoric of the French Revolution was based on the false assumption that man was both inherently good and rational. Secondly, the rhetoric served to disguise the frightening aims of France for domination in world affairs. And, finally, much to his horror, too many Americans had been ensnared by the French sycophants who praised human nature while they acted on the premise that every man could be deluded.

Adams dismissed the idealism of the French Revolution as the bait set out to tempt weak minds. The bait had lured the soft headed for twenty years. A few weeks before his inauguration he replied to a resolution adopted by the clergy of Boston expressing confidence in him. "Too many individuals in our beloved town of Boston," he wrote, "have been infected with this infernal spirit of fanaticism and the bodies you mention [the clergy] have prevented the contagion from spreading to more."[20]

Adams was pleased by the expressions of good will from Thomas Jefferson in the weeks before he took office. He wrote that he had never questioned Jefferson's integrity and his love of country, but Jefferson's associations with the French supporters clearly disturbed him. To his friend Tristram Dalton he confided: "I may say to you that his patronage of Paine and Freneau and his entanglements with characters and politiks which have been pernicious are and have been a source of inquietude and anxiety to me as they must have been to you but I hope and believe that his advancement and his situation in the Senate, an excellent school, will correct him. He will have too many French about him to flatter him but I hope we can keep him steady. This is entre nous."[21]

"To a Frenchman the most important man in the world is himself and the most important nation is France. He thinks that France ought to govern all nations and that he ought to

govern France," Adams once observed.[22] Two months before
he took office he lamented "that our citizens have been so
little informed of the true temper and character of French
policy towards this country." "For twenty years," said Adams,
"many important facts have been concealed from them lest
they should conceive prejudices or entertain doubts of their
disinterested friendship and the whole character of their government since their revolution has been tinged with false
colours in the eyes of our people by French emissaries and
disaffected Americans."[23]

Adams' brutally realistic appraisal of the French had not
carried him over to a pro-British position. His nationalism
and his belief that imperialism was present in all human societies, including the British, kept him from good standing
in the pro-British circles. When a friend suggested that Hamilton had intrigued to prevent his becoming President, Adams
shrewdly observed that if it were true it was because "he
wishes for closer connections with Britain than he believes
me disposed to. This I know to be the case with the Essex
Junto."[24]

The most frightening aspect of the American political
scene to Adams was the development of parties attached to
Great Britain and France. "You may perceive," he wrote, "by
what has been said the different gradations of attachment
and aversion to me in different parties." "It all proceeds from
foreign attachment," he observed. To a nationalist, such as
Adams, no stronger evidence of the folly of mankind could
be offered: "The difference between France and England occasions the differences here. This is to me a frightful consideration." His pessimism carried him dangerously close to
complete despair. It seemed during the days of his darkest
forebodings that partiality for France or England had corrupted all save a very few. In fact, on March 10, after a few
days in the presidency, he confided: "I believe that Gerry and
I are the two most impartial men in this respect almost in
the Union." And before another year had passed he wondered
about Gerry.

With the fate of the nation in the hands of Adams, at least there was no danger of the nation betraying its own interests while under the illusion that a foreign government could be its generous friend. Nor did Adams' antipathy for France cause him to yield to a frustrating cynicism and let events take the course to war. He worked for peace, but he also perceived that to attain it he would have to play the dangerous game of assuming a belligerent posture.

He detested those who thought peace was to be secured by kowtowing. That is why he despised James Monroe. When his close friend Gerry suggested that Monroe had been dealt with unjustly by the previous administration, Adams replied that, as a member of the Senate, Monroe was so "dull heavy and stupid a fellow as he could be consistently with Malignity and Inveteracy perpetual." Concerning the appointment of Monroe, Adams observed, "A more unfit piece of wood to make a Mercury could not have been called from the Forest."[26]

Peace would be sought, he told Gerry, but not at the price of independence or national honor. On March 25, 1797, he wrote to General Knox:

> I have it much at heart to settle all disputes with France and nothing shall be wanting on my part to accomplish it Excepting a Violation of our faith and a Sacrifice of our honor. But old as I am, War is even to me less dreadful than Iniquity or deserved disgrace.[27]

Adams' policy consisted of negotiating on the one hand and, on the other, preparing the popular mind and the defenses of the country for war. The day before he took office he asked Jefferson if he would go to France as a special envoy. Jefferson declined, and within a few weeks Adams concluded that the refusal had been fortunate. In characteristic fashion he decided that it would have been degrading to national honor to send a man occupying such a high position.[28] Before the end of May he had completed arrangements for the sending of three envoys, Pinckney, John Marshall, and Elbridge Gerry.

On May 16 he delivered a message to a special session of Congress and reported alarming news from France. On the occasion of Monroe's departure the President of France, said Adams, had delivered a speech that had for its main purpose dividing the American people from their government. "Such attempts," he said, "ought to be repelled with a decision which shall convince France and the world that we are not a degraded people, humiliated under a colonial spirit of fear and sense of inferiority, fitted to be the miserable instruments of foreign influence, and regardless of national honor, character, and interest."[29]

To counteract the French belief that American commerce could be attacked with impunity Adams recommended the creation of a navy, provisions for convoys, and the arming of merchant ships. To prevent incursions at home he asked Congress to consider additions to the artillery and cavalry and the organizing, arming, and disciplining of the militia. To Jefferson and Madison the President's speech had the ring of a war message. Given the French decree of March 2, which Adams promised to make public, his stern tone was certainly warranted. That decree announced that neutral ships, carrying in whole or in part merchandise belonging to the enemy were to be seized. The decree specifically repudiated Article II of the Treaty of 1778 on the ground that the Jay Treaty granted concessions to Great Britain that made the original provision for "free ships make free goods" an intolerable limitation on French practice.

Adams did not act without giving careful consideration to the configuration of power in Europe. Early in May he had written to Gerry: "Your brief of the formidable position of France is very true as it appears at present, but intelligence of the surest kind which is not laid before the Public shows it to be hollow at home and abroad; in Spain, Holland, Italy, and even France itself." Gerry feared English bankruptcy and subsequent revolution, but Adams thought "she would be more dreadful to France after going through all the horrors that France has experienced than she is now."[30]

But by July 1 Adams expressed alarm because of the prospect of British defeat. He wrote to his friend Dalton:

The situation of the United States is uncommonly Critical. If a peace is made between France and England as it is already known to be made with the Roman Emperor, and France is not in a better temper, or Conducted by different Governors, this Country has before it one of the most alarming prospects it ever beheld.[31]

By the end of October the President had recovered his feeling of confidence. He shrewdly analyzed French policy in words almost identical with Talleyrand's description of that policy. France, he said, did not want war. He advised Secretary of State Pickering: "A Continued Appearance of Umbrage, and Continued Depredations on a weak defenceless Commerce, will be much more convenient for their Views."[32] There is no evidence in his voluminous correspondence that he ever changed this interpretation.

French depredations certainly warranted the strong language employed by the President. In an incomplete list of American ships taken by the French prepared by Secretary of State Pickering in June, 1797, no fewer than 316 American vessels appeared.[33] The encouragement given to privateering by the French government brought a swarm of French privateers to the West Indies. French officials authorized the capture of all neutral vessels bound to British ports.

On October 4, 1797 John Marshall and Elbridge Gerry arrived in France where Charles Cotesworth Pinckney joined them. Their instructions called for a new treaty and a settlement of American claims. When the story of a bid for a bribe to members of the Directory is set aside, and attention is focused on significant facts of the negotiation, then the basic positions of both the United States and France become clear. The Americans carried on negotiations over a period of five months. The original proposal for a bribe did not come up after the very earliest meetings with Talleyrand's agents. However much the American commissioners resented this request, the fact is that they continued their negotiations for months thereafter.

These facts emerged out of the negotiations. France clearly

did not want a war with the United States. Secondly, she laid down as a requirement for entering upon treaty negotiations that the United States grant a loan, the money to be used to finance the purchase of supplies from the United States.[34] Such a loan would in ordinary times have been good business, but in time of war a government loan to one belligerent could only result in a declaration of war by the other belligerent. The price that Talleyrand demanded then was not a loan but a full 180 degree shift in American policy that would involve her in war. Secretary of State Pickering clearly preferred war with France to peace and his denunciations of France glowed with the red heat of anger and political passion, but he approximated the truth when he said that France expected to impose a treaty on the United States in the same way she had forced small European neighbors at the point of her sword to accept treaties that reduced them to tools of France.[35]

The American position in these negotiations served notice to Talleyrand that he was dealing with a proud and unbending people. The commissioners rejected a loan on two grounds. Their instructions did not allow it and a loan could only result in a war with England.[36] They had come to protest American grievances against France, and they made their errand so clear that Talleyrand scolded them for overlooking the fact that France had grievances against the United States.

More important, confronted with the full implications of the French alliance, they stated politely but boldly why the United States must maintain peace with Great Britain. She could not give her consent to the French decree that stipulated that any ship carrying as any portion of its cargo any article originating in England should be deemed lawful prize and that any vessel which had entered a British port would be barred from entering a French port. "In possession of a rich, extensive, and unsettled country," the commissioners explained, "the labor of the United States is not yet sufficient for the full cultivation of its soil, and, consequently, but a very small portion of it can have been applied to manufactures." The American people, they said, could not readily change their economy from agriculture to manufactures "on the mere passing of a decree." "It is, therefore," they told Talleyrand, "scarcely possible for them to surrender their foreign commerce." And given the actual state of the world, it was difficult to believe that the supplies they needed could be "completely furnished, without the aid of England and its possessions."[37] They concluded with a statement that summed up the very basis of the foreign policy that Hamilton had put into operation:

A variety of other considerations, and especially the difficulties individuals must encounter in suddenly breaking old and forming new connexions, in forcing all their commerce into channels not yet well explored, in trading without a sufficient capital to countries where they have no credit, combine to render almost impossible an immediate dissolution of commercial intercourse between the United States and Great Britain.[38]

John Marshall and Charles Cotesworth Pinckney left Paris in March, but Elbridge Gerry remained because Talleyrand warned that his leaving would provoke an immediate rupture. Gerry divested himself of his official role as a representative of the United States. For the next several months he met with Talleyrand and exchanged notes with him frequently, but always with a clear understanding that he was acting in a private capacity. If the French foreign minister suffered any illusions that Gerry would allow his desire for peace to lead him into sacrificing American interests, Gerry soon disappointed him. Gerry defended the position of his country with considerable spirit. At the same time he urged the importance of France sending a minister to negotiate in the United States. Talleyrand, on May 26, agreed.[39] Then, on the following day, the French newspapers told of the publication of the XYZ papers.

Gerry's hopes crashed. In his letter to the President upon his return he observed that Talleyrand appeared "sincere and anxious to obtain a reconciliation." He had, noted Gerry, proposed an assumption of the debts due to American citizens, and he had withdrawn the proposition of a loan.[40] The publication of the XYZ papers, Gerry thought, had led Talleyrand to believe that the American people would be so resentful that negotiations were hopeless. Gerry concluded that France would still make peace.[41]

Talleyrand had cared little about a treaty in the early days of the negotiations. In the spring of 1798 he had written:

> It would be attended only with serious inconveniences to break at once with the United States, while our present situation, half friendly, half hostile is profitable to us, in that our colonies are still provisioned by the Americans and our cruisers enriched by captures made from them.[42]

Talleyrand played an insulting game up to the time that he became convinced that the game might very well prove costly. His threat of war should Gerry leave suggested that his aim was not a settlement but a continuation of the suspense so profitable to France at the moment. It suggested too that Talleyrand sought to divide the American people from their government. He had repeatedly sought to negotiate separately with Gerry, probably because, as John Quincy Adams, then at Berlin, thought, he wished to convince the Republicans in the United States that only their own executive and his party stood in the way of peace.[43] Whether he hoped to make an ally of the Republicans in the event of war as John Quincy Adams and William Vans Murray, representative at the Hague, concluded at the time, or whether he merely saw a division in the United States as strengthening his hand in diplomacy, makes little difference.[44] A friendly nation could scarcely expect to settle its difficulties amicably using these tactics.

Talleyrand did not command French policy. The Directory formulated the policy and left it to Talleyrand to implement. The United States must have seemed of minor importance to the Directory, for Europe presented more pressing dangers. To be sure French arms dominated the entire continent, but French military victories solved no problems. She had conquered in the name of liberty and human rights, but everywhere her conquering armies left hatred and disillusion. Those who had originally sympathized with the French call for a new order found that the French armies plundered and robbed in order to subsist and to replenish the ever empty treasury in Paris. Just as the Directory was the master of Talleyrand so were the French armies the masters of the Directory for it had no substantial popular support. It ruled with the permission of the armies who stood between its continued rule and its overthrow.

Great Britain, complete master of the seas by the summer of 1798, had managed to survive the greatest danger from popular unrest and financial crisis. The French knew only too well that she would strive to form new coalitions among the powers and that her finances and mastery of the seas were capable of rallying the great powers to a new effort. Herein lay one major explanation of French attempts to ruin the trade between Great Britain and the United States. It was one way to weaken England.[45] Many French leaders also contemplated an empire in the West Indies and the Mississippi Valley, but this was not a project that could be achieved while Great Britain ruled the seas. That many Americans came to expect a French invasion in 1798 only serves to show how fear had blotted out a realistic appraisal of their situation. The miserable showing of the French expedition to Ireland in 1796 should have put their fear to rest.

The French question set off one of the most dangerous political battles in all of American history. A deep distrust between Federalists and Republicans engulfed the country. To the extreme Federalists, men of the stripe of Timothy Pickering, Theodore Sedgwick, and Oliver Wolcott, the Republicans symbolized ignorance, political demagoguery, and a loyalty to France that superseded their loyalty to the United States. Extremist Republicans harbored equally dangerous suspicions of the pro-British and anti-Republican sentiments of the Federalists.

The Federalists quickly grasped the fact that hostile relations with France would weaken the Republicans who had become identified with that country. The Republican leaders saw this too, and, worried about the fate of their party, came to see in every Federalist measure an effort to provoke France and drive her into war so that the Republican party would lose all popularity as the party of treason.

The Republicans had long been opposed to an army and navy. They viewed these as too likely to be used to put down opposition at home. This view owed something to their dislike of the taxes that would be made necessary to equip and support an armed force. John Quincy Adams suggested the major factor when he ascribed the Republican opposition to defense measures to their "confounding the principles of internal government with those of external relations." "We dread the force of the executive power at home, and leave it therefore without any power to withstand force from abroad," he wrote. The difficulty, he said, lay in the faith "that men were susceptible of being governed by *reason alone.*" Young Adams warned that "whoever in this world does not choose to fight for his freedom, must turn Quaker or look out for a master."[46]

His father was neither a Quaker nor a fit subject for a French master, and he was prepared to use force. But he desired peace. After the release of the XYZ papers he renewed and extended his earlier call for defense measures, and Congress responded with appropriations for more frigates, more troops, and improved harbor defenses. Patriotism became the order of the day. Timothy Pickering and a host of Federalist speakers and writers whooped up the war cry. Parades and mass meetings sang *Hail Columbia* while the President denounced the French and warned against their allies in the United States. Well might Thomas Jefferson write: "At this moment all the passions are boiling over, and one who keeps himself cool and clear of the contagion, is so far below the point of ordinary conversation, that he finds himself insulted in every society."[47]

Jefferson had no illusions about France. John Quincy

Adams, in November, 1796, had written that he had no fears should Jefferson be elected for he felt confident "that he will inflexibly pursue the same general system of policy which is now established."[48] Immediately after the publication of the XYZ papers Jefferson wrote to Madison deploring the French conduct of the negotiations. The arguments of the French he considered "calculated to excite disgust & indignation in Americans generally, and alienation in the republicans particularly, whom they so far mistake as to presume an attachment to France and hatred of the Federal party, & not the love of their country, to be their first passion."[49]

James Madison, more introspective and so often fearful that he or his country might be wrong, in the summer of 1797 drafted a memorandum, apparently for his own use, entitled "Questions concerning the possible grounds of Dissatisfaction on the part of France against the United States."[50] In it he listed the many reasons why France might reasonably object to the Jay Treaty. It reflected his desire to believe the best about France. When he heard the first vague reports about the failure of the negotiations of Marshall, Pinckney, and Gerry, he feared that France might not leave us any choice but to go to war. The prospect of war frightened both him and the Republicans he had talked to in Norfolk. He wrote:

It seemed to give extreme uneasiness to the warm & well informed friends of Republicanism, who saw in a war on the side of England, the most formidable means put into the hands of her partizans for working the public mind towards Monarchy.[51]

Throughout the crisis Madison wrote of the degeneracy of the public councils and never appeared to feel any deep resentment toward the nation whose highhanded treatment had made Federalist measures possible.

But Madison was not alone in his inclination to emphasize the danger from the domestic political enemy. The Federalists welcomed the opportunity to attack the Republicans as the tools of a foreign power. In his excellent book, *The*

Presidency of John Adams, Stephen G. Kurtz has shown that
a considerable part of the Federalist party desired an army to
put down the dangers at home.[52] The Alien and Sedition Acts
constituted an effort to stamp out political opposition.

The new navy had just begun its campaign against French
privateers when Talleyrand on June 1 undertook to bring
about a change in policy by a memorandum to the Directory.
The firmness of Gerry, the reports from the United States indicating a determination to resist, and the complaints of
French merchants that the profitable trade with the United
States was being ruined had all worked toward convincing
Talleyrand that the mongrel peace could no longer be
sustained. Victor Du Pont returned from the United States
and landed at Bordeaux on July 3. Talleyrand turned to him
for arguments with which to persuade the Directory of the
necessity of making peace. On May 31, prior to leaving the
United States, Du Pont had a long interview with Jefferson
who had urged upon him that French practices were driving
the United States into the arms of England. Du Pont wrote a
bold reply to Talleyrand citing the abuses committed by
French privateers in the Antilles, how the owners of privateers
sat on the tribunals that heard prize cases, and how French
privateers carried on depredations in American waters. The
great danger was, said Du Pont, that the United States and
Great Britain were already consulting about a joint expedition against the French and Spanish colonies to the southward. Du Pont's letter strengthened the hand of Talleyrand.[53]

Before he ever received Du Pont's report Talleyrand dis-
patched Pichon to consult with William Vans Murray at the
Hague about negotiations. Pichon assured the American minister that France would receive an American minister and
treat him with the respect due a representative of an independent nation. Word of this probably reached John Adams
sometime in late September. Now arrived another letter from
Richard Codman of Boston, who resided in Paris, to Harrison
Gray Otis, prominent Federalist Congressman, stating that
Du Pont's memoir had convinced the Directory that France

could no longer delay coming to terms.[54] Early in October Elbridge Gerry landed at Nantasket Roads and found himself an object of contempt. No one would deign to speak to him. Federalists became uneasy when they saw him visiting frequently in the home of John Adams. Gerry very wisely refrained from public pronouncements but privately he urged the President that France would make peace.

Rumors of a French conciliatory gesture had reached James Madison early in June. By late summer the new direct taxes made themselves felt and sapped the prospect of war of some of its glory. On August 1 Nelson destroyed the French fleet at Aboukier Bay and deprived Napoleon of any striking power he may have had. Fear of a French attack had sharply declined by the close of 1798.

Adams now found that he had to deal with intrigue in his own cabinet. Alexander Hamilton, operating behind the scenes, had drafted the papers presented by certain members of the cabinet. In the summer of 1798 he sought the position of second in command to George Washington, and he looked forward to achieving glory on the field of battle. Secretary of War McHenry made several appointments on the same day, including that of Hamilton, and placed Hamilton's name first on the list. Adams signed the appointments whereupon McHenry argued that as Hamilton's name appeared first, Hamilton outranked the others. Adams made it clear that he had signed believing "that the nomination and appointment would give Hamilton no command at all, nor any rank before any Major Gen." At the close of his letter to the Secretary of War he warned: "There has been too much intrigue in this business both with Gen. Washington & me."[55] He resented the attempt to use the name of Washington in order to impose decisions on himself and warned that although he was President by only three votes that as long as he shouldered the responsibilities of the chief executive he would insist on the right to make the decisions.

Unlike several members of his official family Adams was determined to arrange a peaceful settlement if that were possible. In October of 1798 he carefully weighed what he should say in his forthcoming message to Congress. He continued to hold to the position that he would not send another minister to France without full assurance that he would be properly received, but he also wished to avoid any unnecessary delay. He wrote to Secretary of State Pickering: "But the question is, whether in the speech, the president may not say that in order to keep open the channels of negotiation, it [sic] his intention to nominate a minister to the French republick, who may be ready to embark for France, as soon as he or the president shall receive from the directory, satisfactory assurances, that he shall be received and entitled to all the prerogatives and privileges of the general law of nations, & that a minister of equal rank & powers shall be appointed and commissioned to treat with him." He went on to name several possible choices and noted that none of them have "been marked as obnoxious to the French."[56]

Adams had spent the summer in Quincy and had been deeply worried over the prolonged illness of Abigail. He delayed his return to Philadelphia until the last possible moment. Away from the immediate pressures exerted by those who were anxious for war he had been able to reach his own conclusions. On his return to Philadelphia the same small group of cabinet members drafted a message to Congress in a way that infuriated him. Secretary of the Treasury Wolcott, probably after consultation with Hamilton, composed the two paragraphs on foreign policy. These closed the door to negotiations in their original form. Adams insisted on a revision that kept the door slightly ajar.[57] The President in his own draft had gone much further. In this he proposed that the Senate agree to the appointment of a new envoy.

The proponents of war won only a temporary victory. On February 18 Adams made his own decision to nominate William Vans Murray minister plenipotentiary to France. The following day he wrote to George Washington: "This I ventured to do upon the strength of a letter from Talleyrand himself giving declarations in the name of his government that any minister plenipotentiary from the United States shall be received according to the condition at the close of my message to congress of the 21st of June last. . . ."[58] A month later he wrote a letter in which he put down his reflections on the reactions to his stepping out ahead of his political advisers. "If any one entertains the idea, that because I am a president of three votes only, I am in the power of a party, they shall find I am no more so, than the constitution forces upon me."[59] The President clearly had his fighting spirits up, and promised that he would resist party pressure to the bitter end.

But it was not only the Federalists he would resist. In his letter to Washington he voiced contempt for those who engaged in "babyish and womanly blubbering for peace." "There is not much sincerity in the cant about peace," he said, "those who snivell for it now, were hot for war against Great Britain a few months ago & would be now if they saw a chance." He concluded by decrying the irresponsibility of political parties who would push for either peace or war as one or the other suited electioneering purposes.

The President appointed Oliver Ellsworth of the Supreme Court and William R. Davie, a former governor of North Carolina, to assist Minister Murray to carry on the negotiations. The opposition sought to kill the project by delaying their departure, but Adams patiently insisted and they left from Newport, Rhode Island on November 3. They arrived in Paris in March where Napoleon Bonaparte was now First Consul. Joseph Bonaparte served as president of the French commission. The instructions to the American envoys called for full payment for damages suffered at the hands of French privateers. Secondly, the instructions called for a new treaty which would change the provisions of the treaty of amity and commerce as regards the right of each nation to take its prizes to the ports of the other and which forbade the outfitting in their ports of privateers belonging to an enemy of either nation. Finally, the obnoxious alliance providing that the United States must aid France in her defense of her possessions in the new world and the consular convention of 1779 giving French consuls unusual powers in American cities were to be abrogated. France held that the old treaties were still in force and sought to set as a price for their abrogation the cancellation of all claims on the ground that she was only liable to pay damages if those treaties were still in effect. The final convention, signed amid a scene of festivity in the home of Joseph Bonaparte, provided for a suspension of both the old treaties and all claims by both parties, and included articles incorporating the traditional doctrine of neutral rights. Napoleon, with an eye to future wars and hopeful of getting the Americans to take a stand against Great Britain, insisted on the neutral rights provisions.

When Adams presented the Senate with the convention in December, 1800, it failed to get the necessary two-thirds vote but he resubmitted it. This time it was ratified but only after the clauses suspending the old treaties and settlement of spoliation claims had been deleted. Bonaparte then ratified the treaty subject to further revisions, the abandoning of claims by both sides. This was accepted by the Senate in December, 1801. Americans recovered only a small part of their losses but this was a low price to pay for emancipation from the unpopular alliance. Their real gain lay in the abrogation of the old alliance.

NOTES

1. Charles Cotesworth Pinckney to Secretary of State Timothy Pickering, December 10, 1796, *American State Papers Foreign Relations*, Vol. II, p. 5.

2. Major Mountflorence's report, given to General Pinckney, December 19, 1796, *ibid.*, pp. 8-9.

3. *Ibid.*, John Quincy Adams to the Secretary of State, February 17, 1797, p. 14.

4. John Quincy Adams to the Secretary of State, October 31, 1797, *ibid.*, p. 251.

5. *Writings of John Quincy Adams,* ed. Worthington Chauncey Ford (New York: The Macmillan Company, 1913), Vol. II, p. 286.

6. Thomas Jefferson to Gouverneur Morris, August 7, 1793, *American State Papers,* Vol. I, pp. 167-171.

7. Monroe to Pickering, February 16, 1796, quoted by Stanislaus Hamilton, *The Writings of James Monroe* (New York: G. P. Putnam's Sons, 1898-1903), II, pp. 454-456.

8. *Ibid.*

9. Arthur Campbell to James Madison, March 23, 1801, James Madison Papers.

10. Thomas Jefferson to James Madison, January 22, 1797. James Madison Papers.

11. Fauchet to Commissioner of Foreign Relations, February 4, 1795, "Correspondence of the French Ministers to the United States, 1791-1797," ed. F. J. Turner, *Annual Report of the American Historical Association for the year 1903*, Vol. II, pp. 559-571. Hereafter cited as "Correspondence of French Ministers to the U. S."

12. For a discussion of Fauchet's recommendations see Alexander De Conde, *Entangling Alliance: Politics and Diplomacy under George Washington* (Durham, N. C.: Duke University Press, 1958), pp. 421-422.

13. *Ibid.*, pp. 446-449.

14. *Ibid.*, p. 426.

15. Stephen G. Kurtz, *The Presidency of John Adams: The Collapse of Federalism 1795-1800* (Philadelphia: University of Pennsylvania Press, 1957), pp. 125-132.

16. Adet to Commissioner of Foreign Relations, October 3, 1796, "Correspondence of French Ministers to the U. S.," pp. 950-952.

17. Charles Cotesworth Pinckney to Secretary of State Pickering, December 20, 1796, *American State Papers Foreign Relations*, Vol. II, pp 7-8.

18. Major J. C. Mountflorence to C. C. Pinckney, December 18, 1796, *American State Papers Foreign Relations*, Vol. II, pp. 8-9.

19. John Adams to Dr. Lathrop, February 20, 1797, *Letterbook*, Microfilm copies of Adams Family Papers.

20. *Ibid.*

21. John Adams to Tristram Dalton, January 19, 1797, *Letterbook*, Adams Family Papers.

22. John Adams to General Knox, March 25, 1797, *ibid.*

23. John Adams to Samuel Griffin, January 19, 1797, *ibid.*

24. John Adams to Dr. Welsh, March 10, 1797, *ibid.*

25. *Ibid.*

26. John Adams to Elbridge Gerry, May 30, 1797, *ibid.*

27. John Adams to General Knox, March 25, 1797, *ibid.*

28. *Ibid.*

29. *The Works of John Adams*, ed. Charles Francis Adams, Vol. IX, p. 114.

30. John Adams to Elbridge Gerry, May 3, 1797, *Letterbook*, Adams Family Papers.

31. John Adams to Tristram Dalton, July 1, 1797, *ibid.*

32. John Adams to Secretary of State Pickering, October 31, 1797, *ibid.*

33. Secretary of State Pickering to John Adams, June 21, 1797, *Report of the Secretary of State respecting the depredations committed on the commerce of the United States, American State Papers Foreign Relations*, Vol. II, pp. 28-63.

34. John Adams to Congress, June 5, 1798, transmitting communications from envoys at Paris, Enclosure A dated March 2, 1798, *American State Papers Foreign Relations*, Vol. II, pp. 185-188.

35. Timothy Pickering to John Adams, January 18, 1799, transmitting *Report of the Secretary of State on the transactions relating to the United States and France, since the last communication to Congress on that subject, American State Papers Foreign Relations*, Vol. II, p. 231.

36. John Adams to Congress, June 5, 1798, transmitting communications from envoys in Paris, Enclosure A dated March 2, 1798, *American State Papers Foreign Relations*, Vol. II, p. 187.

37. John Adams to Congress, June 18, 1798, transmitting communications from envoys to the French republic, Enclosure, "The Ministers Plenipotentiary and Envoys Extraordinary from the United States to the French republic to the Minister of Exterior Relations," *ibid.*, p. 198.

38. *Ibid.*

39. John Adams to Congress, January 18, 1799, transmitting correspondence of Elbridge Gerry, Gerry to Secretary of State, October 1, 1798, p. 206.

40. *Ibid.*, p. 207.

41. *Ibid.*

42. James Alton James, "French Opinion as a Factor in Preventing War between France and the United States," *American Historical Review*, XXX (October, 1924), p. 52.

43. In a letter to his father, John Quincy Adams warned that France was determined to go to war with the government of the United States and expected "to derive support from a part of the American people." He believed that they expected to form a southern republic. He acknowledged that he had formerly held the view that they had no idea of sending an army to America. He wrote: "But various circumstances now lead me to a different opinion, and with respect to the marine, they are preparing to turn all their exertions towards it, as may be collected clearly from the pamphlet of Theremin which I sent you a few days ago." John Quincy Adams to John Adams, April 3, 1797, *The Writings of John Quincy Adams*, Vol. II, pp. 155-156.

44. J. Q. Adams to William Vans Murray, April 19, 1798, *ibid.*, pp. 278-279.

On April 27, 1798 John Quincy Adams wrote to William Vans Murray: "It is no doubt very apparent that *at present* they prefer this mongrel condition between peace and war, in which they plunder us as enemies and we continue defencless [sic] as friends, to a state of direct and open hostility, in which they could injure us very little more, perhaps not so much, and in which we could do some harm to them." *Ibid.*, p. 281.

45. "It seems to be understood that the French government have determined to arrest and intercept all our commerce to and from the ports under the dominion of Great Britain. I have conversed with several intelligent men here, engaged in the public affairs at this time upon the subject. They do not hesitate in conversation with me to avow that they approve this policy; they say that the loss of the American commerce will

compel Great Britain to make peace." J. Q. Adams to John Adams, February 16, 1797, *The Writings of John Quincy Adams*, Vol. II, p. 121.

46. J. Q. Adams to William Vans Murray, July 22, 1798, *The Writings of John Quincy Adams*, Vol. II, p. 344.

47. Thomas Jefferson to James Lewis, Jr., May 9, 1798, *The Works of Thomas Jefferson*, ed. Paul Leicester Ford (New York: G. P. Putnam's Sons, 1894), Vol. VII, p. 250.

48. J. Q. Adams to Joseph Pitcairn, December 2, 1796, *The Writings of John Quincy Adams*, II, p. 42.

49. Thomas Jefferson to James Madison, April 6, 1798, Papers of James Madison.

50. James Madison, "Questions concerning the possible grounds of Dissatisfaction on the part of France against the United States," Papers of James Madison.

51. James Madison to Thomas Jefferson, January 21, 1798, Papers of James Madison.

52. Stephen G. Kurtz, *The Presidency of John Adams,* p. 314.

53. James Alton James, "French Opinion as a Factor in Preventing War between France and the United States," *American Historical Review*, XXX (October, 1924), p. 53.

54. Samuel Eliot Morison, "Du Pont, Talleyrand, and the French Spoliations," *Massachusetts Historical Society Proceedings*, Vol. XLIX (1915-16), p. 76, fn. 3.

55. John Adams to Secretary of War James McHenry, August 29, 1798, Adams Family Papers, *Letterbook.*

56. John Adams to Secretary of State Timothy Pickering, October 20, 1798, Adams Family Papers, *Letterbook.*

57. *The Works of John Adams,* ed. Charles Francis Adams, Vol. IX, p. 131, fn. 1.

58. John Adams to George Washington, February 19, 1799, Adams Family Papers, *Letterbook.*

59. John Adams to Attorney General Charles Lee, March 29, 1799, Adams Family Papers, *Letterbook.*

Jefferson and Madison
Formulate Foreign Policy
VIII

HISTORIANS, pointing to the modest changes that ensued in domestic policies, usually reject Jefferson's judgment that his election constituted a revolution. Jefferson's own yardstick, a change in attitude and spirit, does justify the term. It was a revolution in terms of a buoyant spirit unencumbered by traditional fatalism. Jefferson expressed the new attitude as he observed the beginnings of the French Revolution: "I have so much confidence in the good sense of man, and his qualifications for self-government that I am never afraid of the issue where reason is left free to exert her force."

The change from Federalism to Republicanism initiated a new approach to foreign policy of notable significance. Whereas Hamilton was distinguished by a tough-minded realism, by prudence, by a disciplining of the national spirit, and by sober calculation of available power, Jefferson and Secretary of State James Madison exhibited an assertiveness, a keen sensitivity to presumed slights, and a full confidence in the nation's capacity to defend its interests and uphold justice. Hamilton and the Federalists started their formulations with a recognition of the existing system of international relations and were willing to work within the framework of current practice. Jefferson and Madison began by rejecting existing realities and sought to implement an ideal.

To understand Jefferson and Madison in foreign affairs one has to begin by making their full faith in the natural rights political theory central to their approach. In every society man was endowed with the natural rights of life, liberty, and the pursuit of happiness. The ideal government was one which served to uphold these rights and the ideal citizen was one who jealously guarded his rights which rested in the natural order of the universe and were above existing man-made contrivances. Only in the United States had the ideal been transformed into practice and embodied in political institutions. This system had its counterpart in international relations. A nation possessed rights that had their origin in the natural order, and these were no less rights because the existing system ignored them. It was the first duty of an enlightened citizen and of an enlightened nation to uphold these rights against the forces of darkness.

Thereby entered the moralistic approach to foreign policy. What was right and justifiable was to be determined by standards derived from an ideal and not by the standards of existing systems. With it entered the imperious assumption that American concepts of what was right and wrong possessed a universal validity. This is what made the American approach to foreign relations unique and in the light of this we better understand both its strength and weaknesses.

The attitude expressed itself spontaneously and Americans never found it necessary to explain its intellectual basis. An interesting illustration of the approach is found in the report of a committee of Congress drafted in 1803 when it was proposed that two million dollars be appropriated for the purchase of the Floridas. The committee observed:

The Government of the United States is differently organized from any other in the world. Its object is the happiness of man; its policy and its interest, to pursue right by right means. War is the great scourge of the human race, and should never be resorted to but in cases of the most imperious necessity. A wise government will avoid it, when its views can be attained by peaceful measures. Princes fight for glory, and the blood and the treasure of their subjects is the price they pay. In all nations the people bear the burden of war, and in the United States the people rule.

High purpose and selfish material interests were thereby blended into foreign policy. The upholder of the higher law inevitably became the uncompromising defender of national interests without suffering any wracking doubts concerning the identity of national interests and international justice. Jefferson and Madison gave expression to widely held views and their approach to foreign policy became the American approach that found its culmination in the moralizing of Woodrow Wilson at Versailles and Cordell Hull's moral and legalistic expositions in behalf of an ideal international order based on law rather than force.

Any profound questioning of the approach was to be postponed until the middle of the twentieth century, but John Quincy Adams' perceptive powers diagnosed the weaknesses as applied to domestic affairs at an early date. Asked for his evaluation of Jefferson, he wrote:

Jefferson is one of the great men whom this country has produced, one of the men who has contributed largely to the formation of our national character—to much that is good and to not a little that is evil in our sentiments and manners. His Declaration of Independence is an abridged Alcoran of political doctrine, laying open the first foundations of civil society; but he does not appear to have been aware that it also laid open a precipice into which the slave-holding planters of his country sooner or later must fall. With the Declaration of Independence on their lips, and the merciless scourge of slavery in their hands, a more flagrant image of human inconsistency can scarcely be conceived than one of our Southern slaveholding republicans. Jefferson has been himself all his life a slaveholder, but he has published opinions so blasting to the very existence of slavery, that, however creditable they may be to his candor and humanity, they speak not much for his prudence or his forecast as a Virginian planter. The seeds of the Declaration of Independence are yet maturing. The harvest will be what West, the painter, calls the terrible sublime.[1]

To these opinions we may add a portion of a letter written by Jefferson to Albert Gallatin only a year later. The Missouri Compromise debate struck Jefferson as an instance where the old Federalist politicians used the slavery issue as a facade for gaining control so that they could put through their favorite measures. Should the northern majority press its advantage, said Jefferson, the South would face the question of its very existence for Congress then would extinguish slavery. And should this take place, he warned "all the whites south of the Potomac and Ohio must evacuate their States, and most fortunate those who can do it first."[2]

Such is the human dilemma that wracks men's souls, but the soul of Jefferson appears to have escaped the wracking. Observing the record of his two administrations, one is prompted to say that in the realm of foreign affairs he made himself the trumpet of an almost chauvinistic nationalism, practiced a policy of unilateralism that paid scant attention to the legitimate interests of other nations, and in the course of carrying out his policy overrode domestic minority interests with a vigor that left deep scars. This is not to condemn him for his inconsistency or to damn the actions themselves, for it is part of the human irony that in terms of the nation's welfare he acted wisely indeed.

The first problem faced by Jefferson was that of the Barbary pirates, who for years had looted merchant ships. The European powers solved the difficulty by paying tribute, a practice that the Federalists adopted. Jefferson rejected this procedure as a reflection on national honor although he did agree to abide by John Adams' arrangement to pay Algiers $30,000 per annum for three years.

Tripoli, whose Bashaw had recently plundered American ships, remained to be subdued. On May 15, 1801 Jefferson put two rhetorical questions before the cabinet: "Shall the squadrons now at Norfolk be ordered to cruise in the Mediterranean?" and "What shall the object of the cruise be?" Two weeks later the squadron set sail. It captured a Tripolitan cruiser, but no decisive action came in 1801.[3]

In 1802 the old problem raised its head again. The Emperor of Morocco added insult to injury by ordering the American consul to leave the country. Jefferson earnestly proposed another naval expedition, but this time the objections of Secretary of Treasury Albert Gallatin in regard to the cost led to an abandonment of the proposal. But the following year Jefferson had his way. Two frigates, the *Constitution* and the *Philadelphia,* accompanied by several brigs and schooners sailed forth under the command of Edward Preble. Morocco came to terms, but action against Tripoli ended in a temporary disaster. The *Philadelphia* ran aground, and the Tripolitans arrested the crew. Jefferson decided at once on a naval expedition strong enough to rescue the prisoners and pound the unruly pirates into submission.

The American representatives, Robert Livingston in Paris and Levett Harris at St. Petersburg, made the mistake of seeking a peaceful solution by appealing for the diplomatic aid of the two European powers. Jefferson held them guilty of "begging alms in every court of Europe." "This self-degradation is the more unpardonable as, uninstructed and unauthorized, they have taken measures which commit us by moral obligations which cannot be disavowed," the President wrote.[4] To Jefferson's relief the European governments ignored the appeals, and the following year his nation's honor was vindicated.

A greatly strengthened squadron subjected the Tripolitan towns to a chastising bombardment, and a daring overland expedition led by William Eaton accomplished what Jefferson so much desired. The adventurous Eaton, a former army officer, had been commissioned to bring about an overthrow of the ruler of Tripoli and to reinstate his exiled brother. Eaton learned that his candidate for the throne had fled to Upper Egypt. Undiscouraged he set out to find him and finally brought him to Alexandria. With an "army" of Greeks,

Italians, and Arabs he recruited along the way, Eaton crossed the Libyan desert and occupied the town of Derne. In all probability he would have succeeded in carrying out the daring scheme, but by this time the American peace commissioners negotiated a treaty and ordered Eaton to withdraw. The treaty, highly favorable, brought about peace. The American prisoners, however, were only released after a payment of $60,000.

It is the Louisiana Purchase that earned Jefferson his greatest claim to being the grand agrarian imperialist. In the light of the developments in the Mississippi Valley and in Europe that had their culmination in that great diplomatic victory, probably no president would have pursued a different course.

The Pinckney Treaty of 1795, with its opening of the Mississippi and its granting of the right of deposit at New Orleans, led to the rapid growth of an economic interest in the Spanish colonies near the mouth of the river. Thanks to wartime demands in the West Indies and Europe, New Orleans had become a significant entrepot. Flour, cotton, sugar, iron ore, cordage, lead, tobacco, and furs passed down the river where they were transported to sea-going vessels and carried to world markets. In 1801 the value of these commodities totalled $1,095,412. More than 73,000 barrels of flour came down the river, most of it on flatboats from Kentucky and Tennessee. Some 550 American-owned boats manned by American crews engaged in the traffic.[5]

In 1803 the river provided the chief outlet to market for the goods produced by the 900,000 Americans living in the Trans-Appalachian states. By the turn of the century the interest transcended this section of the country. In the words of Arthur P. Whitaker, the United States had become "Mississippi minded." The East also had an interest for a prosperous West bought eastern manufactures. By 1802 seventy-four American ships sailed from New Orleans to other ports in the United States. That this Mississippi interest would be given up by Americans in either the East or West is difficult to believe, and it played a major role in the final days of the Paris negotiations.

The French government had long been interested in Louisiana. Before 1763 the great wilderness beyond the Mississippi belonged to France. Spain acquired it at the end of the Seven Years' War when she refused to make peace unless France promised some compensations. Some Frenchmen criticized the decision but Louisiana aroused but little interest again until 1787 when the controversy between the United States and Spain directed French attention to it.

From this time forth French representatives in the United States did their best to awaken the government at home to an appreciation of the possibilities of building an empire in the Carribbean based on the Mississippi Valley. Eléonore François Elic Moustier, Minister to the United States, presented the French foreign office with a 330 page memoir outlining the arguments in favor of recovering Louisiana.[6] This impressive document pointed to the great commercial advantages for France in having an area which could supply its highly prized colonies of Guadaloupe and Martinique with the goods they needed. The political advantages to France seemed no less important. Spain, too weak to defend the area itself, would involve its ally, France, and thereby bring the nation into conflict with its other ally, the United States. Thereby the latter would be forced to fall back on Great Britain. Finally, the Americans and the many French settlers at the mouth of the river would welcome France for they believed that France would inject new life into the colony and develop New Orleans into a flourishing commercial center.

Moustier's enlightening brief probably furnished the future advocates of an American empire with the necessary information and arguments. In 1793 Genêt, who had written his own instructions, organized expeditions against the Spanish colonies to the south and west, but his boldness made him *persona non grata* with the Washington administration and brought about his recall. When the Jacobins took over control in Paris, problems at home were too pressing to allow them to give any attention to remote areas in the new world, but on the accession of the Directory to power the recovery of Louisiana became one of the lodestars of French diplomacy.

Efforts to have Spain cede the territory began with the negotiations of the Treaty of Basle in the spring of 1795. Charles Delacroix and Talleyrand, successive foreign ministers, continuously instructed their representatives in Madrid to convince the Spanish that Louisiana in the hands of France would provide the best possible barrier against British and American expansion.[7]

It remained for Napoleon to close the deal. On October 1, 1800 the Treaty of San Ildefonso transferred Louisiana to France in return for a Spanish kingdom based on territory in Napoleon's hands in Italy, plus six warships. When peace was established in Europe in 1802 by the Treaty of Amiens, Napoleon turned his attention to building his empire in the new world. The program began with a campaign to reestablish French control in Santo Domingo where the former Negro slaves, under the leadership of Toussaint Louverture, had established an independent republic.

A French army of 20,000 under General Leclerc quickly subdued the local government only to be decimated by yellow fever in the ensuing months. The failure in Santo Domingo led to the postponement of the occupation of Louisiana.

In October, 1802 Spain issued the orders for the transfer of Louisiana to Napoleon and Napoleon made ready an expedition under General Victor to occupy the newly acquired territory. In the last minute the launching base was transferred fom Dunkirk to Helvoet Sluys, near Rotterdam. Before the expedition was ready, the winter season had embedded it in ice.[8] In the early spring there was a further delay when a British squadron patrolled the coast. Finally, on the April day when the French were ready to sail, a courier arrived announcing the sale of Louisiana to the United States.

Historians have differed as to what was the decisive factor in Napoleon's decision. The failure in Santo Domingo, the recently arrived information from the United States that military preparations were underway, and the prospect of an early renewal of the war in Europe and the consequent need of Napoleon for funds, have all been cited as factors. The early renewal of war appears to have been the most weighty. If so, then it may be said, as Samuel Flagg Bemis has written, that once again Europe's distress worked to the United States' gain.[9] Irving Brant, however, gives great weight to James Madison's skillful brandishing of a threat of war.

The grand transaction had been known to Jefferson for some time. In November, 1801 Rufus King, United States minister in London, sent James Madison a copy of the treaty. Jefferson's immediate reaction was one of calmness, but in April, 1802 he wrote a letter to Robert R. Livingston, minister to France, stating in clear and bold terms his views of French control of Louisiana. "There is on the globe one spot, the possessor of which is our natural and habitual enemy," Jefferson declared. Reviewing the importance of the Mississippi River as an "outlet for the produce of three-eighths of our territory," he saw no other alternative, should France take control of New Orleans, but to "marry ourselves to the British fleet," build a navy, and "make the first cannon, which shall be fired in Europe, the signal for tearing up any settlement she may have made. . . ."[10]

Robert Livingston set energetically to work to dissuade the French and, failing that, to protect the rights which the United States gained in the Pinckney treaty. When he approached Talleyrand on the question of the cession, Talleyrand rebuked him in tones bristling with hostility. Livingston then prepared a memoir setting forth the disadvantages to France should she take possession of Louisiana and circulated copies among French officials. The American minister received instructions from Secretary of State Madison that he should seek to purchase the Floridas and New Orleans. Livingston did not know that Spain had refused to include the Floridas so he approached the French with the proposition.

In October, 1802 occurred an event of marked importance, the suspension of the right of deposit at New Orleans by

Spain. Both Jefferson and the American people assumed that France was responsible. Their attitude toward France changed from passive hostility to a belligerent demand for action. On February 16, 1803 Senator Ross, of Pennsylvania, introduced a set of resolutions authorizing the President to call out 50,000 troops and seize New Orleans.

The dispatches of the French *chargé d'affaires* in Washington, Louis A. Pichon, reported the increasing hostility toward France since the news of Louisiana first became known.[11] After the suspension of the right of deposit, James Madison warned Pichon that short of definite assurances from France that American rights would be respected, there was likelihood of war. On January 14, 1803 Madison bluntly told Pichon that anything short of a change of boundaries that would free the United States of foreign control of the lower reaches of the Mississippi, would be unsatisfactory.[12] Madison made a bid for purchasing the Floridas, stating that the free navigation of the rivers entering into the gulf were essential for "the very existence of the United States." He expressed the hope, in careful diplomatic language, that France would not push the United States into a war. Pichon warned the French foreign office that popular demand would drive the administration into an alliance with England and into war at the first opportunity.[13]

In January, 1803 Jefferson appointed James Monroe as Minister Plenipotentiary and Extraordinary to France and Spain, a move aimed at assuring the turbulent spirits in the West that the administration would do all in its power to protect their interests. Monroe did not sail until March 2 and did not reach Paris until April 12, the day after Livingston had received Napoleon's offer to sell Louisiana to the United States. During the next week Monroe and Livingston haggled casually over the price. The treaty provided that the United States should pay $11,250,000 plus another $3,750,000 with which France would pay American claims.

No uncertainty clouded the joyous reception of the news of the purchase of Louisiana in the United States. Both Jefferson and Madison approved of the transaction without any reservation, but the President at first held the opinion that it would be necessary to amend the Constitution giving the federal government specific authority to acquire new territory, to incorporate its people as citizens and admit it to statehood. Jefferson, long time advocate of a strict interpretation of the Constitution, hesitated to revamp his approach to fit the needs of the hour although his colleagues, James Madison and Albert Gallatin, expressed the opinion that the Constitution already provided the necessary power. In August a letter from Livingston warned that Napoleon was on the verge of changing his mind whereupon Jefferson concluded that "the less we say about constitutional difficulties respecting Louisiana the better." Still, he thought it would be best if some amendment were worked out regarding citizenship and statehood but the President dropped this, too, after his cabinet held it unnecessary.[14]

Spain had ample reason to protest. She had consented to the cession in considerable part because France would provide a buffer state against American expansion. Now the Floridas were encircled by the United States and Mexico lay exposed to the Americans. Carlos Yrujo, Spain's minister in Washington, felt especially sensitive for he had personally advocated cession to France. He protested that France could not transfer Louisiana except with Spain's approval and then went on to argue that Napoleon had not fulfilled the conditions laid down in the Treaty of San Ildefonso concerning the Kingdom of Etruria and therefore the transfer to France of Louisiana was invalid.

Madison found no difficulty in demolishing these arguments, at least to his own satisfaction. The promise not to cede, he noted, was not in the Spanish-French treaty and Spain, moreover, had not chosen to inform the United States earlier. Consequently, he concluded, the United States had made the purchase in good faith. As far as the Kingdom of Etruria was concerned, he replied to Yrujo, that territory was now in the hands of the Spanish and the fact that Great

Britain and Russia refused diplomatic recognition did not alter the case. Yrujo understandably charged Madison with bad faith, but he could scarcely have expected the United States to have been deterred from achieving so great an object by essentially squeamish objections. Madison gave the matter little thought, only being concerned that Spain might gain support from either France or England. Napoleon had already accepted a first payment and was only concerned about getting the remainder as soon as possible. England had no reason for supporting Spain. Had the Spanish government declined to complete the actual transfer to France, Jefferson, with the approval of his cabinet, was ready to use force.

The special session of Congress commenced in October and after only two days of debate the Senate ratified the treaty by a vote of 22 to 7. Some Federalists raised objections but no serious opposition developed. On December 20, 1803, New Orleans was in a festive spirit. The colony had been transferred to France on November 30. General James Wilkinson and William C. C. Claiborne, the governor of the Mississippi territory, accepted the new territory in behalf of the United States. A party arranged by the French prefect lasted from three in the afternoon until nine the next morning. The event in remote New Orleans took place after Spain had resolved to raise no further objections. Her restraint grew out of her concern for the Floridas which now lay at the not so tender mercy of a people who identified expansion with the unfolding of nature's beneficent plans for the future.

No nation can increase its territory by one hundred per cent and not be changed. Its economy, its responsibilities, and its power are affected. The Louisiana Purchase gave to the United States one of the world's richest agricultural areas. The national government, possessed of this vast domain, leaped into a position that, compared with any single state, made it a giant. The hackneyed phrase "nothing succeeds like success" now applied. The central government not only met the liveliest anticipations of those who dreamt of empire; it went far beyond.

From a strategic point of view the acquisition had tremendous implications. Both banks of the great Mississippi River belonged to the United States. The country now had an opening on the Gulf of Mexico, and it would inevitably become the dominant power in that area. The importance of this may be most clearly seen if one speculates as to what United States foreign policy might have become had France held Louisiana. Could there have been a war with Great Britain a few years later? Or suppose that Great Britain after Waterloo had taken over Louisiana. Would not this have catapulted the United States into a search for European allies? The questions suggest that the United States would have been compelled to seek another orientation to world affairs than the one it chose in setting forth the Monroe Doctrine.

Thomas Jefferson no sooner received the good news of the Louisiana Purchase on July 3, 1803 than he retired to his library to determine the extent of the purchase. The negotiators in Paris had been under instructions to purchase the Floridas, an area judged of greater value than Louisiana. Jefferson approached the question with the hope of finding that the purchase included some part of the area east of the Mississippi. Taking the words of the two treaties, he concluded that Louisiana included all of the area which France had earlier transferred to Spain. The magic word "retrocession" could mean nothing else. Given this foothold, he proceeded to an examination of old maps and confirmed the fact that Louisiana under French rule prior to 1763 included the territory as far east as the Perdido River.[15] He informed Secretary of State Madison of his finding who, in turn, wrote instructions to Robert Livingston in Paris to examine the same question in the archives there. "The proofs countenancing our claim to a part of West Florida may be of immediate use in the negotiations which are to take place in Madrid," wrote Madison.[16] Before this instruction reached Livingston, he and James Monroe had already searched the materials in Paris and had come to the same conclusion.

James Madison's correspondence during July confessed to the indeterminate nature of both the eastern and western limits of Louisiana. For the time being Madison avoided making precise claims. On the other hand, he urged the necessity of Spain ceding all of the Floridas. Spain was to be advised that the Floridas, separated from the rest of the empire, were now of less value to her than ever while to the United States they had a peculiar importance because the navigable rivers constituted a road to market for American products. Secondly, in the event of war, Great Britain would seize the Floridas. Finally, continued possession by Spain endangered amicable relations with the United States. There must be an arrangement on this subject, Madison warned, "which will substitute the manifest indications of nature, for the artificial and inconvenient state of things now existing."[17]

By early October the United States assumed a more advanced position. Monroe now received word that Louisiana, on the basis of the recent state of evidence, extended as far as the river Perdido.[18] Jefferson and Madison had made up their minds on that point; from this time forth they looked upon Spanish arguments to the contrary as further evidence of Spanish perversity while complimenting themselves on their forbearance in not making an immediate seizure.

The transfer of Louisiana to France on November 30 and then to the United States in December, 1803 opened the door to a frank statement of American demands. Jefferson set out to get the Floridas in a spirit of overbearing righteousness. Madison, Pinckney, American minister at Madrid, and James Monroe, who was under instructions to help Pinckney when the moment appeared opportune, shared Jefferson's belligerent attitude.

The first of a series of explosions occurred early in March, 1804 after Congress passed the Mobile Act giving the President power to establish a customs district within the area under dispute. To be sure, Jefferson, who had promoted the bill, did not contemplate immediate action and was prepared to wait what seemed to him a reasonable time, but Marquis

Yrujo, the Spanish minister, called on the Secretary of State and angrily denounced the law. No explanation of the discretionary features served to assuage him. Yrujo understandably viewed the Mobile Act as aggression.[19]

Madison held firmly that the territory as far east as the Perdido constituted a part of the Louisiana Purchase, but retreated to the position that Congress had never intended that a customs district should be established south of the boundary set by the Pinckney treaty of 1795 until the United States had negotiated the question of the disputed territory.

The rift between the Secretary of State and Minister Yrujo in Washington coincided with an equally unpleasant eruption of ill feeling in Madrid. Charles Pinckney exceeded his instructions to wait for Monroe's arrival before pressing matters at Madrid. Early in 1804 he raised questions about the Floridas and Spanish failure to ratify the Claims Convention negotiated in 1802.

This agreement provided for the settlement of claims arising out of Spanish seizures of American ships during the closing years of the century. The United States Senate did not ratify it until 1804 and then with the stipulation that Spain must also pay for the damages done by France within Spanish jurisdiction. Spain charged that the convention of 1800 between France and the United States had settled all outstanding claims between those two countries and therefore declined to ratify the convention of 1802 unless these latter claims were excluded. Pinckney, notified of this stand and of Spain's refusal to give further consideration to the question until the objectionable parts of the Mobile Act had been revoked, blundered into making a bluff. He would, he said, have to warn all Americans to leave the country within the time allowed by treaty in event of war. The Spanish foreign minister called his bluff, and Pinckney, fully exposed, had to sit in Madrid knowing that he had destroyed his own usefulness.[20]

In July, 1804 Jefferson referred the Spanish question to his cabinet. Out of that discussion Jefferson drew the following set of conclusions: (1) acknowledgment of the Perdido River as the eastern boundary as a *sine qua non* of negotiations, (2) no relinquishment of territory west of the Rio Bravo del Norte in exchange for the Floridas, and (3) that an agreement barring settlement in the western portion of the Louisiana Purchase for twenty years would be acceptable.[21] The United States would be willing to relinquish Texas and pay $2 million for the Floridas but under no consideration was the area between the Perdido and the Mississippi, already claimed, to be considered as a part of the prospective purchase.[22]

Shortly afterwards Minister Yrujo notified the Secretary of State that the king had declared that he would not cede either the whole or any part of the Floridas. This did not deter those charged with responsibility for American foreign policy. Spain, now at war with Great Britain, would soon be more amenable, and, in any case, chief reliance rested on French willingness to influence the Spanish.

In the spring Talleyrand and Robert Livingston had discussed a project for bringing about the desired Spanish decision, but the French foreign minister had stipulated a price for his influence. This had the endorsement of Livingston, but Jefferson and Madison, although bent on getting the Floridas, were not men to stoop to a corrupt bargain. Both of them finally rejected it, and Madison wrote a lengthy letter to John Armstrong, Livingston's successor, in which he said, "The United States owe it to the world as well as to themselves to let the example of one Government at least, protest against the corruption which prevails."[23]

James Monroe embarked for Paris in the fall of 1804, eager to win French support for the forthcoming negotiations in Madrid. On his arrival he learned that France had thrown her support to Spain on the question of the boundary issue. In his brief stay Monroe met with no success, but he continued on to Madrid where he and Pinckney spent five months presenting Madison's draft of a treaty and his arguments supporting it.[24] Making no progress, the frustrated American negotiators joined hands in recommending that the United States use force. Armstrong in Paris gave the same advice.

Amid the quiet scenes at Monticello that summer of 1805, Jefferson meditated upon the course to be pursued. He regretted the bungling manner of Monroe and Pinckney in asking for all or nothing when they might have settled for an agreement on the status quo barring Spanish reinforcements in the Mobile area. That was to be regretted, but the doggedness of the Spanish, backed up by France, troubled him still more. Their demeanor suggested that upon the restoration of peace in Europe these two allies would join hands in a campaign against the diplomatically isolated United States.

Jefferson now seized upon the idea of an alliance with Great Britain.[25] Fear proved a strong stimulant, and he wrote letters at once to Madison and Gallatin. Neither of them gave him any encouragement, but he stuck to his proposal and early in October secured the tentative approval of the cabinet. He wrote to Madison, who was in Philadelphia, that assuming an alliance with England, he thought Congress should pass resolutions authorizing the executive to suspend intercourse with Spain, to dislodge the establishments of Spain in the western part of Louisiana, and to appoint commissioners to examine and ascertain all claims for spoliation.[26] Not until sometime between October 11 and 23 did he drop the idea. When he did so, he attributed his decision to the news that a new coalition was now fighting Napoleon. With an air of relief he speculated that the United States would be granted at least two years of peace.

Not long before Jefferson dropped the notion of an alliance with Great Britain he had received from his Secretary of Treasury, Albert Gallatin, a brilliant and exhaustive analysis of the question of relations with Spain.[27] Jefferson, having worked himself into a state of mind where everything Spanish appeared as intrigue, dishonesty, or machination, discovered that one man in his cabinet held sharply different opinions. The Spanish minister had written a similar statement in the previous January without making any impression on either

Jefferson or the Secretary of State. Madison had earlier found reasons for breaking off all negotiations with Yrujo on grounds of his ill temper and his seeking to influence Americans by supplying them with information on Spain's case.

Gallatin took up each point in Jefferson's charges. The western boundary of Louisiana, he held, was much too uncertain a matter to provide a basis for war. He considered the claim to the Perdido better founded, "yet it must again be repeated that the claim is not self-evident, but constructive. . . ." He might at this point have said what Yrujo had written; that interpretation of a treaty rests with the contracting parties and it had never been the intention of either France or Spain to include this area, and that it was not permissible to twist the language of a treaty to mean that which was quite beyond anything intended.

Gallatin put the argument more strongly. The United States had acquired Louisiana without demanding any stipulation of boundaries from either France or Spain. He thought the manner in which the treaty had been drawn up "betrays either unpardonable oversight or indifference to that object, and a disposition to trust to a mere contingency for securing it." Gallatin continued: "We cannot deny that we had before the ratification of the treaty a knowledge of the intentions of the parties to the Treaty of St. Ildefonso, so far as related to the eastern boundaries. For we knew that Laussat was instructed to demand and the Spanish officers to deliver, east of the Mississippi, that part only which is in our possession." Gallatin admitted the justice of Spain in opposing Jefferson's demands.

In his masterfully dispassionate way Gallatin went on to point out that Spain only declined to ratify the Claims Convention because the United States insisted on including an expression in favor of future claims on the basis of French depredations against American property in Spanish ports. Such an expression guaranteed no future indemnification nor did omission of the expression destroy any basis for pressing them in the future. This, then, said Gallatin, could not be made a just cause for war.

Analyzing the costs of a war in terms of the losses in trade, revenue, and of the property of Americans which would be seized in foreign ports, Gallatin concluded that a war would be most unprofitable. "Still," he admitted, "there is a point where forebearance is no longer possible" because of the train of injuries it would invite. Yet, he doubted that point had been reached. National honor had been more severely strained by Great Britain's blockade of ports and policy of impressment.

Nor were the prospects in a war that would involve France and Spain bright. After the Floridas and "the miserable establishments of Santa Fe and San Antonio" had been taken, Napoleon might still think it proper to persevere. To force a peace then, it would be necessary to take Cuba—a project requiring some British naval cooperation, an army of fifteen or twenty thousand men, a six months' siege, and from ten to twenty million dollars. Then "our fate becomes linked to that of England, and the conditions of our peace will depend on the general result of the European war. And this is one of the worst evils which the United States could encounter; for an entangling alliance, undefined debts and taxes, and in fine a subversion of all our hopes, must be the natural consequence."

Financially, Gallatin explained, the United States was in no position to go to war. The government was committed to heavy payments into the sinking fund for the next three years. If war could be postponed until 1809, it could be faced with more equanimity.

Gallatin, whose recognition of the bargaining nature of diplomacy stood him in good stead, then outlined a series of compromises which would serve the interests of both countries and would have a reasonable prospect of being acceptable.

Gallatin's presentation influenced the administration but slightly. A cabinet meeting on November 14 resolved in favor of the purchase of the Floridas and the collection of spoliation claims making only two concessions to Spain. The western boundary was to be drawn at the Colorado River and then due north to highlands whose waters emptied into the Missouri and Mississippi rivers. To calm Spain's fears of American encroachment, the western part of Louisiana was to be closed to settlement for thirty years.[28]

Jefferson's message to Congress, December 3, 1805, held Spain guilty of attacks on American commerce, refusal to settle spoliation claims, interference with American commerce at Mobile, and making inroads into the territories of Orleans and the Mississippi.[29] Three days later, in a secret message to Congress on relations with Spain, Jefferson cited the unsuccessful negotiations of Monroe and Pinckney, Spain's refusal to settle both the spoliation claims and the boundary questions and contended that Spain's course authorized "the inference that it is their intention to advance on our possessions."[30] He still held hope that France would support an overall settlement between Spain and the United States. Jefferson closed by advising Congress that the present crisis in Europe was favorable for pressing a settlement. "Should it pass unimproved," he thought, "our situation would become much more difficult. Formal war is not necessary. It is not probable it will follow. But the protection of our citizens, the spirit and honor of our country, require that force should be interposed to a certain degree."

Jefferson had sent Gallatin a draft of the proposed message. The Secretary of Treasury fixed his attention on the fifth resolution—that citizens support the resolutions with their lives and fortunes. Gallatin objected that the complaints against Spain did not justify the "solemnity" of that resolution.[31] Jefferson went over Gallatin's memo, removed some of the strongest language, and sent Gallatin the revised edition which he said conformed to most of his ideas.[32] The secret message fell far short of Gallatin's ideas.

The two men had basically different approaches. Jefferson twisted the facts so as to make a general charge against Spain and then invited Congress to use force. He did not want war, but he was quite willing to gamble that an aggressive posture would bring Spain to terms. There was an element of risk, but not as great as if Spain had not been absorbed in a major European war.

Gallatin, with a genius for diplomacy, disliked the bluster and regretted the absence of a give-and-take spirit. The Secretary of Treasury had familiarized himself so thoroughly with the position of the diplomatic opponent that he could present the opponent's side with as much, if not greater skill, than the Spanish minister. Unlike the President, he was less obsessed with the rightness of the American position than with the hard realities.

A committee in the House of Representatives headed by John Randolph presented a report favorable to Jefferson's policy, and on January 14, 1806 the House adopted three resolutions supporting the President.[33] The first of these authorized the President to raise such troops as necessary to protect the southern frontiers "from Spanish inroad and insult, and to chastise the same, . . ." The second resolution approved the spending of $2 million for the purchase of the Floridas. The third approved of an exchange of territory, some part of western Louisiana in return for the Floridas.

Jefferson's war-like proposals led to a sharp split in Congress. The first resolution passed by a vote of 72 to 58, the second by a vote of 74 to 57. The third enjoyed a slightly wider margin. The majorities did not show a united nation in support of Jefferson's measures, a dangerous situation should his policy lead to war and one which Gallatin had warned would be the case.

By April Jefferson faced a split in his own party. John Randolph, who had helped carry the measures through Congress, turned on Secretary of State Madison with a vengeance when he discovered that France would in all probability extract the purchase price from Spain. In his split with the administration, Randolph also fought the proposed renewal of the non-importation act against Great Britain on the ground that it would be wholly ineffectual.

Randolph, a master of invective, poured out his wrath in a series of speeches which put the administration in the role of bribing Napoleon to bully Spain into submission to the United States. The administration, he charged, had no valid claims to the territory of West Florida. Time and again, Randolph drove home that the real issue was "whether we should have a territorial accommodation of our differences with Spain, whether we should have an accommodation which did not merely suit Spain and us, or a moneyed accommodation which neither suited us or Spain, but France."[34]

Madison's friends rallied to his support charging that Spain as an independent country would do as she pleased with the funds. If France obtained the money, that was no concern of the United States and certainly did not conform to Randolph's charge that Jefferson and Madison were seeking to bribe France. Randolph, who had been fighting in behalf of a resolution to make Jefferson's secret message public, lost. A man less given to rancor, with a better command of the facts, and able to approach his audience in a spirit of restraint, might have hurt the administration. The debates of early 1806, however unsuccessful Randolph was, showed that Jefferson's shirt sleeve diplomacy did not have the support of the country to the degree which was desirable if Spain was to be forced into a settlement. His policy was dividing the country at the very time a more patient course could have united it.

Jefferson's bluster worked no miracles in Madrid. Spanish questions drifted on without a settlement and without Jefferson resorting to force. He continued to seek the aid of France but without success, and, indeed it is difficult to perceive why France should have wounded her ally in order to please the United States although Napoleon's highhanded measures in Spain did offer proof of the contempt he had for the Spanish.

A year after the Randolph volcano erupted in Congress, Jefferson continued to urge the American minister to Spain to use every effort "to accommodate our differences with Spain, under the auspices of France." Concerning Spain, Jefferson wrote:

Never did a nation act towards another with more perfidy and in-justice than Spain has constantly practised against us. And if we have kept our hands off her till now, it has been purely out of respect for France, & from the value we set on the friendship of France. We expect therefore from the friendship of the emperor that he will either compel Spain to do us justice, or abandon her to us. We ask but one month to be in possession of the city of Mexico.[35]

Unfortunately, Spain offered no positive program. Power-less to defend her colonies in North America, she relied on giving negative answers to American demands and resorted to ruffling American feathers further by claiming that the Louisiana Purchase extended only a few miles west of the Mississippi River. She would have fared better had she bar-gained in 1806 rather than in 1819, for there is every reason to believe that she could then have secured a boundary well to the east of the Sabine River and along the eastern ridge of the Rocky Mountains.

NOTES

1. *Memoirs of John Quincy Adams,* ed. Charles Francis Adams (Phila-delphia: J. B. Lippincott and Co., 1875), Vol. IV, pp. 492-493.

2. *The Writings of Albert Gallatin,* ed. Henry Adams (Philadelphia: J. B. Lippincott and Co., 1879), Vol. II, p. 178.

3. Nathan Schachner, *Thomas Jefferson: A Biography* (New York: Thomas Yoseloff, 1951), p. 685-686.

4. *Ibid.,* p. 782.

5. Arthur Preston Whitaker, *The Mississippi Question 1795-1803, A Study in Trade, Politics, and Diplomacy* (New York: D. Appleton-Cen-tury Co., 1934), p. 139.

6. E. Wilson Lyon, *Louisiana in French Diplomacy 1759-1804* (Norman: University of Oklahoma Press, 1934), p. 65.

7. *Ibid.,* p. 91.

8. *Ibid.,* p. 139.

9. Samuel Flagg Bemis, *A Diplomatic History of the United States* (New York: Henry Holt and Co., 1955), 4th Edition, p. 137.

10. Lyon, *op. cit.,* pp. 152-153.

11. Irving Brant, *James Madison: Secretary of State 1800-1809* (Indian-apolis: The Bobbs-Merrill Co., 1953), p. 105.

12. *Ibid.,* p. 116.

13. *Ibid.,* pp. 117-118.

14. *Ibid.*, pp. 141-145.
15. *Ibid.*, p. 150.
16. *Writings of James Madison*, VII, p. 52.
17. *Ibid.*, p. 54.
18. *Ibid.*, p. 70.
19. Brant, *op. cit.*, pp. 192-199.
20. *Ibid.*, p. 209.
21. *The Writings of Thomas Jefferson*, ed. Paul Leicester Ford, Vol. VIII, pp. 309-312.
22. Spain had bestowed large sections in land grants which the United States hoped to be free to cancel.
23. *Writings of James Madison*, VII, p. 183.
24. Brant, *op. cit.*, p. 259.
25. *Writings of Jefferson*, Vol. VIII, p. 374.
26. *Ibid.*, p. 379.
27. *Writings of Albert Gallatin*, ed. Henry Adams (Philadelphia: J. B. Lippincott & Co., 1879), Vol. I, pp. 241-254.
28. *Writings of Jefferson*, Vol. VIII, pp. 383-384.
29. *Ibid.*, pp. 385-396.
30. *Ibid.*, pp. 397-402.
31. *Writings of Gallatin*, I, p. 280.
32. *Ibid.*, p. 281.
33. *Annals of Congress, Ninth Congress, First Session*, p. 1127.
34. *Ibid.*, p. 959.
35. *Writings of Jefferson*, IX, pp. 381-382.

Idealism in Crisis

IX

THE FOREIGN POLICY of Jefferson and Madison reflects their idealism, their solicitous feeling for the interests of the nation, and an optimistic estimate of the capacity of the United States to retaliate against any impositions by others. Their strong nationalism and idealism led to repeated crises and eventually to war because they did not have the power to achieve their ambitious goals. The weakness stemmed in part from lack of a navy and reliance upon a militia system, but the more important source of weakness was the hazardous ambivalence that is likely to characterize any foreign policy that must wait upon the slow and uneven advance of public opinion to a position where leaders are free to act.

In ascribing an idealistic approach to Jefferson and Madison it is not intended to suggest that they were moved only by high ideals. They could shift to take advantage of the power struggle in Europe and could and did take steps justified only in terms of national interest. Nor were Jefferson and Madison Don Quixotes seeking to impose their standards on the world at large. Their lack of power saved them from this. The significance of the course they pursued lies in the fact that in spite of their moralistic position they eventually frankly professed that they would be guided on the issue of peace or war by what served the national interest. It was precisely because Great Britain and France observed such standards for determining policy that Jefferson and Madison condemned the two belligerents.

From the beginning, realistic considerations entered into their calculations. A consistent aim of their diplomacy was a solution to the question of the Floridas. Their fear that either Great Britain or France might acquire the territory was not unreasonable in view of Spain's involvement in the Napoleonic wars. Great Britain, allied to Spain, might compel her ally to cede the Floridas in return for aid against Napoleon. A French victory over Spain raised the spectre of Napoleon compensating himself in a peace treaty by taking the Floridas. There was less to fear from Spain's retention of the territory, but Spanish control of the lower reaches of the rivers that furnished a natural outlet for the produce of the frontier regions of the southern states caused them deep concern.

For example, the realism that intertwined itself with the idealism of the President and Secretary of State sometimes originated in pressure from Congress. The uprisings in Congress in early 1803 when Americans were deprived of the right of deposit at New Orleans and the violent reactions to the prospect of having France as a neighbor inspired Jefferson's and Madison's first move to acquire the Floridas. They would have much preferred to secure the territory by negotiation, and in 1804, when Spain expressed her ire over the establishment of a customs district in West Florida, the President and the Secretary of State professed a willingness to negotiate. When Spain refused to negotiate, Jefferson held her guilty of injustice and perfidy.

Balked in their efforts, Jefferson and Madison watched the developments in Europe with an eye to taking by force what they could not secure by other means. After the Chesapeake Affair of June, 1807, when war with Great Britain appeared probable, Jefferson wrote to Madison that the conflict would provide occasion for seizing the Floridas.

While war with England is probable, everything leading to it with other nations should be avoided, except with Spain. As to her, I think it the precise moment when we should declare to the French government that we will instantly seize on the Floridas as reprisal for the spoliations denied us, and, that if by a given day they are paid to us, we will restore all east of the Perdido, & hold the rest subject to amicable decision. Otherwise we will hold them forever as compensation for the spoliations.[1]

In the summer of 1808, when Napoleon invaded Spain and there appeared some possibility of peace with Great Britain, Jefferson once again sought to turn Spain's misfortune to the advantage of the United States. "Should England make up with us, while Bonaparte continues at war with Spain," he notified the Secretary of War, "a moment may occur when we may without danger of commitment with either France or England seize to our own limits of Louisiana as of right, & the residue of the Floridas as reprisal for spoliations." His anxiety to be ready for such an occasion prompted him to instruct the Secretary of War "to have an eye to this in rendezvousing & stationing our new recruits & our armed vessels, so as to be ready, . . ." The opportunist note closed with the further advice: "Mobile, Pensacola, & St. Augustine, are those we should be preparing for. The enforcing the embargo would furnish a pretext for taking the nearest healthy position to St. Mary's, and on the waters of Tombigbee."[2] The same day Jefferson advised his Secretary of State of his plans.

James Madison could enter into the President's plans without hesitation for he had long sought to exploit every opportunity to bring about this result. His instructions to James Monroe, when the latter was sent to Spain in November, 1804, to seek a settlement of differences with that country, proposed that he make use of other arguments than those founded upon reason.

You are aware, I presume, that the Prince of Peace will claim your special attention. Mr. Short inculcates the policy of it. He says that he governs the Court absolutely, and may be managed by his weaknesses, particularly his vanity. Such a resource is not to be neglected.

But the main one will lie in a skilful appeal to the fears of Spain, and the interest which France, as well as Spain, has in not favoring a coalition of the United States with Great Britain.[3]

Three years later, in May, 1807, Madison, still adamant on the question of the Floridas, sought to enlist the aid of France in obtaining Spain's consent to a settlement. The delays and pretexts put forth by Spain, he wrote to the United States minister to France, "have put the patience of the United States to a severe trial." He warned that a crisis could not much longer be postponed because Spanish interference with the trade of Americans desiring to send their goods down to Mobile was "kindling a flame which has been with difficulty kept under, and must in a short time acquire a force not to be resisted." The time was approaching, he warned, when the United States would have no other choice than "between a foreign and an internal conflict."[4] In slightly more than three years Madison as President gave way to that pressure and seized West Florida.

The realism of Jefferson and Madison on the Florida question sharply contrasted with their appeals to idealistic considerations in the controversy with Great Britain over the question of neutral rights. In 1805, when the dispute with Great Britain first assumed serious proportions, neither Jefferson nor Madison considered the differences beyond settlemen by negotiation. "No two countries on earth have so many points of common interest & friendship; and their rulers must be bunglers indeed, if, with such dispositions, they break them asunder." So wrote Jefferson in May, 1806 concerning relations between Great Britain and the United States.

Prior to that time the two countries were involved in lesser issues of impressment, blockade, and the rights of a neutral to enter the carrying trade between Britain's enemy and that enemy's colonies. Some settlement of these issues was within the realm of possibility. As it turned out, they were not settled and contributed to the two countries' becoming involved in a more basic dispute. The reasons for the failure lay in considerable part in the nationalistic and idealistic approach of Jefferson and Madison although it is not to be denied that British practices provided a peculiarly trying test for a proud people.

What Americans regarded as the obvious injustice and tragedy of impressment has obscured the problem that led the British to pursue the practice. Desertions from their merchant marine and navy numbered into the thousands. According to Secretary of the Treasury Albert Gallatin, a careful observer, the desertion of British seamen to American ships was a major factor in the rapid growth of the American merchant fleet. Seeing a threat to their security in this development, the British sought to check it by boarding American ships and retrieving their seamen. The apprehensions of the British in the midst of a war are easily understandable, but in ferreting out the deserters, the British captains resorted to the scoop rather than the tweezers. Naturalized Americans found themselves in British holds and condemned to separation from their families. Their fate was decided by navy captains who took little care to determine whether the seaman was a British deserter or an American. Yet it should also be noted that in November, 1804, when the House of Representatives asked Secretary of State Madison for a report, he set the number of Americans impressed since the renewal of the war at forty-three.[5]

Serious as was the question of impressment it did not lead to any great public excitement until 1805 when it took on a new importance after the British threatened to clamp down on the American re-export trade. The British threat did not take place until the spring of 1805. Relations between the two countries remained good until that time.

After months of tedious negotiations with the British during 1805, James Monroe, the American minister, before leaving London to undertake his special mission to Spain, analyzed relations with Great Britain. His report was marked by a spirit far more realistic than that of Jefferson and Madison. Monroe observed that his negotiation had by no means failed although no agreement had been reached. Measured in terms of the true interest of the United States, wrote Monroe, relations with Great Britain left little to be desired in spite of impressment and the unsettled boundary questions. Our commerce, he observed, "was never so much favored in time of war, nor was there ever less cause of complaint of impressment."[6] While Europe was suffering the uncertainties of war, "the United States are prosperous beyond the example of any other nation, and more might be lost at home and abroad by an appearance of hostility with any Power than could be expected from a formal concession of the points contended for."[7]

Monroe proposed to take up the negotiation upon his return from Spain. It would then be time, he said, to decide what course to pursue. He suggested to the Secretary of State that the United States would be free to press for its rights or to postpone issues until they could be pursued with greater assurance of success.

If it is deemed expedient, in pursuing our just rights, to profit of time and circumstances, and, in the interim, unless they be secured by a fair and equal treaty, to act with moderation till the occasion invites to a more decisive and hazardous policy, the state of things permits it; or, if it should be deemed more advisable to adopt the latter course at present, the opportunity is fair for such a measure.[8]

The United States minister in London appreciated that the United States was prospering as never before, and he did not want to endanger her prosperity by a peremptory insistence on her "just rights." He foresaw that to press forward now seeking to settle issues of lesser import might be highly injudicious.

By March, 1805, however, James Madison was prepared to hazard present prosperity for the chance of reaching an agreement on impressment. He explained his course as one dictated by pressure from Congress. The action of the House of Representatives in asking for a report on impressments, the resolution introduced by Jacob Crowninshield, and the recent enactment by Congress of a law against British officers committing trespasses or torts on board American vessels, furnished proof, as Madison saw it, "of the public sensibility to those aggressions on the security of our citizens and the rights of our flag."[9] The Secretary of State appears to have exaggerated the pressure from Congress for Crowninshield's resolution had been laid on the table, and the House had manifested little interest in it.[10] James Madison was certainly not seeking to provoke a war, but his anxiety to reach a settlement so as to remove causes for future difficulty was far outweighed by a deeply held conviction that "the United States are, in a manner, driven to the necessity of seeking some remedy dependent on themselves alone." Madison found impressment inhuman, a violation of national sovereignty, and a wholly arbitrary practice contrary to the true interests of Great Britain. His decision to press forward was strengthened by his conclusion that "such were the ideas and feelings of the nation on it, that no Administration would dare so far to surrender the rights of the American flag."[11]

The summer of 1805 saw a new crisis emerging out of an abrupt change in British policy concerning the American indirect carrying trade between the colonies of Great Britain's enemies and the mother countries. In some twenty cases, including the well known Essex case, the British admiralty courts suddenly ruled that neutral vessels carrying goods between the West Indies and the mother country were subject to seizure even though they stopped in the United States. James Madison stated that these re-exportations averaged more than thirty-two million dollars in the three years ending in September, 1803.[12] The new rulings clearly threatened ruin to the American commercial interest. James Madison and James Monroe responded with alacrity to the challenge, ably arguing that the decisions violated the law of nations, conflicted with earlier rulings of the British courts, and did not harmonize with British practice in opening her own colonies to neutral vessels in time of war.[13]

For a few weeks the excitement was intense, but by late

summer the British were clearly softening their policy and Monroe, in late September, notified the Secretary of State of the change. "It is evident to those who attend the trials," he reported, "that the tone of the judge has become more moderate; that he acquits whenever he can acquit our vessels, and, keeping within the precedent of the Essex, seizes every fact that the papers or other evidence furnish, in the cases which occur, to bring them within that limit."[14]

The new British sufferance of the American re-export trade impressed Monroe as a temporary maneuver calculated to postpone the issue. He saw in the deep British jealousy of American prosperity a force not easily put aside and he fully expected a renewal of seizures when the occasion suited the British.[15] The former policy of tolerance was not based on generosity but on the necessity of not frightening the northern powers, especially Russia and Sweden, into opposition. Now that Russia and Sweden had joined the coalition against France they would be faced with difficulties overriding their concern with trade.[16] Therefore the British would face the United States alone in seeking to limit neutral rights. He did not have to guess at the fundamental British position. Lord Mulgrave had said that the United States should not engage in any trade with enemy colonies except in goods to be consumed at home.[17]

Monroe concluded that Great Britain was committed to destroying the American re-export trade. "It is certain," he wrote to Madison, "that the greatest jealousy is entertained of our present and increasing prosperity, and I am satisfied that nothing which is likely to succeed will be left untried to impair it."[18] The recent seizures proved that Great Britain was much less concerned with establishing a basis of friendship with the United States than she was in checking the prosperity of the rapidly growing commercial rival. This was her primary object.

Precisely the same conclusion as regards British aims embittered Madison and caused him to denounce as immoral their efforts to protect their commercial interests by invoking the Rule of 1756. Monroe did not approve of British policy, but he did not view it as immoral. Consequently he remained capable of dealing with the challenge in realistic terms, whereas Madison assumed a self-righteous position, gave way to a deep hostility toward the British, professed to seek an adjustment but called for the most powerful nation in the world to sacrifice her own interests in order to abide by a generous ideal.

In one significant respect both Monroe and Madison deluded themselves. They both believed that the United States was capable of united and firm resistance. The British thought otherwise. Monroe reported that they entertained prejudices concerning the United States "which the experience of multiplied and striking facts ought long since to have swept away." "Among these it is proper to mention an opinion, which many do not hesitate to avow," Monroe stated, "that the United States are, by the nature of their Government, being popular, incapable of any great, vigorous, or persevering action: that they cannot, for example, resist a system of commercial hostility from this country, but must yield to the pressure."[19] The ambivalence of United States policy in the years ahead demonstrated how correct the British were.

James Madison's grossly exaggerated estimate of the power of the United States to resist was at the heart of his failings as a diplomat. His belief that the American people would unitedly support strong measures even when these involved temporary but very real personal sacrifices was only one of his mistakes. His strong nationalism led both him and Jefferson to count too heavily on the importance of the American market to British manufactures, on the reliance of the British West Indies on American food supplies, on the dependence of the British population on the agricultural produce of the United States, and the need of the British navy and merchant marine for American naval stores, especially if the war in Europe should cut off supplies from the Baltic area.[20] All of these were of some importance, but in failing to take into account the hardships that measures to deprive the British of these advantages would impose on major interest groups in the United States, he erred as he had erred in the 1790's.

His error plus his deep conviction that the United States occupied a position of righteousness explain why he made impossible demands when the time came for serious diplomatic negotiations. Two developments conspired to bring these about in 1806: a movement in Congress to assert American rights on the high seas and more particularly to bring an end to impressment gained great strength late in 1805 and early in 1806. This coincided with a change in the British government which brought Lord Grenville to the front and made Charles Fox the foreign minister. Congress, after much debate, vented its feelings in the enactment of the Non-Importation Act giving the executive the power to prohibit the importation of a long list of British manufactures if the British failed to cease impressments and to stop their seizure of American ships. The rise of Charles Fox to power gave new hope to the protracted negotiations. He had long been known as a friend to the United States, and it was assumed that he would cultivate American friendship. The Non-Importation Act came at a most inauspicious time and threatened to ruin the negotiations by introducing the element of menace, thereby stiffening British resistance. Both Monroe and Madison found it necessary to explain away the act as a popular expression aiming at no more than calling attention to their grievances and that it in no way controverted the basic American friendship toward Great Britain.

The anxiety of Congress also led to a call for a special mission. James Madison appointed William Pinkney, a successful Maryland lawyer who had served in England on the joint tribunal established by the Jay Treaty for the settlement of seizure cases. Pinkney arrived in London in May. Madison's instructions to Monroe and Pinkney reflected Madison's view that the United States asked only for what was just and humane. The President and the Secretary of State laid down two necessary requirements, a British surrender on impressment and a revocation of the Rule of 1756 to the extent that goods landed in the United States from the West Indies and paying the regular duties should be considered a part of the stock of the United States and therefore not subject to seizure when re-exported to Europe.[21] To these he added a long list of desirable provisions including indemnity for past seizures, a stricter definition of blockade, a more limited list of contraband, and a restraint on British ships of war from "seizing, searching, or otherwise interrupting or disturbing vessels to whomsoever belonging within the distance of four leagues."

James Madison was an expert on international law, the history of treaties, and the rulings of British courts in cases involving seizures and blockades. An indefatigable worker, he wrote in the early months of 1806 a lengthy pamphlet on the Rule of 1756, entitled *An Examination into the British Doctrine concerning Neutral Trade*. The volume entitles him to a place among the most notable authorities on international law. In graceful style and with devastating logic he built up the case against Great Britain. On the points at issue he cited the opinions of all the great writers on the laws of nations, Grotius, Vattel, Pufendorf, Bynkershoeck, Cocceius, Grongingius, and Martens. His minute examination of treaties entered into by Great Britain over several centuries showed that Great Britain herself had recognized the principles for which the United States now contended. British admiralty courts, he demonstrated, reached their decisions on the basis of expediency rather than on principles of law.

Madison saw in the behavior of England and France an illustration of the lessons of history as to the causes of war. "The wars which afflict mankind," he wrote, "are not produced by the intrigues or cupidity of the weaker nations, who wish to remain at peace, whilst their neighbors are at war." Wars, he concluded, "are the offspring of ambitious, and not infrequently commercial rivalships, among the more powerful nations themselves." "This," he asserted, "is a fact attested by all history." The road to peace, he said, lay in circumscribing the practices of the powerful, ambitious to exercise their power and extending the rights of the weaker nations who were not tempted to infringe on the rights of others. At the base of Madison's argument lay the appeal to human reason and a call to contribute to the progress of humanity. It would be wise, he thought, for the nations now at the pinnacle of their power to remember the proof offered by history that no nation was privileged to occupy the place of power over any great period. Those who were all powerful now would some day be weak and would then depend upon a system of international law for their security. Therefore it was to their own interest to forfeit temporary advantages gained by lawlessness and to aid in the establishment of a system of international law.[22]

The negotiations were delayed by the illness of Charles Fox, who became a victim of dropsy and died the following September. He was, in the words of a British historian, a man who "had always lived with that intensity of which only a certain idler is capable. He had drunk the cup of life to the full. Travel, drinking, gambling, women, art, literature, popularity, the senate, domestic happiness, . . . he had drained them all." He departed this life uttering as his last words, "I die happy."[23] His departure was viewed as a particularly unfortunate blow to the negotiations, but it is doubtful that Charles Fox would have been lured into making the sacrifices necessary to meet the austere requirements laid down by James Madison.

What was lacking was not a conciliatory spirit but the imagination to bridge the gap between two proud nations enmeshed in intense commercial rivalry. The representatives of the British cabinet who conducted the serious negotiations beginning August 22, 1806, were the nephew of Fox, Lord Holland, and Lord Auckland. Though both men were understanding in their attitude toward the Americans, they were firm in their defense of British interests.

The question of impressment occupied most of the attention of the negotiators for two months. At the second meeting with the two British negotiators the Americans received a proposal on impressment. It called for providing the crews of ships of both nations with documents of citizenship, completely protecting those who carried them. Auckland and Holland argued that this device would accomplish the purpose of the United States to protect its own seamen. The British were still to be free to examine the crews on American vessels and to impress those who were determined to be deserters.[24] In reply to the American assertion that nothing short of a surrender of impressment would meet the demands of the United States, the British negotiators stated that to give up impressment presented the alarming danger that the American merchant marine would become a "floating asylum for all the British seamen who, tempted by higher wages, should quit their service for ours."

The American negotiators came prepared with a plan whereby Great Britain would surrender impressment in return for a treaty provision binding both parties not to permit the employment on its ships of deserters from a vessel of the other party and providing that consuls who discovered deserters from the ships of their own nations might arrest them and return them to the service of their own country.[25] The British rejected this on the ground that it was doubtful that it could be effectively enforced.

Early in November Auckland and Holland proposed the enactment of a law in the United States making it a penal offense to take British deserters aboard and providing that the government of the United States should restore such deserters. This proposal failed to gain the approval of the Grenville cabinet.[26] In its place the cabinet proposed that laws be passed by both parties "whereby it should be made penal for the commanders of British vessels to impress American citizens on board American vessels on the high seas, and for the officers of the United States to grant certificates of citizenship to British subjects." The right to search American ships for deserters was not withdrawn by this proposal and was therefore unacceptable to Monroe and Pinkney.[27]

181

The exchange of proposals came to an end on November 8 when it became clear that regardless of what other devices might be adopted for preventing the loss of seamen, the British government would not surrender the right of impressment. As a ban on impressment was a *sine qua non* in their instructions, Monroe and Pinkney pleaded that it would be necessary to break off the negotiations. Thereupon the British representatives proposed that a note be attached to the treaty that would allow each party to adhere to the principle it avowed but which committed the British government to surrender in practice what it could not surrender as a principle. The salient paragraph read:

That His Majesty's Government, animated by an earnest desire to remove every cause of dissatisfaction, has directed His Majesty's Commissioners to give to Mr. Monroe and to Mr. Pinkney the most positive assurances that instructions have been given, and shall be repeated and enforced, for the observance of the greatest caution in the impressing of British seamen; and that the strictest care shall be taken to preserve the citizens of the United States from any molestation or injury; and that immediate and prompt redress shall be afforded upon any representation of injury sustained by them.[28]

The note, the British commissioners explained, was as far as any ministry dared go at present because of long standing national feeling on this issue of deserters and because of the precarious situation of the nation at this moment. The practice, however, would be limited to such extreme cases as deserters from a warship fleeing to a merchant vessel that was close by. The British government accordingly issued orders embodying the new policy.[29]

Monroe and Pinkney accepted the note as a satisfactory solution to the problem of impressment. They believed that the British would so limit the practice that British insistence on retaining the right was not an adequate cause for terminating the negotiations. They not only accepted the note as a great gain, but they weighed what they judged to be a minor disadvantage, namely British refusal to yield on the principle, against the commercial gains they expected to achieve if negotiations were continued and a treaty agreed upon. However, their specific instructions stating that no treaty should be negotiated which did not include a provision expressly prohibiting impressment troubled the two American envoys. To protect themselves they attached the condition to their continuing negotiations that the United States would be under no obligation to ratify the treaty. Monroe and Pinkney arrived at this decision on the basis of realistic considerations. Jefferson and Madison were soon to reject their decision on idealistic grounds.

The final treaty was not signed until the last day of 1806. Any realistic appreciation of the hard facts in the background of the negotiation must include the undisputed naval supremacy of Great Britain, the firm determination of her people to resist what they deemed impositions, a determination strengthened by their involvement in a life and death struggle with Napoleon, and the fact that on one point the British could unite with greater feeling than on any other, that her supremacy rested upon her navy, that her navy was peculiarly dependent upon her merchant marine—the great nursery of seamen—and that the war imposed handicaps on her merchant fleet which the Americans were exploiting effectively and thereby rising rapidly to challenge British commercial prosperity. Given these facts, the treaty negotiated by Monroe and Pinkney must be viewed as a diplomatic victory.

The greatest gain was a treaty provision that protected the American re-export trade. It did not permit trade directly between the colonies of Great Britain's enemies and Europe, but not even Madison expected such a concession. It did allow the trade subject only to the conditions that the ships land in the United States and that the import duties be paid. These duties must be the equivalent of one per cent on goods in transit from the mother country to the islands and two per cent on goods on their way from the islands to Europe.[30] These conditions would not greatly handicap American merchants who enjoyed great advantages over their British competitors, who paid the high insurance rates incident to war and whose ships were barred from entering most of the ports of Europe.

The other provisions were less favorable but did not seriously threaten injury. One gain was a provision that British ships of war should not engage in actions within a distance of five marine miles of the coast.[31] No provision was made for indemnification for past seizures, a desirable rather than a necessary item in Madison's instructions. The American representatives argued strenuously in favor of indemnification, but the omission did not impose heavy losses. At the close of the negotiations Monroe expressed the opinion that the claims amounted to much less than had been assumed.[32] A new limitation was added to the right of Americans to trade with the British East Indies. The Jay Treaty included only the limitation that American ships must not carry goods from the Indies to any other part of the world than the United States. The new treaty specified that the American ships going to the Indies must sail directly from the United States.[33]

James Madison, in a letter to the two envoys on February 3, was highly critical of what he assumed would be included in the treaty. Aside from the failure to provide against impressment, he objected to a limitation on the re-export trade that would have required the goods to be stored in the United States for thirty days. Such a limitation was not included in the treaty. He saw in the restrictions on the re-export trade a trick by which the British sought to protect themselves against American competition. Madison pronounced such an object as quite illegitimate.[34] He likewise objected to the failure to provide for indemnification of Americans whose ships had been seized.

In the final days of the negotiation Napoleon issued his Berlin decree declaring England in a state of blockade, ordering the seizure of all goods of British origin that might be carried by neutrals, and excluding all neutral ships from harbors under his control if they had entered a British port. This policy could scarcely be effectively enforced by France and the decree constituted more a piece of braggadocio than a serious threat, but it stung British pride and created a desire to retaliate. If Napoleon was to ride roughshod over neutral rights, then, reasoned the British, the neutrals ought to manifest resentment. It was this which led the British government to attach to the treaty with the United States a proviso that held Great Britain bound by the treaty only if the United States resisted the pretensions of Napoleon. To add such a stipulation was not only a highly undiplomatic move but one which made the treaty less than binding on the British while the United States would be obligated to observe its provisions. Monroe and Pinkney did their best to have the note deleted but without success. Jefferson and Madison found it a highly objectionable feature. However, James Madison and Thomas Jefferson did not know of this note when they first rejected the proposed treaty.[35]

In his lengthy letter of May 20, 1807, giving his reasons for rejecting the treaty, the Secretary of State paid no attention to the note on impressment. The treaty, as he saw it, surrendered the rights of seamen and violated "both a moral and political duty of the Government to our citizens."[36] Instead of viewing the provisions concerning the re-export trade as a gain, he denounced this section of the treaty on the ground that it restricted the re-export market to Europe and provided that only goods from the continent of Europe could be carried on American ships to the West Indies. That the treaty actually included such restrictions is extremely doubtful. James Monroe denied that it did, and nowhere in the two envoys' reports of the negotiations was it ever suggested that any part of Article XI could be interpreted to this effect.[37] It would appear that Madison read into the treaty objections that were not there. He found the limitation of trade with the East Indies an insuperable objection and was highly critical of the British because they refused to provide for indemnification of Americans who had suffered losses by British seizures.[38]

The replies written by Madison and endorsed by Jefferson provide ample evidence for the conclusion that unless they could have a treaty that met all of their preferences they would rather have no treaty. Free of treaty restrictions they could combat what they termed British pretensions by means of their pet scheme of commercial retaliation. Their view of their demands as based on international law, their assumption that they were asking only for what was just, their unwillingness to accept anything less than what suited them rested on a full confidence that the United States could achieve its goals by other means than treaties involving compromises. Their attitude is indicated in Madison's comments on Article XI dealing with the re-export trade. Rather than agree to that article, he wrote, the President prefers "an unfettered right of the United States to adapt their regulations to the course which her policy may take."[39]

Idealism was only one factor in the failure of the United States and Great Britain to arrive at a treaty settlement. An overestimate of the capacity of the United States to adhere to a coercive commercial policy probably played the greatest role in Jefferson and Madison taking so unyielding a position as they did, but idealism led them to approach the difficult diplomatic issues in terms of American "rights." This element greatly strengthened their rigidity.

NOTES

1. Thomas Jefferson to James Madison, September 1, 1807, *The Writings of Thomas Jefferson*, Vol. IX, p. 134.

2. Thomas Jefferson to the Secretary of War, *ibid.*, August 12, 1808, Vol. IX, pp. 203-204.

3. James Madison to James Monroe, November 9, 1804, *Letters and Other Writings of James Madison* (Philadelphia: J. B. Lippincott & Co., 1867), Vol. II, p. 209.

4. James Madison to John Armstrong, May 22, 1807, *The Writings of James Madison*, ed. Gaillard Hunt (New York: G. P. Putnam's Sons, 1908), Vol. VII, pp. 447-448.

5. In his report James Madison estimated that forty-three impressments had been made by December, 1803. Appendix, *Annals of Congress, Eighth Congress, Second Session*, p. 1259.

6. James Monroe to James Madison, October 3, 1804, Appendix, *Annals of Congress, Tenth Congress, First Session*, p. 2399.

7. *Ibid.*

8. *Ibid.*, p. 2402.

9. James Madison to James Monroe, March 6, 1805, *ibid.*, p. 2402.

10. *Annals of Congress, Eighth Congress, Second Session*, p. 1006.

11. James Madison to James Monroe, March 6, 1805, *Annals of Congress, Tenth Congress, First Session*, p. 2403.

12. James Madison to James Monroe, April 12, 1805, *Annals of Congress, ibid.*, p. 2411.

13. See letter of James Madison to James Monroe, April 12, 1805 and James Monroe to James Madison, October 18, 1805 in the Appendix, *Annals of Congress, ibid.*, p. 2418.

14. James Madison to James Monroe, September 25, 1805, *ibid.*, p. 2418.

15. James Monroe to James Madison, October 18, 1805, *ibid.*, p. 2421.

16. *Ibid.*, p. 2420.

17. *Ibid.*, p. 2421.

18. *Ibid.*, pp. 2421-2422.

19. *Ibid.*, p. 2422.

20. James Madison to James Monroe, May 20, 1807, *ibid.*, pp. 2586-2588.

21. James Madison to James Monroe and William Pinkney, May 17, 1806, *ibid.*, pp. 2452-2465.

22. *The Writings of James Madison*, ed. Gaillard Hunt (New York: G. P. Putnam's Sons, 1908), Vol. VII, p. 367.

23. A. F. Fremantle, *England in the Nineteenth Century, 1806-1910* (London: George Allen & Unwin Ltd., 1930), Vol. II, pp. 174-175.

24. James Monroe and William Pinkney to James Madison, September 11, 1806, *Annals of Congress, Tenth Congress, First Session*, p. 2486.

25. James Monroe and William Pinkney to Commissioners of Great Britain, September 11, 1806, *ibid.*, p. 2495.

26. James Monroe and William Pinkney to James Madison, November 11, 1806, *ibid.*, p. 2498.

27. *Ibid.*, p. 2499.

28. British Commissioners to James Monroe and William Pinkney, November 8, 1806, *ibid.*, pp. 2503-2504.

29. James Monroe to James Madison, February 28, 1808, *ibid.*, pp. 2591-2593.

30. A copy of the treaty appears in the *Annals of Congress, Tenth Congress, First Session*, Vol. II. See Article XI, p. 2528.

31. *Ibid.*, Article XII, p. 2528.

32. James Monroe and William Pinkney to James Madison, January 3, 1807, *ibid.*, p. 2521.

33. Article III of Treaty, *ibid.*, p. 2524.

34. James Madison to James Monroe and William Pinkney, February 3, 1807, *ibid.*, p. 2543.

35. James Madison to Lord Erskine, March 29, 1807, *ibid.*, p. 2553.

There is no reason to believe that Jefferson and Madison would have accepted the treaty had this note not been attached. Events thereafter soon complicated the relations of the two countries and made any agreement with the British infinitely more difficult. A British order in council issued early in the year and delivered in Washington on March 12 declared illegal all trade of neutrals carried from one port in Europe to another if that port were in the possession of Napoleon. James Madison replied that this ruling would destroy American commerce with the continent of Europe. It did just that and Madison's reject was justified.

This development makes it more difficult to form a judgment on his final reply to Monroe and Pinkney on the treaty that had been signed on December 31, 1806.

36. James Madison to James Monroe and William Pinkney, May 20, 1807, *ibid.*, p. 2571.

37. James Monroe to James Madison, February 28, 1808, *ibid.*, p. 2598.

38. James Madison to James Monroe and William Pinkney, May 20, 1807, *ibid.*, p. 2575.

39. *Ibid.*, p. 2574.

The Embargo:
A Study in Frustration

X

IDEALISM played only an indirect role in that daring experiment whereby Jefferson and Madison tried to defend the national interest by cutting off commercial relations with the outside world. Idealism, admittedly, was an important ingredient of the nationalism that motivated their resistance to the belligerents' decrees, but the measure itself was as earthbound as the business transactions it confined within the national borders.

The Embargo rested upon a carefully calculated choice among submission, peaceful resistance and war. The failure of the Embargo did not discredit the calculations of the President and Secretary of State. It merely revealed the limited ability of even sober and wise statesmen to foresee all the consequences of their acts. They would have been superior indeed had they fully understood the complexity and multiplicity of the forces at work. They could not know that a revolution shortly to break forth in Spain would diminish the effects of the measure upon which they relied. Most understandable is their inability to see that the ministry in London could not alter the Orders in Council without being toppled from power or that Great Britain could not retreat without impressing prospective allies with the weakness of her position. Nor is it a reflection on the prudence of their calculations that they did not foresee the time when enforcement of the Embargo would require the imposition of regulations upon the daily activities of citizens wholly inconsistent with their own understanding of the principles of a free society.

Desiring to exhaust diplomacy before resorting to more extreme measures, Jefferson and Madison continued the Monroe and Pinkney negotiations throughout the spring of 1807. Jefferson's good faith is to be seen in his postponement of the Non-Importation law. His sincere desire for a settlement is likewise affirmed by his efforts to find some solution to the problem of impressment. Jefferson and his cabinet hoped that the United States might so assure the British on the problem of deserting seamen that they would yield the right to remove suspected deserters from American ships. Contrary to this hope, the discussion in the cabinet brought facts to view that complicated the negotiations still further. For example, Albert Gallatin, investigating the probable effects of a law prohibiting the employment of British seamen, found that since 1803 the tonnage in foreign trade was increasing at a rate of 70,000 tons a year, requiring an additional 8400 sailors every two years. British deserters, Gallatin estimated, supplied from one-half to two-thirds of that increase. To dismiss the British already employed would involve a loss of at least 5,000 seamen and "would materially injure our navigation much more indeed than any restrictions which, supposing no treaty to take place, they could levy upon our commerce."[1]

The Chesapeake Affair of June, 1807, provoked such a crisis that war seemed more appropriate than economic coercion. Public meetings from Boston to Norfolk protested the outrage, and Jefferson and his cabinet considered war inevitable. Not since Lexington had the country been so aroused, wrote Jefferson, but hostilities were postponed until Congress could convene. Gallatin explained that Congress was the arbiter of war under the Constitution, that waiting for Congress would produce the necessary unanimity, and that a four month delay would enable American ships to return to port and escape British seizure.[2] Jefferson confined himself to issuing a proclamation ordering all armed British ships to leave American ports at once and to making a strong protest to London.

The intention of the administration was to postpone going to war for a short time only. Albert Gallatin admitted that the war would entail destruction, debts, taxes, and the necessity of an increase of the executive power, but he concluded that "all those evils" should not "be put in competition with the independence and honor of the nation." "The awakening of nobler feelings and habits than avarice and luxury" might be necessary to prevent "our degenerating, like the Hollanders, into a nation of mere calculators."[3] Jefferson reflected with pleasure on what a galling enemy the British would find in the United States. American privateers, 250 of them manned by the 20,000 Americans still on the high seas, would reap a rich plunder.[4] Canada would be seized and held until the British accorded the nation its rights. Jefferson also proposed to engage Spain and settle the Florida question.[5] And if war must come, it could come on no better issue. Czar Alexander and Napoleon, he wrote, would eventually destroy the British monopoly of the seas and protect the rights of neutrals, but impressment was an issue on which the Americans must fight alone. Reflecting upon the divided opinion as to the proper course in the past, Jefferson was thankful that the British had now "touched a chord which vibrates in every heart." "Now then," he observed, "is the time to settle the old and the new."[6]

The fuller view of the unprepared state of the nation that time kindly provided quieted the belligerent spirit. Gallatin by August found the citizenry of New York so appalled by the inability of the city to defend itself that they early opposed war.[7] Naval defenses were scarcely existent and their absence had its effect all along the coast. When the *Constitution* docked at Boston, money was not available to pay the crew, and the frigate was ordered to New York in the hope that funds might be conjured up in the meantime.[8] Secretary of the Navy Robert Smith could not send a ship to the East Indies to warn merchantmen of impending danger because he had no funds.[9] The Secretary of War reported that the militia was wholly unready.[10] Concerning the defense of Washington, Gallatin warned that the enemy "might land at Annapolis, march to the city, and re-embark before the militia could be collected to repel him."[11]

When Congress convened, Jefferson limited himself to recommending a series of defense measures. The administration, at the peak of its popularity, put through its bills with large majorities. On December 11 the House of Representatives passed the administration gunboat measure 111 to 19.[12] Opposition was limited to a few Federalists and Virginia Quids. The opposition showed no greater strength in seeking to block the putting into operation of the Non-Importation Act. A petition from the merchants of Philadelphia calling for repeal was denounced as unpatriotic and was not received.[13] A Boston petition, phrased more diplomatically, asking for repeal, modification, or suspension, was received, but the arguments in the House rested largely on the right of petition rather than on the merits of the arguments contained in the petition.[14] Feeling ran strongly in favor of defense measures, but the war spirit had wilted.

Foreign relations entered upon a new stage on December 18, the day on which Jefferson called for the Embargo. The emphasis shifted from impressment and hostile British actions in American ports to the question of British trade restrictions. Ever since the beginning of the Wars of the French Revolution the prosperity of the United States in the carrying trade had aroused deep enmity among the British. In 1805 James Stephens published his *War in Disguise, or the Frauds of the Neutral Flags*. Stephens viewed the American gains in the carrying trade as threatening the very existence of Great Britain. If the trade were permitted, the Americans would not only carry goods to France but would carry French manufactures on the return voyage. Napoleon would insist on that. Thereby the American market for British manufactures would be lost, and not only the market in the United States, but the market of the whole new world for many of the British manufactures carried in American ships were re-exported to the West Indies and South America. In addition the British would lose the profits from the large re-exports of American goods from England to the continent. In this way France would soon replace England as the great commercial entrepot.[15]

Napoleon's Berlin decree of November 1806 lifted the argument of James Stephens out of the realm of fears conjured up by a lawyer into the realm of British policy. The decree proclaimed a blockade of the British Isles and ordered the seizure of British ships entering ports under his control. In retaliation, in January 1807, the British issued an Order in Council prohibiting neutrals from engaging in coastwise trade on the continent. Prior laxness in enforcement gave way to a sharp clamping down on American trade in the summer of 1807. For the first time the United States faced actual exclusion from carrying on any trade with the continent.

The most sweeping Order in Council followed on November 11. This declared illegal all trade with France, her allies, and any country which did not permit the entry of British goods. All trade with the continent must pass through a British port, and American ships would have to purchase a license before proceeding to ports in another country. The British described the purpose as retaliatory and justified by the French decrees, but Americans could only view its purpose as that of delivering a blow against them rather than France. In considerable part this was the case, but the order was also inspired by a patriotic urge to strike back against Napoleon. Once the order had been issued it could not be withdrawn without arousing the hostility of the merchants against the ministry and without undermining the confidence of those nations whom the British hoped to rally to their side in the battle against Napoleon.

Before he was officially notified of the new order Jefferson learned of it through a newspaper account. He seized upon the report to present a special message to Congress calling for an embargo. Jefferson presented his proposal as a defense measure that would protect the nation's merchant marine from seizure. The step could readily be defended on this ground. Even before news of the new Order in Council there was considerable expectation of hostilities because the Chesapeake Affair had not yet been settled. The new order added to the expectations of a wave of seizures that would lead to war. To lay an embargo prohibiting American ships from leaving for foreign ports was a justifiable measure of national defense which would prevent the loss of millions of dollars of shipping. The Embargo met a second need, the psychological need to strike back against injury. That it filled this need is amply illustrated in the debates over the proposal. Thirdly, it aimed at coercing the British. This aim is embodied in Section I which prohibited foreign vessels to take on goods beyond what were already on board when notified of the act.[16] It placed no prohibition on imports. The only limitations on imports were those prescribed by the Non-Importation law. That law did not exclude the most important British imports, cottons, cheap woolens, and iron and steel products. The original Embargo bill lacked effectiveness as a coercive measure because of failure to prohibit imports in foreign vessels and by omission of a prohibition against exports of specie in foreign ships to pay for imports.

The strength of the majority party and the recent eruption of resentment against the belligerents assured easy passage. The Senate suspended its rules to permit passage on a single day, and the vote was 22 to 6. Because local strongholds of Federalism and Old Republicanism enjoyed greater strength in the House, the opposition in the lower chamber was able to prolong the debate for three days and mustered 44 negative votes. Merchant groups did not at this time or for many months to come oppose the Embargo. The fishery interests filed the first protest, and that did not come before Congress until April 11. The first opposition to the Embargo grew out of political motivations rather than economic grievances. Because of the stagnation of commerce since the previous summer, the Embargo did not greatly change the status of the maritime interests.

A fuller debate on the Embargo began in February when supplementary legislation was introduced to make it more effective as a coercive measure. The new bill prohibited exports of goods to adjacent foreign territory, placed new restrictions on coastwise shipping, and prohibited the export of specie.[17] Strangely, the bill did not extend the prohibitions against British imports although it was generally observed that depriving the British of the American market for manufactured goods would be one of the most effective ways of putting pressure upon her.

The supplementary legislation passed both houses with as comfortable margins as those enjoyed by the original bill, but the minority now began to employ arguments that would eventually help to undermine confidence in the measure. Barent Gardenier of New York, a representative whose every speech lashed the administration with charges of deceit and ignorance, maintained: "Between the original measure and this, there is no connexion: the principle of the one is totally different from the other. Nay, sir, this bill is totally at variance with the President's embargo Message." After quoting from Jefferson's message of the previous December, Gardenier said the alleged purpose of the original bill was to protect American vessels from seizure whereas the new bill aimed at coercing Great Britain. Gardenier charged that from the beginning Jefferson's aim was to coerce the British. He held that Jefferson's purpose was no other than to tie the nation to Napoleon. "Do not go on forging chains to fasten us to the car of the Imperial Conqueror," he warned the House.[18]

Edward St. Loe Livermore, of Massachusetts, saw in the Embargo the deep seated prejudice of the agrarians against commerce. He warned that "commerce is of such service to agriculture that agriculture is of little service without it." The Embargo, recommended on other grounds, he said, had as its real purpose forcing merchants into bankruptcy.[19] Significantly, even Livermore admitted that merchants accepted the Embargo as a wise measure, but the real motives of the administration and of the majority had been hidden from their view.[20]

In April the debate reached new heights of intensity when a resolution was introduced that gave to the President the power to suspend the act as it applied to one of the belligerents if one of them withdrew the obnoxious edicts. The minority challenged the proposal as an unconstitutional delegation of legislative power to the executive. The resolution likewise presented the minority with an opportunity to expand upon the arguments against the Embargo. They asked how a contest with Great Britain over the issue of maritime rights could justify surrendering those rights in the wholesale manner provided for by the obnoxious Embargo. They cited the decline in prosperity and attributed it to the policy of the administration. The majority's reply that the decline was due to the belligerents' orders carried less and less weight as the depression continued.

To the majority's explanation that there could be no trade even though there was no Embargo the opponents retorted by asking why there must be an Embargo if there could be no trade anyway. The same representatives of the Northeast argued that the merchants, if freed of the Embargo, would find ways to circumvent the orders and decrees. Much was made of the fact that the measures of the belligerents did not bar American ships going to non-European parts of the world. Why then, they asked, should Americans prohibit themselves from profiting from the channels of trade that were still open?

To these annoying questions the opponents of Jefferson added charges that rested on half truths or no truth at all. The Monroe-Pinkney negotiations were re-examined in detail and the conclusion reached that Jefferson and Madison did not wish a settlement. This charge was made to rest upon the administration's earlier threat of putting into operation the Non-Importation Act. The critics of Jefferson, many of whom had once been in the vanguard of those denouncing impressment, now maintained that the importance of this evil had been exaggerated. At any rate, they argued, the British had been willing to make satisfactory arrangements on this issue. They cited the note of the British negotiators offering to issue orders to naval commanders to exercise extreme caution.

The argument that carried greatest weight in the long months ahead stressed the futility of resisting the belligerents. The nations of Europe were engaged in the greatest struggle of all history. The issue was whether Napoleon should control the continent and perhaps the world. Given the importance of the issues, it was not to be expected that the belligerents would endanger their chances of victory by making concessions. The Federalists, strongly pro-British, added that it was in the interest of humanity at large and of the United States in particular that Napoleon should be defeated.

Not until April 14, in the debate on a resolution granting to the President the power to suspend the Embargo, during the absence of Congress, did any administration supporter present in full the arguments in favor of the Embargo. George W. Campbell of Tennessee, long close to both Jefferson and Madison, devoted the larger part of the day to examining the arguments of the critics of the Embargo and to showing that it was a wise measure.[21] Campbell denied that the Embargo was dictated by France, a charge based upon an extremely loose interpretation of a phrase from Jean Champagny, Minister of Foreign Affairs to General Armstrong, United States Minister to France.[22] Campbell rested the case for the Embargo on three considerations. First, the driving of American commerce from the seas since the summer of 1807 followed by the British Order in Council of November showed that it was the intent of the belligerents to enrich themselves by seizing American ships and goods. This confronted the nation with three choices, submission, war, or embargo. The first amounted to acceptance of colonial status. War presented the danger of hostilities with both belligerents, and the weak state of the nation's defenses gave but slight hope of victory. To permit American ships to continue sailing the high seas where they would be seized would certainly bring on war. Except to a small number of political dissidents, the Embargo appeared to be the only way to save the nation's shipping from seizure, and the most feasible way to exert pressure on the belligerents. Campbell cited the alarm that had been aroused in Parliament. Imports of British goods, estimated at sixty millions of dollars annually, had been almost entirely stopped. The results could be clearly foreseen:

This immense sum will therefore no longer flow into that country, in supplies or specie; their goods will remain in the hands of the manufacturers, and not in their warehouses, there being no other part of the world to which they can send them for consumption. This will carry the effects of the Embargo home to every class of society in that country; the people will sensibly feel them, will see the causes that produced them, and speak to their government in a tone of language that will command their attention. In addition to this that country will be deprived of about fifteen millions of pounds of cotton, which she annually received from us, being about one-half the amount of the article required to supply her manufactories.[23]

Commercial non-intercourse would bring widespread unemployment and scenes of ruin and distress to England.

Campbell met the Federalist criticisms at other points. They had described the Embargo as a measure that turned over all trade to Great Britain. Campbell replied:

It is true, sir, we have abandoned our commerce *with* Great Britain, but not *to her;* we have retired from the ocean, and in retiring, have carried with us almost the whole commerce of the European world. The belligerent Powers cannot carry on commerce with each other, and there are no neutrals in Europe with which they can trade—what commerce then, is abandoned by us to Great Britain?[24]

He rejected the Federalist contention that the Monroe-Pinkney treaty should have been ratified. To have accepted the arrangement on impressment would have compromised our position that impressment was wholly unjustified under the law of nations. Secondly, the note annexed to the treaty left Great Britain free to disregard the provisions whenever she found it opportune to retaliate against France in ways contradicting the treaty provisions. Finally, Campbell cited the treaty provision which prohibited any interference with exportations or importations by either party. In words reminiscent of James Madison's arguments against the Jay Treaty, Campbell saw this provision as depriving the nation of the power to counteract hostile British measures.[25]

When Congress reconvened in November, 1808, all of the attacks made on the Embargo the previous spring were repeated. Extremists like Josiah Quincy, Barent Gardenier, and John Randolph in the House and Timothy Pickering in the Senate played constantly on the theme of conspiracy. Pickering, chief spokesman for the Essex Junta, the Massachusetts diehards whose political partisanship carried them close to treason, gave a speech in the Senate on November 30 in which he attributed sinister motives to the President.[26] Not until the opponents of Franklin Roosevelt plumbed even greater depths, did a President find himself the target of such invective. Pickering began by repeating the old charge that the Embargo rather than the orders and decrees was the cause of commercial stagnation. He cited figures on insurance rates that minimized the danger of seizure and set forth statistics purporting to show that only a small percentage of ships leaving Boston had been seized, but his figures referred only to ports largely unaffected by the orders and decrees.

Secondly, Pickering contrasted the success of the Washington administration in negotiating with Great Britain in 1794 and with Spain in 1795 with the failures of Jefferson and Madison. These failures he attributed to unrealistic demands of Jefferson and Madison. Thirdly, he justified the British Order in Council of November 1807, closing all ports controlled by France. The Emperor had highhandedly ordered all states to close their ports to British commerce, a measure designed to ruin England by cutting off all trade. In dread fear of the Emperor all countries except Sweden had complied. Could England then be blamed for striking back? Finally, Pickering purported to show that Jefferson's call for the Embargo was not a response to the British Order in Council but a compliance with orders from Napoleon. Jefferson, he maintained, could not have known of the British order at the time he called for the Embargo. Jefferson was acting on orders from the French minister Champagny to Minister Armstrong. The Embargo was nothing less than an act called for by Napoleon who saw that his continental system could not be successful unless the British also lost their American market.

The partial truths and final daring conjecture added up to a distortion, but many New Englanders undoubtedly accepted the thesis. That they believed it is an indication of how deeply they feared that the agrarians would, under the banner of national honor, align themselves on the side of France in order to seek the destruction of both England and the commercial interests at home.

Not all opponents of the Embargo resorted to charges of conspiracy. Calmly and without invective men like Timothy Pitkin, of Connecticut, presented reasonable arguments as to why the Embargo was unlikely to have the desired coercive effects.[27] These more reasonable men argued with some force that a settlement with England would have been possible had not Jefferson and Madison been unrealistic in their demands.

The votes were in the hands of the administration but time was on the side of the minority. In 1808 there was no solution to the grievous difficulties faced by the nation. Not negotiation, not war, and not an embargo—even an embargo that would have barred British imports and wholly sealed off exports—could have driven Great Britain to acknowledge before the world that she was wrong in her policy or that she was not sufficiently strong to uphold it. In 1812 an embargo caused the British to repeal the Orders in Council but not in 1808, when the British ministry teetered uneasily and could ill afford to align the shipping interests solidly against it, and when prospective allies on the continent watched warily for evidence of British weakness and would be guided by it in deciding whether to accept the dominance of Napoleon. This would at first glance appear to justify the Federalists' fatalism and their ridicule of the Embargo as an effective instrument, but they underestimated the economic power the nation held in its hands. Even the Embargo as carried out in 1808 injured the British.[28] Parliament was faced with petitions carrying 50,000 signatures, and opponents of the ministry took up the cause of the United States. Amidst changed circumstances on the international scene and a stronger ministry at home four years later the United States did demonstrate how powerful the economic weapon could be.

The action of the Republicans in laying an embargo is not to be fully explained in terms of their faith in the policy of economic coercion. Albert Gallatin always questioned the wisdom of adhering to the Embargo for any length of time.[29] By early summer of 1808 Jefferson clearly had doubts about its effectiveness and acknowledged that the time would come when it would be in the national interest to give up the policy and resort to force.[30] The adherence of the Republicans to the Embargo rested quite as much on other grounds as it did on faith in its effectiveness as a weapon. British measures deeply hurt the United States economically and hurt it even more psychologically. Republicans believed as firmly as they believed in republican principles that British action was unjustified by the law of nations, that it was equally unjustified by military necessity, and that British action was motivated more by commercial jealousy than anything else. To submit without protest to such action would be to accept the equivalent of colonial status. To maintain national self-respect it was necessary to resist. The majority dismissed the arguments of the Federalists as based on nothing but an unwarranted prejudice against Jefferson. When the opposing party could believe the impossible, namely that the "Great Enchanter," as the Federalists called him, was scheming to ally the nation with France, help defeat England, and then make war on the commercial interests at home, their arguments were scarcely to be taken seriously.

In the fall of 1808 the Republicans marshalled as many votes for the Embargo as they had in the dark days of December 1807, but they carried on their shoulders the heavy burden of a measure that gave no promise of success. The Embargo rested upon careful calculation but it became increasingly clear that the logical predictions of the previous winter were not to be fulfilled. The Republicans explained the failure as a result of Federalist evasion of the law and of British reliance on the dissident political elements to change the law, and they made much of the fact that Spain's revolution against Napoleon opened a new market for the British and thereby diminished the effect of the Embargo.

By December 1808, both parties talked of the possibility of open rebellion and civil war. The majority decried the lack of national honor and resolved to meet the threat with further legislation to make the Embargo more effective. They decided that it was necessary to give customs officers the authority to seize goods merely on suspicion that the goods were bound for foreign territory. They likewise believed it necessary to protect customs collectors against hostile action in the state courts where those who evaded the law successfully brought actions against collectors seeking to enforce the law. Finally, the majority decided to call up the military to aid in enforcement. All of these measures were recommended by Albert Gallatin in a letter to Senator William B. Giles, chairman of the committee dealing with questions relating to the Embargo.[31] Congress passed the necessary law in late December, a law that, as the Federalists pointed out, extended the power of government far beyond the limits deemed proper in a society dedicated to republican principles. The majority party was now face to face with a situation in which they would have to go to war with their own people if they were to continue making war against the belligerents by the mild weapon of the Embargo.

The stringent law passed by substantial majorities. It was a

Pyrrhic victory for the party in power. What thoughts passed through the minds of the majority during the succeeding days the documents of history do not reveal, but it is clear that the majority split. Some preferred to adhere to the Embargo to the bitter end, and others believed that the time had arrived for a change in policy. On February 8, 1809, the day of the counting of the votes for President, William Giles introduced a bill in the Senate providing for the repeal of the Embargo except as to Great Britain and France.[32] It was a recognition of the fact that the widespread evasions and the deep schism in the political councils nullified the coercive element of the Embargo and that the British seeing this would scarcely give way.

On January 24 Wilson Gary Nicholas of Virginia introduced a resolution in the House calling for repeal of the Embargo and defense of navigation of the high seas against any nation "having in force edicts, orders, or decrees, violating the lawful commerce and neutral rights of the United States."[33] Three days later Ezekiel Bacon of Massachusetts introduced a resolution authorizing the arming of merchant ships and armed resistance to seizure attempted under the British orders or French decrees.[34] On January 30 Nicholas introduced an amendment to his original resolution providing for the issuing of letters of marque and reprisal against Great Britain and France.[35]

These resolutions pushed the question of the Embargo into the background and substituted the question of war. The resolution of Bacon was viewed as probably leading to war by those opposed to war and objected to by others because they had no faith that the merchants would resist. They would, it was said, pay the British licenses and abide by British regulations, actions deemed tantamount to submission.

Daniel M. Durell of New Hampshire introduced a third resolution in the House on February 6. This stated that if the belligerents seized a ship owned by citizens of the United States under the authority of the objectionable edicts the action should be considered a declaration of war against the

United States.[36] Durell argued that this would clearly specify that the United States was willing to take extreme measures to resist the decrees and orders and separate this issue from the older disputes over impressment, blockades, and the Chesapeake Affair, disputes the United States would willingly postpone until a later time. Durell objected to issuing letters of marque because this would be the same as declaring war. Because the country had faced no new invasion of its rights for over a year, the people were now apathetic and would not be unified. His proposal would place the onus of having fired the first shot on the belligerents. This would unite the people and make possible effective prosecution of the war.

After further debate the House voted down the resolution calling for letters of marque by a vote of 57 to 39.[37] The House, it was clear, was not ready for war, but the following day it took a step of major importance when it sent the three resolutions back to committee and called on that body to submit a bill embodying the earlier Non-Intercourse proposal. The committee promptly complied by reporting the Non-Intercourse Bill providing for repeal of the Embargo, and no commercial relations with Great Britain and France, including a prohibition of imports from these two countries.

It was widely recognized that the Non-Intercourse measure would be even more difficult to enforce. No one claimed that it would coerce the belligerents. The new proposal, however, was the only one that the nation could agree upon, the opponents of the Embargo because it got rid of that law and because it would be ineffective, the former supporters of the Embargo because it fell short of submission. In a society based upon republican principles it was necessary to reach a substantial consensus of opinion; a majority of votes, even a large majority, was not sufficient on matters that evoked resistance and, in turn, created a need for extensive police action. In this lay a major consideration in the formulation of foreign policy in a free society.

Probably at no time in its history has the United States presented a more ambivalent picture. The major factor in this ambivalence was the minority's fear that Jefferson contemplated an alliance with France and looked forward to establishing what was vaguely known as "French principles."[38] This fear had its origins in the well known libertarian views of the President, his willingness to experiment, and his suspicion of the merchant class. Jefferson's great skill in rhetoric and devotion to general principles of liberty created an image that tended to obscure Jefferson the practical and hard-headed statesman from the public view.

The economic effects of the Embargo further divided the country. Not until the close of the debates that occupied Congress over thirteen months did anyone point to one of the vital differences between the commercial interests and the agrarians. William Burwell, of Virginia, on several occasions presented the most factual economic analysis of the situation of any speaker in either house of Congress. In February Burwell arose to reply to the plea of Gardenier that the Embargo should be lifted so that the merchants of the Northeast might derive some profit. Burwell, in answering the New York Congressman, stated explicitly what helps to explain the adamancy of the agrarians:

Does the gentleman for New York wish, because a particular portion of the country could carry on a lucrative commerce, notwithstanding the Orders in Council, by selling their product in the British markets, that the whole interest of every other section of the Union should be given up? Are the great interests of the country to be completely given up, because one class of people would receive relief from it? Of what consequence is it to us to cultivate the soil, if we are restricted to a particular market, which, it has been shown, does not consume one-seventh of our product?[39]

The merchants, if the laws were changed to permit them to go to sea, might enjoy a limited trade with Great Britain and with ports in those parts of the world not affected by the orders of the belligerents, but this would not help the agrarians whose products would remain at ruinous prices as long as the belligerents shut off those parts where the bulk of their produce was consumed. Burwell cited the aid in the form of drawbacks that the agrarians had granted to the carrying trade. If the shipowners were not to support the agrarians in the fight for access to the markets where the greater part of their produce was consumed, why then, asked Burwell, should not the agrarians withhold the favor provided by the system of drawbacks?

The supporters of the administration began with a bias in favor of the President. They were right in their assumption that Jefferson was first an American, dedicated to national interests, and an opponent of Napoleon. They spoke much of national honor, were traditionally hostile toward Great Britain, and their economic situation made them less willing than the merchants to compromise on the issue of the British orders. They were fully aware that as long as Great Britain closed the ports of the continent, prices on the agricultural products they produced would be too low to permit them a profit.

The problem was further complicated by the fact that no one could be dogmatically certain that any proposed measure would be successful. The Embargo was an untried experiment. It was costly not only to the merchants but to the government which suffered heavy losses in revenue. It offered even less hope of success after the revolt of Spain against Napoleon gave some hope to the British of a new market.

The alternatives to the Embargo were equally uncertain of success. War was widely discussed. Supporters of the administration saw no difficulty in conquering Canada and the maritime provinces, but the opponents of war pointed out the difficulties encountered during the War for Independence in attempting to conquer Canada. Those opposed to war likewise made much of the difficult nature of the country, and they ridiculed the idea that Great Britain would endanger her maritime supremacy by yielding her policy as to navigation of the high seas in return for the colonies to the north. They added to this a heavy emphasis on the lack of an army and questioned whether the states would permit their militia to serve beyond national boundaries. Given these considerations, Benjamin Tallmadge, representative from New York, might well say that "sound policy may sometimes dictate an endurance of smaller evils for a time, rather than expose a nation to the calamities of war. . . ."[40]

In a free society all of these fears and frustrations enjoyed free rein. The result was the ambivalence that ended in the Non-Intercourse law, a measure that contained within it greater dangers than the nation foresaw in March of 1809.

NOTES

1. *The Writings of Albert Gallatin*, ed. Henry Adams, Vol. I (Philadelphia: J. B. Lippincott & Co., 1879), p. 332 and p. 336.

2. *Ibid.*, p. 338.

3. *Ibid.*, p. 339.

4. *The Works of Thomas Jefferson*, ed. Paul Leicester Ford, Vol. IX (New York: G. P. Putnam's Sons, 1898), p. 119.

5. *Ibid.*, pp. 124-5 and 134.

6. *Ibid.*, p. 120.

7. *Writings of Gallatin*, Vol. I, p. 353.

8. Irving Brant, *James Madison Secretary of State* (Indianapolis: The Bobbs-Merrill Co., 1953), p. 392.

9. *Writings of Gallatin*, Vol. I, p. 357.

10. Brant, *op. cit.*, p. 393.

11. *Writings of Albert Gallatin*, Vol. I, p. 343.

12. *Annals of Congress, Tenth Congress, First Session*, p. 1171.

13. *Ibid.*, p. 982.

14. *Ibid.*, p. 1176.

15. For further information on James Stephens see *The Memoirs of James Stephens Written by Himself for the Use of His Children*, ed. Merle Bevington (London: Hogarth Press, 1954) and *The Correspondence of William Wilberforce*, eds. Robert Isaac and Samuel Wilberforce (London, 1854).

16. See *Annals of Congress, Tenth Congress, First Session*, pp. 1222-1223.

17. *Ibid.*, Appendix, pp. 2815-2816.

18. *Ibid.*, pp. 1653-1654.

19. *Ibid.*, p. 1702.

20. *Ibid.*

21. *Ibid.*, pp. 2137-2172.

22. The conspiracy theory was based upon a dubious interpretation of a letter from Champagny to Armstrong written on October 7, 1807. Because a great part of the Federalist opposition based their charges on this letter the pertinent paragraph deserves to be quoted: "The decree of blockade has been now issued eleven months: the principal Powers of Europe, far from protesting against its provisions, have adopted them.

They have perceived that its execution must be complete to render it more effectual, and it has seemed easy to reconcile these measures with the observance of treaties, especially at a time when the infractions by England of the rights of all maritime Powers render their interest common, and tend to unite them in support of the same cause." The Federalists interpreted this paragraph as a threat which led Jefferson to call for the Embargo. The evidence does not support the charge. Jefferson did learn of the British Order in Council of November 11 prior to his call for the Embargo although Federalists made much of the fact that he did not receive official notification of it until some weeks after his special message to Congress.

23. *Annals of Congress, Tenth Congress, First Session*, p. 2158.

24. *Ibid.*, p. 2153.

25. *Ibid.*, p. 2161.

26. For Pickering's speech see *Annals of Congress, Tenth Congress, Second Session*, pp. 175-194.

27. For Pitkin's speech, *ibid.*, pp. 1214-1229. It is interesting to note that Pitkin took occasion to deny that he believed that the Embargo had been enacted in order to meet the wishes of Napoleon. See p. 1223.

28. *Cobbetts Parliamentary Debates*, (London: T. C. Hansard, 1808) Vol. X, (January-April 1808) pp. 889-895, 930-932, and 1240-1241.

29. *Writings of Gallatin*, Vol. I, p. 368.

30. Thomas Jefferson wrote to Doctor Thomas Leib on June 23, 1808: "It is true, the time will come when we must abandon it. But if this is before the repeal of the orders of council, we must abandon it only for a state of war. The day is not distant, when that will be preferable to a longer continuance of the embargo." *The Writings of Thomas Jefferson*, Vol. IX, pp. 196-197.

31. Albert Gallatin to William B. Giles, November 24, 1808, *Annals of Congress, Tenth Congress, Second Session*, pp. 232-236.

32. *Ibid.*, p. 345.

33. *Ibid.*, p. 1172.

34. *Ibid.*, p. 1189.

35. *Ibid.*, p. 1232.

36. *Ibid.*, p. 1377.

37. *Ibid.*, p. 1421.

38. William Burwell, one of the most thoughtful members of the House, on February 1 remarked: "I believe that the uneasiness in the Eastern country proceeds entirely from an idea that the embargo originated in an intention to destroy commerce, and to favor one foreign nation in preference to another: and that, if they had not their feelings excited by this perversion of fact, they would bear the measure as well as other citizens." *Ibid.*, p. 1279.

39. *Ibid.*, p. 1281.

40. *Ibid.*, p. 1201.

Negotiations That Ended
in Frustration

XI

Historians have asked the question, "What caused the War of 1812?" If this is turned about and we ask: "Why was not a settlement reached between Great Britain and the United States?", the inquiry is directed into a more specific channel of investigation.

The redirecting of the inquiry flows out of the shift that has taken place in recent writings on the coming of the war. While Julius Pratt's thesis placing primary responsibility on American expansion enjoyed general acceptance, it could be assumed that the determination to acquire Canada and the Floridas provided a conflict of interests not amenable to settlement by diplomacy. Now historians minimize expansionism and place the blame for the war on maritime grievances. Were the questions that divided the two nations as to neutral rights of such a nature that they could not be settled by diplomacy? The answer is no.

There was a conflict of national interests but a reasonably satisfactory compromise was within reach. By far the most important of the grievances centered on the British Orders in Council of January and November 1807 and their revised form in the Order of April 1809. The first barred American ships from participation in the coastwise trade of Europe, the second forced American ships bound for the ports of the enemy or ports controlled by the enemy to go by way of Great Britain and to purchase licenses before proceeding. The final one of 1809, considerably less confining, limited the application of the earlier orders to the coastline from Holland to Italy. In June, 1812, these orders were revoked in their entirety. The most serious grievance of the United States, although not the only one, was thereby removed.

The failure to reach a settlement earlier was not due to irreconcilable national interests but to the circumstances under which the negotiations were conducted. In 1812 the tide of war had turned sufficiently in Great Britain's favor so that she could make the concession without appearing to make it under duress. Earlier the British found no way to meet the demands of the United States without seriously weakening her political position in Europe. But this was not the only cause for the failure of diplomacy. The bitter party conflict within the United States and the strong national bias of James Madison also hindered the reaching of a diplomatic settlement, but it is the first of these factors that provides the subject of inquiry in this chapter.

The breakdown of diplomacy became apparent after the Chesapeake Affair of June, 1807. The incident would not have left such deep scars had not British apologies and reparations been delayed until 1811. The immediate reaction of George Canning to reports of hostilities portended an early and satisfactory settlement. Canning, upon the first incomplete accounts of what had taken place, approached Minister Monroe and gave him a note expressing "sincere concern and sorrow" and assuring him that "if the British officers should prove to have been culpable, the most prompt and effectual reparation shall be afforded to the Government of the United States."[1] Monroe, after expressing appreciation of Canning's friendly assurance of amends, called for a frank disavowal of the principle that warships might be subject to search for deserters.[2] Canning, although he did not yet have an official account of what had taken place, promptly assured Monroe that "His Majesty neither does nor has at any time maintained the pretension of a right to search ships of war, in the national service of any state, for deserters."[3]

This auspicious beginning of negotiations concerning the Chesapeake Affair came to an end when Monroe delivered Secretary of State Madison's official demand for reparations. Monroe's instructions called on the British to yield the right of impressment in regard to merchant ships as well as warships, thereby inserting into the negotiation a problem which three years of laborious negotiations had failed to solve.[4] By the time that Monroe met with Canning to discuss the demands of the United States, the foreign secretary had learned of Jefferson's Proclamation of July 2 prohibiting entry into American ports of British ships of war. Canning protested that this placed France in a favored position, and he also objected strongly to the President taking redress into his own hands without waiting for an explanation from the British government.[5] The introduction of the impressment issue and the President's proclamation impeded further progress. By October Canning informed Monroe that his government would send a special envoy to the United States to negotiate.

In February, 1808, George Rose arrived in Washington to represent the British government. The instructions to Rose made British disavowal and reparation contingent upon the United States' prior withdrawal of the President's proclamation. Jefferson and Madison sought to circumvent this obstacle by proposing that the Proclamation should be withdrawn the same day as the British made their disavowal and extended promises of reparation, but Rose rejected this as contrary to his instructions.[6] The British now regarded the question as closed. The United States deplored the failure of the British to make reparations but did not press the question in ensuing negotiations.

Beginning in February, 1808, attention focused on the Orders in Council issued in 1807. In his first diplomatic note on the orders of the previous November, James Madison took a moralistic and legalistic approach. The British, he wrote, justified the orders in terms of military necessity, but the orders went beyond military necessity and prohibited to the United States all commerce with the enemies of Great Britain, "now nearly the whole commercial world," and were "too evidently fashioned to the commercial, the manufacturing, and the fiscal policy of Great Britain."[7] Madison viewed the orders as aiming more at establishing a British monopoly over the seas than retaliation against France.

Secondly, Madison rejected the British contention that failure of the United States to take action against the French decrees justified British action. The French decrees, wrote Madison, had two aspects. The first, prohibiting the entry of British ships and goods into the ports of France and her allies, was merely a municipal regulation.[8] However injurious, this aspect was no different in principle from the British navigation acts. No foreign power had any right to protest against the act of a sovereign nation when that act was confined to its domestic jurisdiction.

Madison, of course, was legally correct, but he ignored the fact that Napoleon was making municipal regulations for the greater part of the continent thereby threatening to destroy Great Britain by destroying her economy. To present this argument to the hard-pressed British government could scarcely be expected to establish mutual confidence. In effect, it condoned the injury done by Napoleon at the same time that it held Great Britain to observing the law of nations while an unscrupulous tyrant conquered neutral nations that did not bow before his dictates.

Madison dismissed as an idle gesture Napoleon's blockade of the British Isles.[9] The French navy did not dare venture beyond the confines of its own ports. Not a single American ship had suffered seizure by the French until the very recent case of the *Horizon*. Therefore the United States could scarcely be expected to take action against France on grounds of injury France was powerless to inflict. In terms of actual injury, of course, James Madison was correct, but his argument was at least partially vitiated by his readiness to tolerate injuries suffered from France under the cover of municipal regulations. In the first case, he argued on legal grounds; in the second case, he argued on grounds of injury suffered.

In his protest against the orders Madison held the British to a strict observance of international law. A neutral nation, wrote Madison, not being a party to the war, should suffer no infringements of its rights to carry on trade as in peacetime except in so far as the law of nations sanctioned curtailments of these rights. He accused the British of conducting "an unprecedented system of warfare on neutral rights and national independence" in a manner "the common judgment and common feelings of mankind must forever protest."[10] Such strong denunciation in a diplomatic note at a time when Napoleon was taking over neutral nations by conquest and denying them all rights of sovereignty was scarcely likely to impress the British as complete impartiality.

Madison's serious search for a settlement with Great Britain did not accord with the contentious spirit manifested in his notes. He seized upon minor phrases of his diplomatic antagonist that could better have been ignored. In communicating the November Orders in Council, George Canning spoke of concessions, especially that yielding to the United States the right to trade with the enemy's colonies. Madison picked up Canning's reference to the "ancient" Rule of 1756 and pointed out that the rule was not ancient, that it had never been a part of the law of nations, that the United States had never recognized it, and concluded his observations by stating that what Canning called a concession was no concession at all but a step dictated by British expediency.[11]

The Secretary of State likewise went out of his way to challenge the British contention that France had been the first to violate neutral rights. He cited the prior British blockades and unwarranted definitions of contraband. In introducing this point, which was not necessary to the defense of the issues at stake, Madison permitted a feeling of pique to intrude.[12]

Madison's note could only have resulted in fruitless wrangling. George Canning and the British ministry cared little about abstract rights interpreted to suit American interests, but they did care about fostering trade with the United States providing that this could be done without any loss to themselves. The passage by Congress, in April of 1808, of a bill authorizing the President to suspend the Embargo against either belligerent who cancelled its orders or decrees, provided Pinkney with an opportunity which he exploited to the full. Pushing aside the question of abstract rights and carefully steering clear of past grievances, he talked to Canning of the great gains that now lay within British reach.

"To have urged the revocation upon the mere ground of strict policy, or of general right, and there to have left the subject, when I was authorized to place it upon grounds infinitely stronger, would have been, as it appeared to me, to stop short of my duty," Pinkney wrote to Madison.[13] He fully developed the gains that would come to Great Britain by revocation of the Orders in Council. Either of two consequences would result. If France followed suit by withdrawal of the decrees, then commerce would once again flow freely, much to British advantage. If France did not do so, the United States would more effectively shut off trade with France than the British could do. Canning did not express any opinion, but his friendly manner encouraged Pinkney to believe that a settlement was in sight.[14] Both men approved of these informal conversations of July, 1808, seeing in them the opportunity to side-step embarrassing questions and to circumvent the necessity of asserting principles that must be included in written correspondence. By July 22 Pinkney was hopeful that the orders would be relinquished.

A week later Canning shifted to insisting upon the necessity of a written proposal. Pinkney replied that he would gladly present a proposal in writing, but he must first be assured of a favorable British response.[15] Canning demurred. The British government, he said, must be free to argue its case. Pinkney, although he agreed to submit a proposal in writing, warned that this would lead to fruitless argument.

The shift in Canning's strategy may have been due in part to the revolt in Spain and Portugal against Napoleon and to the prospect of the United States seeing in this development an opportunity to open trade with these two nations. Pinkney observed that the idea was now widely entertained that the United States would shortly repeal the Embargo so as to take advantage of the new commercial opportunities. He wrote to Madison urging several arguments against a repeal of the Embargo and closed with the observation: "The embargo and the loss of our trade are deeply felt here, and will be felt with more severity every day."[16]

Two days later, on September 23, Canning indulged his flair for cleverness in two highly undiplomatic notes rejecting Pinkney's proposal. Canning sought to turn the negative reply to his own advantage by distorting what Pinkney had said in the conversations of July. His sharp phrases, later released by James Madison, added to Americans' deep distrust of Canning. The importance of the note, however, lies in Canning's explanation as to why Pinkney's proposal could not be accepted.

The basis of the British decision, aside from the fact that they now expected a repeal of the Embargo, was political. The note spoke of "surrender" and "concessions" to France as impossible. Referring to Napoleon's Continental System, Canning wrote a British determination to defeat it, "knowing that the smallest concession would infallibly encourage a perseverance in it." To the British it appeared that the Embargo was a part of Napoleon's Continental System. This, said Canning, was not the intention of the United States "but, by some unfortunate concurrence of circumstances, without any hostile intention, the American embargo did come in aid of the 'blockade of the European continent,' precisely at the very moment when, if that blockade could have succeeded at all, this interposition of the American Government would most effectually have contributed to its success."[17]

Canning's reply is of utmost importance in explaining why diplomacy eventually failed. The British position was that the orders could be revoked but they could be revoked only under circumstances whereby the repeal did not appear to be a concession. To concede would be a sign of weakness that would encourage France and further depress any will among the other nations on the continent to resist Napoleon.[18] Only if the United States aligned itself on the side of Great Britain at the time of the revocation of the Orders in Council could Great Britain, given her precarious situation prior to 1812, afford to meet the demands of the United States. Herein lies the explanation of the failure of the Erskine negotiations of 1809, a failure that had disastrous effects on relations between the two countries.

Late in 1808 negotiations took a new turn. The newly elected president, James Madison, hoped to terminate the situation of half-war and half-peace. The turbulent debates over the Embargo made it difficult to present a bold front, but the effort was made. Congress passed a resolution announcing that the United States would not submit to the edicts of Great Britain and France and a second resolution calling for the raising of 50,000 volunteers.[19] The British minister, David Erskine, was sufficiently impressed by the show of determination to ask James Madison for an explanation. Madison gave him little comfort. However desirous the United States might be of preserving peace, warned the president-elect, "the situation in which they found themselves made it their obvious and indispensable duty to be prepared for war."[20] On February 10 Madison instructed Pinkney that if the belligerents should engage in depredations on American commerce after repeal of the Embargo, "the next resort on the part of the United States will be, to an assertion of those rights by force of Arms, against the persevering aggressor or aggressors."[21] That this show made any significant impression upon the British ministry seems doubtful.[22] The sharp divisions in Congress and in the country over the question of repealing the Embargo must have confirmed the long held British suspicion that the United States would not be able to maintain a united front.

George Canning did not suddenly alter his position early in 1809. He had consistently favored negotiations, and he had long been willing to come to an agreement with the United States if it could be done without the appearance of making a one-sided concession. In January, 1809, he had reason to believe that this might be achieved. Erskine's reports of conversations with James Madison and Albert Gallatin suggested that the United States was ready to assume a more flexible policy concerning such past issues as the Rule of 1756. The proposed Non-Intercourse Bill included a provision whereby the warships of both belligerents would be excluded from American ports, thereby placing Great Britain on the same basis as France. Likewise a new non-importation bill was under discussion that would treat Great Britain and France on an equal basis. Pinkney's conversations with Canning in February, 1809, must have confirmed his hope that a situation had now developed which could be turned to British advantage. Great Britain, wrote Madison, might feel that she could not yield on the Orders in Council without an express avowal on the part of the United States to go to war against France if that nation failed to rescind her decrees. In the latter case, Madison explained, it should be made clear that only Congress could declare war. However, if Great Britain should be satisfied with an executive opinion on the subject of war against France, Madison was prepared to give it.[23] This did not mean more than that if France should continue her depredations on American commerce the President was of the opinion that Congress would eventually declare war.

Canning responded to Pinkney's overtures and directed Minister Erskine to enter into preliminary negotiations. These were to be followed by more formal negotiations looking towards a treaty between the two countries. President Madison and Robert Smith, his Secretary of State, carried on the negotiations. In the meantime, Congress repealed the Embargo and enacted the Non-Intercourse law. This reopened trade except with the belligerents and gave the President the power to restore trade with either of them in the event one of them rescinded the restrictive decrees against neutrals.

The instructions to David Erskine promised a repeal of the Orders in Council providing the United States met three conditions: The United States must agree to continue the ban on trade with France; secondly, she must assent to the Rule of 1756, and finally she must accept the right of the British navy to seize American ships heading for ports which the United States herself had placed under ban.[24] Neither Madison nor the Secretary of State saw the instructions until Canning later released them. When they did see them, they expressed astonishment and concluded that Canning had never been sincere in seeking a settlement.[25] In April when they met with Erskine, the British minister only suggested these points in the vaguest terms and gave no hint that they constituted a *sine qua non*. Erskine, in failing to make clear his instructions, violated orders from Canning. Carried away by his desire to reach a settlement and also confused as a result of the conversations and correspondence that had preceded the negotiations, Erskine decided to withhold his precise instructions believing that they would be unacceptable.

The correspondence of Pinkney shows that Canning in reality had laid down only one stipulation on which he demanded a firm guarantee, that the United States not resume trade with France for the duration of the war.[26] He had not intended to require, in the form of a treaty provision, that the United States agree to the British navy enforcing the American law against trade with France.[27] What he sought was some assurance that the President would not make an issue of some American ship caught violating the law by the British navy. This was no more than Secretary of State Robert Smith had suggested in a conversation with Erskine.[28] Nor did Canning intend to demand of the United States an acceptance of the prohibition of indirect trade as part of the price for a repeal of the Orders in Council. Some sort of compromise on the Rule of 1756 similar to that in the abortive treaty of 1806 was contemplated.[29] On this point Canning had been given some encouragement by Erskine's report of a conversation with Albert Gallatin who had intimated that the United States might temporarily forego any claim to carry on a direct trade between the French colonies and the mother country. Gallatin had been careful not to suggest that the United States would be willing to surrender the right to carry on an indirect trade.

The third point of Canning's instructions, that the United States would not restore trade with France for the duration of the war, provided the real obstacle to a settlement in 1809. Canning had repeatedly emphasized this requirement in his conversations with Pinkney who had, in turn, fully informed Madison. Erskine did not press the point, and thereby led Madison to believe that this was not a *sine qua non.* Canning, finding no assurance on this point in the agreement negotiated by Erskine, found it necessary to repudiate the agreement.

During the weeks that Erskine was engaged in negotiations with President Madison and Secretary of State Robert Smith, a development of vital importance took place in London. George Canning had repeatedly stated that the ministry was prepared to alter the Orders in Council so as to bring greater pressure upon France and, at the same time, bring relief to neutrals. On April 27 the new Order in Council was signed by the king. It made a series of concessions. The countries north of Holland were declared open to trade and the prohibitions against trade with the enemy and countries controlled by her were limited to the stretch of coast from Holland to Italy. This opened Germany and the Baltic countries to American trade. In addition the new orders reduced license charges and abolished duties on goods in transit to the continent by way of Great Britain. The new orders restored essentially the situation as it existed in 1806 prior to the orders of 1807. In reply to a question from the Opposition, Perceval stated that while the orders of 1807 had not been rescinded, "they were put in a state of modification which amounted to nearly the same effect."[30] William Pinkney took the same view.[31]

James Madison was chiefly perplexed by the British move. Reports of the new orders arrived while he was still contemplating with pleasure the success of the negotiations with Erskine. The new order fell considerably short of what he thought had been achieved. Holland and France were still subject to blockade and the principle underlying the old orders was still maintained. The questions raised by the late news disturbed him deeply. If he saw that the United States had made a real gain, he did not record his observation.

The announcement of the Erskine agreement in London immediately gave rise to angry protest. The *London Times* stated that the "concessions have unhappily been all on our side, who have even conceded that most singular of all concessions, that Holland is a free and independent country, to which America may trade directly."[32] In the House of Commons, Lord Henry Petty questioned Canning on the report of a new arrangement with the United States. Canning promptly assured the House that Erskine had violated his instructions and the agreement would not be ratified.

So strong was the feeling against any concession to the Americans, that even a temporary relaxation of the orders was denounced. Canning had issued an order permitting American ships to enter continental ports from June 9 to August 9 so that those that had left American ports, believing that the Orders in Council had been repealed, should not be seized, a move made to protect the British government against charges of acting in bad faith. Even this modest concession elicited loud protests. A deputation of British merchants called on the Board of Trade to complain that the large stock of goods already in Heligoland would be made worthless when Americans, their warehouses full with goods that sold at a lower price than the British, would send in such a supply to Holland that the British merchants would be deprived of the market for years to come. The *London Times* thought Canning's order was much like saying to the Americans, " 'Gentlemen, make the best use of the intermediate time: hurry all the goods you can possibly get on board, into the European Continent; and thus do the greatest injury you can to the traders of Great Britain, of whom their own government has made a temporary sacrifice for your advantage.' "[33]

After the agreement with Erskine, Madison had basked in the warmth of sudden popularity. On April 19 he issued a proclamation suspending the Non-Intercourse Act as of June 10 as it related to Great Britain. He now relaxed and gave his thoughts to the pending negotiations of a treaty. To Jefferson he confided: "The B. Cabinet must have changed its course under a full conviction that an adjustment with this country had become essential and it is not improbable that this policy (?) direct the ensuing negotiation; mingling with it, at the same time, the hope that it embroil us with France."[34]

The happy reconciliation lasted until July when word reached Madison that Canning had repudiated the agreement on the ground that Erskine had violated his instructions. Finding it necessary to defend his action, Canning released to the public the instructions he had given. Madison, reading the instructions for the first time, expressed amazement and concluded that Canning had never seriously entertained reaching an agreement. His increased bitterness did not augur well for the future. If he had possessed fuller information, some of his bitterness would have been mitigated. As it was, he believed he had been made the victim of a hoax.

At first glance Madison's expression of surprise at the repudiation of the Erskine agreement may appear less than genuine. Indeed, one may wonder why he should have expected George Canning to accept an arrangement that contained no provision concerning the United States agreeing to abandon trade with France. In January, 1809, Canning had carefully stipulated that repeal of the orders would be contingent upon the United States continuing the Non-Intercourse Act against France and her allies.[35] Madison then, it might appear, should have known that this constituted a *sine qua non* and that repudiation was inevitable.

But Madison had good reasons for believing the contrary. He thought that recent adversity had led Canning to surrender the point. And, in Madison's view, Canning was only yielding a device for giving British merchants a monopoly of the trade with the continent.

Canning had good reason for insisting on the stipulation that the United States should not trade with France for the duration of the war. The Non-Intercourse Act, as Canning pointed out, would expire in December. He needed assurance that the United States would not reverse its policy at that time. At home he would be less vulnerable to attack by the shipping interests if the United States gave a firm guarantee of a policy that clearly obviated all reasons for persisting in the orders. Jealousy of American commercial success was general. In September, 1808, Pinkney had described the temper of the British:

The spirit of monopoly has seized the people and Government of this country. We shall not, under any circumstances, be tolerated as rivals in navigation and trade. It is in vain to hope that Great Britain will voluntarily foster the naval means of the United States. Even as allies we should be subjects of jealousy.[36]

This jealousy increased because of the Embargo, a measure viewed by the British people as partial to France.

The British ministry were in all probability even more influenced by the consideration that to have accepted the Erskine agreement would have appeared a concession. Napoleon was at the pinnacle of his success in 1809. It was a time when the British could ill afford to present an appearance of retreat. George Canning observed that Erskine had acted "as if His Majesty had proposed to make sacrifices to propitiate the United States, in order to induce it to consent to the Renewal of Commercial intercourse."[37]

Madison failed to see the real reason for Canning's action. At a loss how to account for it, he attributed it to Canning's haughtiness and cunning. Madison faced war with Great Britain with much less reluctance than if he had not been embarrassed by the repudiation of the Erskine agreement.

Throughout the south and west a wave of hostility led to resolutions. John G. Jackson wrote:

I do hope in God notwithstanding the profligacy of Randolphism, Pickeringism and all other factions combined: the patriotism of the people will excite them to express in language alike audible, and unequivocal; their honest indignation at this flagitious outrage, and their firm determination to rally round their public functionaries in support of their insulted honor and independence.[38]

A meeting of citizens in Charleston, South Carolina, passed a resolution expressing "the highest indignation and resentment at the manner in which the United States have been treated in the late negotiation; nor will those feelings be allayed by the belief that the conduct of the British Ministry in the transaction, was not characterized by the guilt of perfidy, for the pretences on which they have acted would not therefore cease to be as unjust as they are incompatible with the pride and honor of an independent nation."[39] At Nashville, Tennessee, a committee of citizens, including Andrew Jackson, denounced the British repudiation of the Erskine agreement and offered support "should Congress in their wisdom determine that arms shall be resorted to against those, who have so often insulted and injured us, . . ."[40] From this time forth a war party labored to arouse the country to resent the injuries it suffered at the hands of the British.

The failure of negotiations gave birth to a war party and eventually to war. A major factor in the breakdown of the negotiations was the British conviction that the settlement of issues must be so arranged that it did not appear as a surrender made under duress. James Madison did not ease the way for the British. His national pride and a cast of mind that tended to see all diplomatic issues in terms of rights deprived his diplomacy of flexibility. However, these traits might have played a lesser role if the domestic political situation had not strengthened them. Much of Madison's diplomacy can only be understood if placed in the context of domestic politics. It is to that topic we now turn.

NOTES

1. George Canning to James Monroe, July 25, 1807, *American State Papers. Class 1. Foreign Relations*, Vol. III, p. 187. Hereafter cited as *American State Papers.*

2. James Monroe to James Madison, August 4, 1807, *American State Papers*, p. 186.

3. George Canning to James Monroe, August 3, 1807, *American State Papers*, p. 188.

4. James Monroe to James Madison, October 10, 1807, *American State Papers*, p. 191.

5. *Ibid.*, p. 192.

6. James Madison to George Rose, March 5, 1808 and George Rose to James Madison, March 17, 1808, *American State Papers*, pp. 214-220.

7. James Madison to David Erskine, March 25, 1808, *American State Papers*, p. 210.

8. *Ibid.*

9. *Ibid.*, p. 211.

10. *Ibid.*, p. 212.

11. *Ibid.*

12. *Ibid.*

13. William Pinkney to James Madison, August 4, 1808, *American State Papers*, p. 225.

14. *Ibid.*, p. 226.

15. *Ibid.*

16. William Pinkney to James Madison, September 21, 1808, *American State Papers*, p. 229.

17. George Canning to William Pinkney, September 23, 1808, *American State Papers*, p. 232.

18. In the letter cited above Canning wrote: "To this universal combination His Majesty has opposed a temperate but a determined retaliation upon the enemy; trusting that a firm resistance would defeat this project, but knowing that the smallest concession would infallibly encourage a perseverance in it.

"The struggle has been viewed by other Powers, not without an apprehension that it might be fatal to this country. The British government has not disguised from itself that the trial of such an experiment might be arduous and long, though it has never doubted of the final issue. But if that issue, such as the British Government confidentially anticipated, has providentially arrived, much sooner than could even have been hoped; if 'the blockade of the continent,' as it has been triumphantly styled by the enemy, is raised even before it had been well established; and if that system, of which extent and continuity were the vital principles, is broken up into fragments utterly harmless and contemptible; it is nevertheless important, in the highest degree, to the reputation of this country, (a reputation which constitutes great part of her power,) that this disappointment of the hopes of her enemies should not have been purchased by any concession; that not a doubt should remain to distant times of her de-

termination and of her ability to have continued her resistance; and that
no step, which could even mistakenly be construed into concession, should
be taken on her part, while the smallest link of the confederacy remains
undissolved, or while it can be a question whether the plan devised for
her destruction has, or has not, either completely failed, or been un-
equivocally abandoned."

19. *Annals of Congress, Tenth Congress, Second Session*, pp. 853-854
and Irving Brant, *James Madison, Secretary of State* (New York: Bobbs-
Merrill Co., 1953), p. 474.

20. *Ibid.*

21. Henry Wheaton, *Some Account of the Life, Writings, and Speeches
of William Pinkney* (New York: J.W. Palmer & Co., 1826), p. 426.

22. Bradford Perkins, *Prologue to War: England and the United
States 1805-1812* (Berkeley: University of California Press, 1961), pp.
210-211. Perkins discounts British fear of the United States using arms
to defend its rights.

23. Wheaton, *op. cit.*, p. 426.

24. George Canning to David Erskine, January 23, 1809, *American State
Papers*, p. 300.

25. James Madison to Thomas Jefferson, August 3, 1809, James Madison
Papers.

26. William Pinkney to James Madison, June 23, 1809, *American State
Papers*, p. 303.

27. *Ibid.*

28. David Erskine to Robert Smith, August 14, 1809, *American State
Papers*, p. 306.

29. William Pinkney to Robert Smith, June 23, 1809, *American State
Papers*, p. 303 and Albert Gallatin to David Erskine, August 13, 1809,
American State Papers, p. 307.

30. Perkins, *op. cit.*, p. 207.

31. *Ibid.*, p. 209.

32. *London Times*, May 31, 1809.

33. *Ibid.*, May 26, 1809.

34. James Madison to Thomas Jefferson, April 24, 1809, James Madison
Papers.

35. Brief account of an unofficial conversation between Mr. Canning
and Mr. Pinkney, on the 18th of January, 1809, continued on the 22nd of
the same month (transmitted by Mr. Pinkney to the Secretary of State),
American State Papers, pp. 299-300.

36. William Pinkney to James Madison, September 21, 1808, *American
State Papers*, p. 229.

37. Perkins, *op. cit.*, p. 216.

38. John G. Jackson to James Madison, August 17, 1809, James Madison
Papers.

39. David Ramsey to James Madison, September 5, 1809, James Madison Papers.

40. William Dickson to James Madison, September 11, 1809, James
Madison Papers.

The Embargo Aftermath—
Factionalism and Drift

XII

THE REPEAL of the Embargo ushered in a period of party factionalism and drift. The immediate reason for politics coming to rest at dead center was the alignment of political forces brought about by the Embargo. The middle of the road Republicans, in helping the Federalists to repeal the law, served notice to James Madison's incoming administration that pursuance of a bold policy would jeopardize party harmony. The success of the Federalists in exploiting the issue of the Embargo likewise increased the awareness of the administration that it was not invulnerable to this small but obstreperous party. Together these assured the triumph of caution, but why the Republicans should have split on the issues at hand and why the Federalists should have been able to paralyze an administration when they commanded so few votes remains to be explained.

Factionalism and drift were not a result of a cancelling out of diverse sectional interests. All sections, agrarian and mercantile, had a stake in neutral rights. All were dependent on Europe for manufactured goods. The agrarians lived upon the receipts from the sale of wheat, tobacco, cotton, and other products of the farm and forest in European markets. The mercantile interests derived their prosperity from trade with the continent and the carrying to market of both domestic

226

produce and the goods of the European colonies in the western hemisphere. Free access to the world's great entrepôts constituted a national rather than merely a sectional interest. All parties might have joined hands in defending it had not other considerations entered.

Both parties, although at different times, did champion freedom of the seas. It was the commercial interests who, when the British in 1805 first threatened serious interference with American trade, took the lead in defending neutral rights. Later, after the agrarians took over the leadership of the fight, the commercial interests took up their political cudgels to oppose what they had earlier taken the lead in advocating.

A part of the explanation for this curious development lies in the subordination of national interests to party interests. The Federalists readily shifted to a course of opposing Jefferson's struggle for neutral rights when they discovered that they might achieve a return to power by exploiting the difficulties faced by the administration in defending the national interest. In attributing the belligerents' restrictions on neutral trade to the mistakes of the party in power at home, they soon learned that they gained a wider audience than when they opposed the administration on domestic issues. Since 1801 the Federalists had been looking for political ammunition. In the memoirs of Senator William Plumer of New Hampshire is recorded the nature of the political motivation of his Federalist colleagues. At the dining room table in his Washington boarding house Plumer heard his Federalist friends acknowledging the merits of proposals and then deciding to oppose them simply because they found in that course of action an opportunity to embarrass the administration.[1] Until the Embargo came along the Federalists gained little by their political expediency. The administration's foreign policy soon provided them with further opportunities.

The Federalists enjoyed one great advantage. There was no satisfactory solution to the problem of how to spring loose the ships and ever mounting surpluses of farm produce from the iron clasp of restrictions imposed by the powerful belligerents. Every proposal could easily be charged with some weakness or be construed as posing some danger. If the proposals were relatively free of other objections, they could always be attacked as futile. No proposal gave any assurance of efficacy. The Federalists made full use of this situation.

The difficulties of the problem at hand weakened the unity of the Republicans at the same time that it provided the Federalists with a political opportunity. Enterprising farmers and their politically ambitious Republican representatives were too activist in spirit and too severely injured economically simply to resign themselves to an acceptance of the belligerents' infringements on neutral rights. All sections of the Republican party, with the exception of the numerically unimportant Virginia Quids, could agree on the necessity of doing something. Beyond that they fell into disagreement. The difficulty of the problem defied unity on actual proposals. It is this that explains why the Republicans, seeking to maintain party unity, were reduced to gesture making and bickering.

Historians have severely criticized the Tenth Congress and the leadership of James Madison.[2] The debates in Congress at first glance appear tedious and the laws enacted futile, but attention to the causes behind the frustration tempers harsh judgments. The length of the debates, the repetition of charges and arguments, and the failure of the President to carry Congress and the country in some particular direction is not an indication of the small stature of the participants but of the magnitude of the problem faced. In the course of the Congressional debates speakers wrestled with basic questions of foreign policy in an able way and occasionally with learning. More important, the politics of 1809 and 1810 illustrate strikingly the impact of foreign relations on domestic politics and the effects of partisan considerations on the handling of foreign affairs. The country was unable to agree on either submission or bold measures that might lead to war. It was this frustration that led to the futile gesture-making that later generations have decried.

In this mood, Congress, late in the winter of 1809, passed

the Non-Intercourse law. To the already existing problems it added the high costs of a circuitous trade and a decline in customs receipts; but as John Randolph observed, the law had no more effect on the belligerents than the placing of a tortoise under an elephant.[3]

Though the tortoise could not impede the progress of the elephant, the act of placing it there provided some psychological satisfaction and it was not without some political value. Although no one liked the Non-Intercourse measure, no other proposal could muster the support of a majority. Neither proposals calling for energy nor those calling for submission enjoyed the support of more than a small minority. The small group of Republicans who had sought to pass a bill providing for letters of marque, had lost. Randolph attributed their failure to "heterogeneous materials—even those who have been designated (I know not why) as ultra-federalists and citra-federalists."[4] The tall Virginian of effeminate features and highpitched voice did not miss the mark. No party, nor faction thereof, favored war. In attributing the breakdown to heterogeneous political elements, Randolph accurately sized up the situation. It is this schismatic political scene that calls for analysis.

Federalists subdivided into ultras and moderates. The ultras, like Josiah Quincy, Timothy Pickering, and Barent Gardenier, with a special talent for a kind of aristocratic billingsgate, judged Thomas Jefferson by the rhetoric he employed in giving wings to the democratic dream and they saw behind it French infidelity, immorality, and the indecent aspirations of agrarians who persisted in discussing problems beyond the limits of their intellectual talent. They adhered to the conspiracy theory of history.

The more moderate Federalists, men like James Bayard of Maryland and Samuel Dana of Connecticut, displayed a greater evenness of temper, depended more upon judicious analysis of the Jeffersonian policy and its shortcomings, and spoke in tones of paternalistic concern. They granted somewhat reluctantly that the British had been unjust, but they attributed the injustice to the necessity imposed upon them by the struggle against Napoleon. Usually the two factions joined hands in voting against all Jeffersonian measures and in favor of those that might weaken the administration. The only real question dividing them was whether Jefferson was a fool or a knave.

The Republicans divided into three factions. The largest minority enjoyed the leadership of G. W. Campbell of Tennessee, John W. Eppes and John Jackson of Virginia, and George Troup of Georgia. They looked upon themselves as those especially entrusted with bearing the ark of revolutionary principles through the wilderness of political expediency. During the life of the Embargo they, like Jefferson, believed that if the Embargo should be lifted, it must be followed by war. They supported the Embargo until its demise and when the ensuing months brought with them further tribulation, they attributed it to the removal of the Embargo. By 1809 the urgency of resisting British infringements became for them a matter both of principle and patriotism. Troup descended to crude and vitriolic denunciation of his opponents, but Campbell (though he fought a duel with Barent Gardenier) and Eppes defended their cause with logic and with an abundance of classical allusions.

A second group of Republicans, commanding a majority of the party on many occasions, were timid when bold measures were proposed, but they were determined to exhibit resistance to the measures of the belligerents. Their ambivalence explains in part the tortuous path Congress pursued. They helped repeal the Embargo, but they adhered to the view that a show of resistance must be maintained. Lack of a program offset their superiority in numbers and, in the end, a growing impatience with timid measures eroded their position. While the first faction of Republicans consistently advocated convoys and letters of marque, steps which would have hastened war, the second faction opposed these moves.

Finally a faction of Republicans, led by John Randolph of Virginia and Matthew Lyon of Kentucky, hated not only war but viewed every effort to counter the belligerents as unrepublican servility to the commercial interests. They voted with the Federalists while denouncing them.

This political configuration, shaped by the difficulties imposed by the belligerents, paralyzed every effort either to accept the unhappy situation or to take steps that might lead to war. Much has been written in criticism of the Tenth Congress and the weak leadership of James Madison, but it does less than justice to the difficulties the leaders confronted. Only two bold courses of decision offered themselves for consideration. The first of these lay in accepting the prevailing situation with all its injuries, but this was to ask that a nation strikingly activist should transform itself into fatalists. The second course was to adopt bold measures of economic coercion that might well lead to war and the perils involved in fighting the most powerful fleet in the world and possibly the mightiest land power in the world at the same time. Only time could render such dread alternatives acceptable. A free society could only debate until the frustrations of the middle road eroded the preference for indecision.

The fact that the major political parties were guided by considerations of how their proposals would affect their fortunes at home is equally important in explaining the attraction of gesture-making. The Federalists favored a policy that would avoid war, but they were equally driven to exploit the foreign policy of Jefferson and Madison for the purpose of driving the Republicans out of office. Likewise, the Republicans were quite as anxious to protect themselves from the attacks of Federalists lurking in the rear as they were anxious to challenge the belligerents who were thwarting national ambitions.

Because James Madison, in the late winter of 1809, turned to another attempt at negotiating, the full frustration of the political situation did not descend upon the country until the autumn of 1809. These negotiations, known under the rubric of the Erskine Affair, at first apparently successful, temporarily lifted the spirits of the country. When they ended in collapse, each faction found its own explanation of the failure and sought to exploit it for party advantage.

When Congress reconvened on November 27, 1809, the foreign policy issue completely dwarfed all others. The Senate no sooner met than a strong supporter of the administration, William Giles, introduced a resolution supporting the action of the administration in breaking off relations with Jackson. Giles held that the resolution would bridge the gulf between the executive, who was charged with the conduct of foreign relations, and Congress, which bore the final responsibility for declaring war.[5] He described the breaking off of communications as an act which "may consequently involve us in war with Great Britain; or, in other words, may serve as a pretext to Great Britain to make war upon us, if she should conceive it her interest to do so, which I think not very improbable."[6] He placed an even greater emphasis upon the need of demonstrating to Great Britain that the country was united. Great Britain, said Giles, had been encouraged to intrude upon the rights of the United States by the lack of unity among the parties. He expressed horror at the thought that America should become "a bleeding victim" because of their own "unhappy divisions and dissensions." Was it not deplorable to confront a war because of "our own unfortunate divisions and dissensions?" The resolution, serving notice that the country was now united, would call forth British respect and make her cautious. Giles summed up his appeal for unity in these words: "For, sir, do you believe that if Great Britain saw the strong arm of this nation stretched out to oppose her unjust spirit of hostility, guided in all its operations by one undivided will, she would so readily encounter its powerful influence, as if she saw it paralyzed in all its efforts from the want of an unity of will and action?"[7] Within three days the Senate passed the resolution by a vote of 20 to 4.

No such happy fate awaited the proposal in the House of Representatives. In place of achieving Giles' aim of manifesting national unity in the face of injury, the resolution opened up an acrimonious debate. The Federalists raised serious questions concerning the negotiations. Did Canning's conditions originate in statements made by officials of the administration? What had been Pinkney's reply to Canning's inquiry the previous January concerning enforcement of the Non-Intercourse Act by the British navy? Did James Madison and Secretary of State Smith know the facts of Canning's instructions at the time of the negotiations? Why had not the American negotiators demanded evidence of Erskine's authority to enter into such an agreement? Speaker after speaker entered into detailed analyses of the diplomatic correspondence. Viewing the transaction with a critical eye, the Federalists detected errors of judgment and exploited them to the full.

Was Jackson's offensive letter adequate grounds for breaking off communications with the representative of one of the most powerful empires in the world? The question served the purposes of the Federalists.[8] They flayed the Republican appeal for unity with the assertion that it was equivalent to the monarchical maxim that the head of the government can do no wrong.[9] Sanctimoniously proclaiming the duty of representatives in a free republic to examine with fairness and candor every subject, the Federalists analyzed in critical spirit every minute detail of the negotiations. Laban Wheaton of Massachusetts did not deny that the British government had done injury but, he said, British actions must be viewed in the context of the struggle the British were waging against Napoleon. And viewing the letter of the British minister, said Wheaton, it seemed injudicious to magnify his remarks into a cause for war. The resolutions, he said, called for war. In tones of alarm made to ring through the House for weeks to come, Wheaton asked:

What, sir, shall we, shall a whole nation go to war, shall thousands of lives be lost, and millions of hard earned property be wasted, because one man imagines, in which imagination he may be, as I think in this case he must be mistaken, that another has made some representations or insinuations that might seem to affect his honor or character? Are you willing, sir, that our sons should thus fall unpitied victims at ambition's shrine?[10]

Wheaton found nothing insulting in Jackson's letter to Secretary of State Smith. The letter only stated the facts; Madison and Smith had known the nature of Canning's instructions at the time of the negotiation and therefore they should fully have expected George Canning to disavow the agreement. "In all this," said Wheaton, "I can see nothing but severe civility. And yet this is made the occasion for suddenly breaking off a correspondence that might have led, however dubious the prospect in the beginning of it, to an amicable adjustment of all the points in dispute between the two countries, and we are now called upon to prepare ourselves for war to avenge the imaginary affront."[11] Wheaton described the futility of going to war with a nation whose fleet could blockade every port from Maine to Georgia while the oaks for an American fleet still stood in the forest. And, if by remote chance, Great Britain should be humbled in the contest, would the United States have done more than make way for Napoleon?[12]

Practically every administration opponent repeated Wheaton's charges. They assumed an air of superiority, asking always how reason could vindicate the program pursued by the administration.[13] The resolution itself was described as crude and bully and as couched in such insulting terms as to give the British no choice but to declare war. Pitkin pleaded that if such a resolution had to be passed "let us do it in language that will show that we are conscious of its worth."[14] All Federalists pronounced it a conditional declaration of war.

Underlying the Federalist note of disgust was the conviction that the British were engaged in an heroic struggle in behalf of a noble cause. Timothy Pitkin warned in grim tones that the Republicans' program would make the United States an ally of Napoleon:

The inevitable consequence must be an alliance with her enemy, and I cannot but view such an alliance with a sort of horror I am unable to describe. No ally of Bonaparte has ever fought, but to increase the power of this military despot, and to lose their own independence. And we cannot expect to share a different fate. It is possible, sir, that in this contest, what has been called the freedom of the seas may be obtained; but it will not be obtained for us; it will only be transferred to him who now commands the freedom of the land.[15]

Jabez Upham of Massachusetts, repeating the same sentiments, declared that it was time to lay aside the grievances against Great Britain. That nation, he said, was "virtually fighting the battles of the civilized world, not indeed for the sake of the world, but to preserve her own existence." Napoleon had trampled upon peace, order, and religion; Great Britain had been contending in their favor "and everything sacred."[16]

Given this pro-British bias, the Federalists found it easy to detect faults in the administration's conduct of the Erskine negotiations. Day after day Federalists charged that Canning's three conditions originated in the ideas suggested by Pinkney and Gallatin, that James Madison and Secretary of State Robert Smith had known that Erskine had no authority to enter into an agreement along the lines settled upon the previous spring, and that, if they had not known the nature of Erskine's instructions, they were obligated to find out the extent of his authority.

The Republican reply pushed aside the merits of the British in the war against Napoleon and equated the Emperor's tyranny on land with British tyranny on the seas. Federalist justifications of the British shocked them and they retorted with the charge that their opponents were lacking in national honor. They refuted the charges that serious errors had been committed by the administration in the Erskine negotiations. The injuries suffered at the hands of the British provided a constant theme. And, the Republicans insisted, a nation which did not stand united in opposing an aggressor could only expect to be the victim of further aggressions.

Richard Johnson of Kentucky expressed the Republican point of view. The resolution, said Johnson, was not a provocation to war but a solemn declaration that this nation had been abused and insulted. In breaking off communications with Jackson, Johnson explained, the President had "maintained the honor, vindicated the rights, and spurned the insults offered to an independent and patriotic people."[17] He dwelt on a favorite point of his fellow Republicans; weakness in the face of injury invites further injury.[18] The wavering course hitherto pursued had already invited the contempt of other nations and it was responsible "for many of the wrongs we have suffered." Johnson reminded his listeners of the long trail of injuries and measured this against the Federalist platform of submission:

You are treated with contumely upon the ocean, your citizens are impressed and held in perpetual bondage. Your commerce is destroyed, your flag was torn down and scattered to the winds of heaven in foreign ports, on the 4th of July, the day of our independence; and now, at our own door, at the seat of the Federal Government, a foreign Minister looks your President in the face, and charges him with falsehood—and we are told to submit to it.[19]

Republicans justified resistance by reciting the wrongs suffered and stressed the danger of internal division in the face of external aggression.

The Federalists replied that it was sometimes better to do nothing than do something. They rested their case on expediency and on considerations of the world situation. War posed greater dangers than did the endurance of the present grievances. These grievances were the product of the great struggle in Europe and they would not be removed until peace had been restored and the belligerents could return to the policies of peacetime.

It was at this point of the argument that the two parties met head on. To the Republicans the war was only a pretext under which the British made commercial war against the United States. Great Britain impaired American neutral rights not because of military necessity but because she was determined to suppress a commercial rival. This was at the heart of the Republican policy. Both Jefferson and Madison shared this distrust of Great Britain. They, unlike the Federalists, dismissed the danger of Napoleon. This is not to say that they either liked or trusted the French Emperor, but they viewed Great Britain as posing an imminent danger and Napoleon only a remote danger. This explains much of the Republican policy.[20]

William Milnor spoke for the whole party when he said:

"She is herself supplying her enemy with the very articles with which she refuses to permit neutrals to supply her, under the plea that her sole object is to deprive her enemy of those articles." Milnor affirmed that the Orders in Council did not grow out of a desire to injure her enemy but rather out of jealousy of "our increasing ability to rival her in commerce. . . ."[21] The view was partly supported by the facts, sufficiently so that from James Madison down to the humblest Republican party politician, this interpretation prevailed. This made the Federalist argument that the British were fighting the battle of civilization against Napoleon seem hollow and led the Republicans to the conclusion that to talk of the inexpediency of resistance was nothing less than an invitation to further duping by the devious British.

The differences in argument are sufficiently clear; the origins of these differences are less easily established, but they sharpen the appetite for speculation. The New Englanders of the extreme Federalist persuasion had long viewed the British with friendly eyes. They had likewise developed a complete distrust of France, and the rise of Napoleon served to confirm their view that Jacobinism must lead to wild disorder and, in turn, to autocracy. They looked upon the Republicans as exponents of the French system. Upon his return to Boston in May, 1808, John Quincy Adams talked with Chief Justice Parsons of the state supreme court. Adams found Parsons

totally devoted to the British policy, and avowing the opinion that the British have a right to take their seamen from our ships—have a right to interdict our trade with her enemies, other than the peace trade—and a right, by way of retaliation, to cut off our trade with her enemies altogether. He also thinks the people of this country corrupted, already in a state of voluntary subjugation to France, and ready to join an army of Buonaparte, if he should send one here, to subdue themselves. The only protection of our liberties, he thinks, is the British navy.[22]

The New England Federalists were engaged in a frenzied crusade to save the country from the infection of French infidelity, and those evils it had spawned, immorality and the Jeffersonian party.[23] The Embargo was something more than a system for counteracting the belligerents' invasion of neutral rights; it was the final culmination of a long attack against all that was sacred, the Church, morality, and the virtuous enterprise of New England merchants. The dynamic of Federalism is to be found less in the arguments employed than in the smug innuendoes that Jefferson's policy was the product of ignorance, that it had its origins in the violent prejudices of agrarians who did not understand commerce, and that Jeffersonianism was underhandedly plotting war against England, and alliance with France, and the destruction of the commercial classes at home. Exploiting the miseries wrought by the belligerents, they sought to turn Republican policy into a symbol of the monumental ignorance of the Jeffersonians and to drive them out of office. All foreign policy issues were viewed with the bias instilled by the domestic scene.

Bias flowing out of domestic politics played a lesser role among the Republicans, but their devotion to resistance, even though this resistance was reduced at times to no more than gesture-making, stemmed in part from their complete hostility to Federalism. Republicans did not harbor any sympathy for Napoleon, but they did resent the British to a degree that went beyond mere opposition to British measures. Republicans, not without reason, viewed their political enemies at home as allies of the British enemy abroad, and thus not really as two separate enemies. To decide to live with British encroachments on neutral rights was to accept the Federalists' position. This hostility explains why the Republicans insisted on maintaining resistance in form even when the measures themselves threatened no injury to the British and could only be interpreted by them as evidence of American imbecility.

The furor Giles' resolution aroused in the House of Representatives illustrates the impact of domestic politics on foreign relations. The declaration itself was innocuous. It charged that the letters written by the British minister were "insolent and affronting" and that they constituted "an insidious attempt to excite" the American people to resentment and distrust of their own government. The resolution pledged Congress "to call into action the whole force of the nation if it should become necessary in consequence of the conduct of the Executive Government in this respect to repel such insults and to assert and maintain the rights, the honor, and the interests of the United States."

The content of the resolution did not justify the Federalists calling it a declaration of war. It committed the United States to nothing specific, and it could scarcely be viewed by the British as a cause for alarm. The Federalist label, however, served the purposes of party warfare.

Nor were the Republicans devoid of political considerations in pushing the resolution. It provided a broad and innocent enough platform to accommodate the two major divisions within their ranks. Their hearty support of it was not due to any illusion that it constituted an effective foreign policy; it must be explained largely in terms of the necessity of maintaining party unity in the face of the Federalist attack. The long debate over the resolution, culminating in a nineteen hour session that ended at 5:30 in the morning on January 4th, ended with the passage of the resolution by a 72 to 41 vote.

In the course of the debate on the joint resolution, Nathaniel Macon of Georgia introduced a bill, drafted in cooperation with Albert Gallatin, entitled the American Navigation Act. The bill prohibited the entry into American ports of British and French ships, either men of war or merchant ships, specified that all imports from the two countries must come directly from their point of origin, in American ships, and finally provided that if one of the belligerents withdrew the orders infringing neutral rights, the United States would withdraw the restrictions on its trade. If passed, it would take the place of the Non-Intercourse Act.[24]

Macon's proposal ideally suited the mood of the majority of Republicans. By continuing a show of resistance, so congenial to their feelings, it met a political need. Failure to do so would have been tantamount to acknowledging that the Federalists were correct.

Aside from party advantage the bill offered little. Nothing much was to be gained by legislating a monopoly when American shipping would dominate the trans-Atlantic carrying trade anyway. British ships, in the years prior to the Embargo, carried few imports from Europe. Secondly, the proposed law would put almost no pressure on the belligerents to open up the continent of Europe to American ships. About the only advantage offered to the Republicans by the bill was that it provided a way out of the embarrassments resulting from the Non-Intercourse law.

Only one exception need be made to this explanation why the Republicans supported the Macon bill. A few of them believed that the British would retaliate by closing British ports to American ships. This possibility pleased them for it would have restored the situation prevailing under the Embargo law. But for the large majority of Republicans the leading considerations in favor of passing the bill were political, namely the preservation of party unity and freeing the party from the burden of hostility imposed by the Non-Intercourse law.[25]

An examination of the reasons why the Federalists opposed the American Navigation Act indicates similar political motivations. The only section of the bill which they approved was that providing for the repeal of the Non-Intercourse law. Their two major objections to it were that it would continue the futile system of trade restrictions and that it would cause the British to retaliate. Neither of these arguments enjoyed any great merit. The bill perpetuated the system of trade restrictions only as regards foreign shippers; it imposed no restrictions on American shipowners. The second reason for opposing it, namely that it would cause the British to retaliate, was vitiated by the Federalists' own claim that American-owned ships would enjoy a near monopoly without the law. A law which would have no deleterious effect on the British would not be likely to lead them to retaliate.

If domestic political considerations had not been paramount, the Federalists could easily have supported the bill, for it would have lifted all restrictions on American merchants imposed by their own government.[26] This is precisely what the Federalists had long proclaimed as their aim. The real source of their opposition was that they found it politically advantageous to oppose this last faint shadow of the old policy of economic coercion.

The most significant response to the American Navigation Act from the point of view of the future lay in the denunciation of the bill by a small but extremely vocal group of Republicans, the first nucleus of the war party. Lemuel Sawyer of North Carolina protested that he was weary of coercive measures. He called for stronger action. It was necessary, he said, to make the British feel the penalty. What could be more chimerical than to assume that restricting trade to American ships would have any effect on the price of the farmers' produce as long as the ports of the continent were closed against American ships? Sawyer favored convoys and the arming of merchant ships.[27]

Gordon Mumford, newly elected representative from New York, denounced the pusillanimity of the bill and called for convoys and the arming of merchant ships.[28] William Burwell likewise sought to attach an amendment to the bill authorizing convoys.[29] Senator James Ross of Pennsylvania called for energetic action.[30] He denounced Macon's proposal as the fourth edition of the Embargo principle and predicted that it would be equally ineffectual in remedying the evils under which the country suffered. Joseph Desha of Kentucky labeled the Macon bill "tantamount to submission" and called on the country to ready itself for war. "I venture to pronounce that your embargoes, non-intercourse, or commercial restrictions, that are now under consideration," said Desha, ". . . have not only humility but imbecility depicted in their countenance."[31] Richard M. Johnson, also from Kentucky, supported the Macon bill but wished to supplement it with energetic measures. Johnson was ready for war. He confessed that he was mortified to hear colleagues "estimate our resources as inadequate for the purposes of war" and that "the people would not support a war in defense of our independence." He did not believe either to be true and warned his listeners that the "people are as willing, and more so than we are, to risk war rather than submit longer."[32] William Anderson, of Pennsylvania, observed: "Sir, we have arrived at a point where it is difficult to remain, dangerous to advance, but infamous to recede—and will the representatives of a free people, by adopting the bill now before us, choose the latter?" He considered "reasoning and commercial regulations . . . poor defence against power. . . ."[33] He found people tired and weary of measures based upon appeals to justice.

These sentiments denoted a change. A segment of Republicans was clearly tired of the policy of economic coercion and was ready for bolder measures. The several attempts to pass bills providing for convoys and the arming of merchant ships testify to their readiness. William Burwell and John W. Eppes, both of Virginia, and both consistent supporters of the administration, introduced bills providing for convoys and the arming of merchant ships.

The change did not yet extend to a majority. Macon argued that his bill would avoid war and a large majority of Republicans supported it. The bill to establish convoys was defeated by a combination of Federalist and Republican votes, but, as far as can be determined, at least thirty-nine Republicans voted in favor of convoys.

The Senate transformed the bill by eliminating those sections which barred British and French merchant ships from entering American ports and which required that British and French imports should only be admitted when carried in American owned ships. Senator Samuel Smith, of Maryland, assumed the lead in promoting these amendments. In the debate Smith maintained that the plan to grant a monopoly to American shipping did not meet the problem, which was to clear the way for ships to proceed to all ports not blockaded. Prohibiting the entry of British ships would not achieve that goal. The prohibition against the entry of French ships would have no effect because French ships did not have access to

American ports in the existing situation. Nor was the law likely to persuade Great Britain to relax her controls. In the three years prior to the Embargo only about eight thousand tons of British shipping entered American ports annually while more than four hundred thousand tons of American shipping entered British ports. In spite of this Smith thought the British would retaliate by closing their ports. Smith put the question: "We should then risk by this law the employment of four hundred thousand tons of shipping; to obtain what? The employment of eight thousand tons now occupied by British ships—what extreme folly! What madness!"[34]

Henry Clay favored the House version and attacked the Senate amendments. These, said Clay, reduced the measure to submission. He preferred making the bill even stronger.[35]

It is significant that the Republican-dominated Senate surrendered the policy of coercion. The Macon bill, as passed by the House, reduced the policy of coercion to one of form only, but the Senate came very close to abolishing even the form. It had, in effect, accepted submission in all but name.

The final prolonged wrangle in the House over the Senate amendments to the American Navigation Act took place in March and April of 1810. It was more than a debate over a measure; it was a grim day of reckoning. Only the Federalists could take any satisfaction in the prevailing recognition that the long effort to bend Great Britain to relax her controls over American trade had now to be given up. The Non-Importation Act, the Embargo Act, and the Non-Intercourse Act had been tried, but the experiment with economic coercion now stood condemned by its own failure. Even the Republicans no longer sought to justify it in terms of effectiveness. They claimed no more than that the policy had the virtue of manifesting to the offending nations how deeply Americans resented their hostile policies. The words of Dana of Connecticut cut to the root of the issue. Dana asked: "The real question for the consideration of the House was, whether they would persevere in a system condemned by experience; whether they would persist in a measure acknowledged to be worse than useless? Some idea of preserving consistency might operate on the minds of some gentlemen; but, from whatever cause, the experiment having failed, why persevere in it?"[36]

Pride in consistency, and a natural dislike of having to swallow personal and party pride by agreeing that the Federalists had been correct constituted strong barriers to a frank and open acknowledgement of the failure of economic coercion. However, it was not pride alone that militated against a fatalistic acceptance of the injuries suffered at the hands of the belligerents. Time and again the representatives of the South and West called attention to the fact that the closing of the continental market explained the low prices of the products produced in their home states. The fact that England consumed only a small percentage of the tobacco these states sent to market was cited with a frequency that made the fact commonplace. Gradually war came to appear a lesser evil than economic ruin. These factors explain why the Republicans clung to a show of resistance even though their resistance in the form of commercial restrictions offered little hope of being effective.

The final revised bill scarcely resembled the original American Navigation Act. Though it carried the name Macon Bill Number 2 it did not even enjoy the support of its original sponsor. It did no more than exclude the public ships of the belligerents from entry into American ports. Only a lingering trace of the old policy of commercial restrictions remained in the bill, a kind of token bestowed on the grave as an act of respect for a noble cause. Section 4 stipulated that in case either Great Britain or France should modify their edicts before March 3, 1811, and the other belligerent should not do the same, the United States would, after three months, apply the provisions of the Non-Intercourse law to that country. This section aroused no debate. It appears that there was little or no expectancy that one of the belligerents would revoke the orders and thereby, if the second belligerent did not do the same, bring into force the Non-Intercourse Act. It was this unforeseen contingency that proved to be momentous and which played a major role in bringing on the war.

NOTES

1. *William Plumer's Memorandum of Proceedings in the United States Senate 1803-1807*, ed. Everett Somerville Brown (New York: The Macmillan Company, 1923), p. 428.

2. Historians have been generally critical of both the Tenth Congress and President James Madison. Henry Adams delighted in exposing the weak leadership of Madison and emphasized the futility of his measures. Irving Brant, in his multi-volume biography of James Madison, restores his subject to a position of leadership. James Madison was not the weak character described by Henry Adams, but this writer cannot agree with Irving Brant's estimate. Bradford Perkins, in his brilliant *Prologue to War: England and the United States 1805-1812*, does not ridicule Madison in the Henry Adams manner nor does he elevate him into a strong leader as does Irving Brant. Perkins' estimate is that the President permitted his own constitutional theory, a clear separation of the executive and legislative branches, to stand in the way of leadership. Perkins speaks of him as not being cut in the heroic mold and, concerning his role in the months prior to the war, writes: "Left to himself, with a Congress like the Tenth, James Madison would have been a complete failure." This strikes this writer as a bit severe. More emphasis on the difficulties of the problem faced by both Congress and the President, and this is the chief purpose of this chapter, does not remove all criticism of either Congress or James Madison, but it does place their shortcomings in a perspective that discourages harsh judgments.

3. *Annals of Congress, Tenth Congress, Second Session*, p. 1508.

4. *Ibid., Eleventh Congress, First Session*, p. 150. On Monday, May 29, 1809, during a debate on a resolution commending President Madison for his promptness in suspending the Non-Intercourse Act as it applied to Great Britain, John Randolph censured his colleagues from Virginia, John Eppes and John Jackson, stalwart supporters of the administration, for seeking to attribute the success of the Erskine negotiations to the Non-Intercourse Act. Randolph seized upon the fact that these two gentlemen had voted against the Non-Intercourse bill because they preferred war if the Embargo were to be repealed. Randolph took note of the several factions that had stopped the "war party": "Now, to be sure, sir, those persons who undertook to stop their wild career were composed of heterogeneous materials—even those who have been designated (I know not why) as ultra-federalists and citra-federalists, if any such there be, united on this vote. There were minority men, caucus men, protesters—in fact, sir, all parties, Catholics, Protestants, Seceders, and all, were united in the effort to prevent the leaders of both Houses from plunging the nation into a war with one power, and knuckling to the other. . . ."

5. *Annals of Congress, Eleventh Congress, First and Second Sessions*, p. 485.

6. *Ibid.*, p. 486.

7. *Ibid.*, p. 488.

In presenting the joint resolution Giles attributed the disavowal to the improvement of the European situation from a British point of view and to the repeal of the Embargo. In linking the resolution to the hated Embargo, Giles invited a fresh outbreak of the party spirits which he professed he wished to set aside.

8. The prolonged debate of the Tenth Congress on this resolution has led historians to charge it with irresponsibility. In the best book on the subject of the causes of the War of 1812, Bradford Perkins is highly critical of the Congress that met in the autumn of 1809 and notes that the forty-one congressmen who voted against the joint resolution voted against their own government. Judged in terms of the unfortunate effects these party divisions had on the British government, he is wholly correct. There is, however, something to be said for understanding the reasons for these party divisions. The debates were repetitious, but they likewise throw much light on the issues that divided Congress into parties and parties into factions. They are especially worthy of study because they make clear exactly how difficult it was to come to terms with a problem that imposed such injuries at home and that was so difficult to solve. One may fret at the factionalism but one may also view it more objectively as the almost inevitable result of a free society where irresponsible political behaviour could be justified under the banner of republican principles. It should also be said that the debates often reached a high level and dealt with serious issues in a way that indicated that a great deal of thought had been given to foreign affairs.

9. See speech of Laban Wheaton of Massachusetts on this point. At the opening of the debate on the resolution other opponents enlarged upon the right of representatives to have full information before deciding a question. For Wheaton's speech see *Annals of Congress, Eleventh Congress, First and Second Sessions*, p. 790.

10. *Ibid.*, p. 792.

11. *Ibid.*, p. 793.

12. *Ibid.*, p. 794.

13. The most thoughtful and convincing attack on the resolution was made by Samuel Dana of Connecticut early in the debate. Dana made two salient points. He compared the difference in the language used by the President in asking for the recall of Jackson and showed how diplomatic in tone it was compared to the resolution. He also argued that a letter of credence to a minister did not vest him with the authority to enter into stipulations in behalf of his government. His discussion of this point was supported with great learning. *Ibid.*, pp. 762-783.

14. *Ibid.*, p. 966.

15. *Ibid.*, p. 987.

16. *Ibid.*, p. 1036.

17. *Ibid.*, p. 803.

18. *Ibid.*, p. 804.

19. *Ibid.*

20. Lawrence S. Kaplan, "Jefferson, the Napoleonic Wars, and the Balance of Power," *William and Mary Quarterly*, Vol. XIV (April, 1957), pp. 196-217; also article by same author "Jefferson's Foreign Policy and Napoleon's Ideologues," *William and Mary Quarterly*, Vol. XIX (July, 1962), pp. 344-359.

21. *Annals of Congress, Eleventh Congress, First and Second Session*, p. 906.

22. *Memoirs of John Quincy Adams*, ed. Charles Francis Adams (Philadelphia: J. B. Lippincott, 1874), Vol. I, p. 534.

23. Sidney Earl Mead, *Nathaniel William Taylor 1786-1858: A Connecticut Liberal* (Chicago: University of Chicago Press, 1942), p. 41. The author presents an excellent picture of the religious controversies in Connecticut and shows the relationship of religious issues to the political controversies. However, caution is in order when discussing the importance of local political issues and their impact on national politics. Oscar and Mary Handlin in *Commonwealth: A Study of the Role of Government in the American Economy: Massachusetts, 1774-1861* minimize party differences on local issues and conclude that it was the difference on national questions that became important. The policy of commercial restrictions adopted by the Republicans on the national scene affected Massachusetts directly because of the heavy concentration of shipowning in that state. Republicans were strong in Massachusetts as is indicated by their election of both James Sullivan and Elbridge Gerry to the governorship. Republicans found it difficult to defend the national policy and Sullivan sought to relieve the pressure by shifting the emphasis from commercial restrictions to the promotion of domestic manufactures. While further studies are very much needed, it is this writer's tentative conclusion that the Federalist objections were not only to the policy of commercial restriction but to the national drift in favor of agrarianism, war with Great Britain, and an alliance with France. Jefferson's and Madison's insistence that Great Britain rather than Napoleon presented the greatest threat fed this fear.

24. *Annals of Congress, Eleventh Congress, First and Second Sessions*, p. 754.

25. On January 8, 1810 Macon said that it had been "acknowledged on all hands that non-intercourse was totally useless." On January 23 Macon delivered a long speech in favor of his bill as a peace measure. He said: "The bill before you has never been considered by me a very strong measure; though not a strong measure, it is certainly very far from submission, and such a measure as can in this nation be carried into complete execution; to say the least of it, it is a fair protest against the acts of both Great Britain and France. And can you do more at this time and preserve peace?" *Ibid.*, p. 1276.

26. A tabulation of the votes on the first reading of the bill shows that six Federalists did vote in favor of the bill.

27. *Annals of Congress, Eleventh Congress, First and Second Sessions*, pp. 1160-1161.

28. *Ibid.*, p. 1250.

29. *Ibid.*, p. 1225.

30. *Ibid.*, p. 1268.

31. *Ibid.*, p. 1306.

32. *Ibid.*, p. 1321.

33. *Ibid.*, p. 1325.

34. *Ibid.*, p. 607.

35. *Ibid.*, pp. 579-582.

36. *Ibid.*, p. 1493.

The Western Hemisphere
Problem
XIII

THE HEMISPHERE QUESTION arose out of the revolutionary movement in South America, a development which swept most of the southern continent and portended an end to Spanish control. Consequently the government in Washington, in addition to the long sought goal of opening up normal trade relations with Europe, aimed at the liquidation of the Florida problem with its danger of European intervention and the prevention of any European nation exploiting the fluid revolutionary situation in South America. Relations with Great Britain and France no longer swung on the lone fulcrum of trade relations but on the larger point of the connections of these two countries to the western hemisphere.

Latin America, for so long the untended but closed reserve of Spain, offered opportunities to which the more commercially and industrially advanced nations of Europe were keenly alert. Great Britain and the United States, well aware that Napoleon was not a disinterested spectator of events in the New World, feared that he might launch some bold enterprise in Cuba or in one of the Spanish colonies to the south. Should Napoleon succeed in Spain itself, he would certainly expect compensation in Latin America.

To the United States the danger of Napoleon intervening appeared less pressing than the danger of Great Britain doing so. She had the fleet and she had the economic machinery for knitting these colonial areas into her economic empire. Whether they should be brought into the sphere of British political domination mattered less to the British than the question of whether the Latin American area should become an economic satrapy of her own or some other power. The United States hoped to prevent either Great Britain or any other nation from winning political or economic dominance in the New World.

Before Jefferson left office in March, 1809, the challenge of Latin America broke in on his absorption with matters of European trade. Not that he had ever been wholly concerned with the latter, for Jefferson's views on the desirability of bringing West Florida into the republic amounted to a fixation, but in the early part of 1809 his eyes stretched beyond Florida and over the entire continent to the south.[1] The broadening of his vision came as a result of a rapidly changing scene. With Napoleon's intervention in Spain the colonial empire of that country collapsed like a plant that has had its root system removed. The amputation of the roots had taken place during the Embargo. A more unhappy coincident could scarcely have taken place for it gave the enterprising British a double advantage in assuming control over Spain's ill tended new world plantation. Immediately, Great Britain, her alertness sharpened by her loss of continental markets, embarked on a frenzied campaign to exploit the markets opened to her by Spain's demise. Jefferson, who in the crisis of 1803 had been ready to marry the nation to the British fleet rather than permit France to take over Louisiana, suddenly discovered that the British merchant marine was about to marry Latin America, and he viewed the approaching marriage with the eyes of a suitor who was on the point of being rejected.

Professor Arthur P. Whitaker, eminent historian, has told the story of Jefferson's and Madison's shift to the larger policy designed to give the United States leadership in affairs of the western hemisphere. Neither a restoration of Spanish control after the close of hostilities nor a transfer of control of any part of the Spanish colonies accorded with the interest of the United States. Only the independence of the Latin Americans would open the door further to trade. The importance of this trade is indicated by the fact that exports to this area had increased from $1,821,000 in 1795-96 to $10,876,000 ten years later.[2] Beginning in August, 1808 Jefferson made efforts to woo the Latin Americans with the assurance that while the United States could not commit itself to rendering them full support in revolutionary movements, the United States would be influenced "by friendship to you, by a firm feeling that our interests are intimately connected, and by the strongest repugnance to see you under subordination to either France or England, either politically or commercially."[3] These views were to be communicated to Spanish officials by James Wilkinson on his return trip early in the spring of 1809 to New Orleans via Havana and Pensacola and also by W.C.C. Claiborne, the governor of the Orleans Territory.

The appealing vision of Pan Americanism, a new world both republican and independent of Europe, led by the United States, received the full support of James Madison. Secretary of State Robert Smith, whose brother was already a leading merchant in the trade with Latin America, gave him hearty cooperation. On April 27, 1809, Robert Smith instructed John Armstrong in Paris to avert any proposal from the Emperor to cut off trade with the Spanish colonies if they revolted. Smith warned that the Emperor had no right to make such a demand and the very attempt would endanger the peace of the two countries.[4] Three days later the Secretary of State advised Armstrong again "that the measure is regarded by the President in such a light as that no countenance is to be given to any hope of attaining it, even by an offer of arrangements otherwise satisfactory, with respect to the Floridas and the Western boundary of Louisiana."[5]

The administration's shift in goals from concentration on the Floridas to the larger policy of Pan Americanism marked such an abrupt change that foreign diplomats in Washington refused to accept it. They viewed the statements on Pan Americanism as harbingers of a new move on the Florida question. Turreau, the French minister, wholly missed the fact that the Americans had moved on toward a larger goal. The repeal of the Embargo denoted to him a rejection of France and a shift toward Great Britain of such proportions that he expected a break in diplomatic relations and consequently he left Washington in an angry mood. He saw in this alleged shift an attempt to win the approval of Great Britain before moving into the Floridas. That the United States had its eyes on Florida and was preparing the way for this move was confirmed to Turreau's satisfaction by Wilkinson's trip, by the sending of military reinforcements to New Orleans, and by the reports of the American settlers in West Florida holding meetings dealing with political questions. Consequently, he sent an urgent message to his superiors in Paris calling for immediate action before the United States blotted out the dream of a French empire in the lower Mississippi Valley and rendered useless the great French asset of having a large French population in the area of New Orleans, an asset on which Turreau had pinned his hopes.[6]

Turreau made no mistake in concluding that the United States wanted the Floridas, but he was mistaken in the early spring of 1810 in believing that the Madison administration was planning to take the Floridas in the immediate future. The President made his position clear on two different occasions. On his arrival in New Orleans Wilkinson forwarded a proposal to Washington calling for the immediate occupation of the Floridas. Madison immediately replied that he wished "no interference of any kind in the affairs and territories of Spain" by any person or persons, whether civil or military, belonging to or under the authority of the United States.[7] Turreau's obvious distrust of the United States provided a second occasion for the President to make known his views. He asked Gallatin to consult with the French minister and, according to Turreau's report of the interview which took place, Gallatin told him that the President did not desire the Floridas, that he had no connections with those Americans in the area who were holding meetings, and that as for Cuba, the United States would not take it as a gift.[8] Gallatin had long held the view that the United States would eventually acquire the Floridas but that it would be a mistake to push the question. Madison had clearly arrived at the same position. The President's correspondence suggests that, with the Spanish empire in South America breaking up, he did not wish to set any precedent which might serve the purposes of a European power bent on taking over some part of the Spanish domain.

Not Florida but the question of South American markets occupied Madison early in 1810. The British moves to capture these markets led the administration in Washington to seek to reverse the trend. The United States had only one diplomatic representative in South America, the minister to the Portuguese court which now resided in Brazil. Madison now appointed three special agents and several new consuls to counteract the British.[9]

The first of these, Joel Robert Poinsett, received a set of instructions in June 1810 which outlined American policy. Secretary Smith wrote of the approaching crisis "which must produce great changes in the situation of Spanish America, and may dissolve altogether its colonial relations to Europe." The geographical position of the United States, "and other obvious considerations," he explained gave this country "an intimate interest" in the destiny of this hemisphere. Therefore, advised the Secretary of State, Poinsett should make it his object "to diffuse the impression that the United States cherish the sincerest good will towards the people of Spanish America as neighbors, as belonging to the same portion of the globe, and as having a mutual interest in cultivating friendly intercourse; that this disposition will exist, whatever may be their internal system or European relation, with respect to which no interference of any sort is pretended: and that, in the event of a political separation from the parent country, . . . it will coincide with the sentiments and policy of the United States to promote the most friendly relations, and the most liberal intercourse." To this was added the less rarified injunction that the "real and ostensible object" of the mission was "to explain the mutual advantages of commerce."[10]

This policy changed abruptly in the early summer of 1810 thanks to developments in Florida. Governor Holmes, of the Mississippi Territory, and other correspondents in the southwest informed Madison that Americans in West Florida were about to take matters in their own hands. These reports similarly made clear what Madison had never really questioned, namely that a majority in West Florida desired annexation to the United States. At almost the precise moment when Madison had decided to put the Florida question on the shelf the people of that area put it directly in his lap.

James Madison, scholar and gentlemanly exponent of high norms of behavior in international relations, viewed the development out of the corner of his eye as a proper gentleman unaccustomed to illicit advances of a paramour might regard the first flirtation, unwilling to encourage it but likewise too charmed by the alluring thought of a final consummation to cut off abruptly the affair. As early as June he accepted Governor Claiborne's plan for intervention. The way was now open for informing the Florida dissidents that the United States would gladly embrace West Florida should its people declare a break with Spain and offer themselves for annexation.[11]

The jealous but cautious suitor had no intention of brooking any rivalry for the prize on the part of Great Britain. A note to Great Britain written on July 13 revealed the lust for territory that had been awakened in the President. The note concerned both East and West Florida, and it referred both to the legal claim of the United States to the territory as far east as the Perdido and to the unsettled claims against Spain growing out of earlier attacks on American shipping. "Under these circumstances," read the note, "it may be proper not to conceal from the British government . . . that any steps on the part of Great Britain interfering with these will necessarily be regarded as unjust and unfriendly, and as leading to collisions, which it must be the interest of both nations to avoid."[12] Madison had no reason to expect an imminent British occupation of the Floridas, but he must have feared that once the United States took over West Florida from Spain, Great Britain, as Spain's ally, might occupy East Florida as a guarantee against American annexation of that territory.

Florida, in the hands of a powerful nation, could be used as a club to keep the United States in line with the interests of the nation which possessed it. Herein, as Governor Vicente Folch of Florida recognized, lay its great value. Not long after the signing of the convention which gave Louisiana to the United States, Folch had urged this upon the government at Madrid. Fearful that his home government might measure the value in terms of trade and revenue only, Folch warned:

By their position they exclude the United States from participation in the navigation, commerce, and communication with the coast of the northern part of the Gulf of Mexico. The Floridas also exclude several considerable rivers, which flow through the settlements of the United States, and subject their commerce to the will of Spain. By their location, the Floridas will have a strong ascendancy over the powerful Indian nations which inhabit that part of the American Union. The position of Baton Rouge on the Mississippi will be a powerful obstacle to the American government of the Mississippi, and it is very suitable, by means of competent forces prudently led for watching, retaining, and preventing all operations of the United States against the interior provinces of Nueva Espana.[13]

Finally, Folch advised, the position of the Floridas left "all the southern frontier of the United States from the Atlantic coast to the Mississippi open to the attacks of a foreign power."

Such strategic considerations did not escape either Jefferson or Madison, but these were largely theoretical as long as the Floridas belonged to Spain. Any possibility of a transfer of the territory aroused fears which were based on the considerations presented by Folch. Such a possibility remained remote rather than immediate when the Americans in West Florida determined to do something about the government of the province.

These Americans constituted a strong majority. West Florida had attracted them because of cheap land, fertile soil and easy access to market. A goodly number had come to escape the law and others had ventured into the province in the hope of retrieving a lost fortune or starting a new career after meeting with failure in the United States. They covered a vast range in types. At the upper level were men like Fulwar Skipwith, former American consul general in Paris, who had married a Flemish countess and who traveled about the district in a coach-and-four, complete with outriders and lackeys. At the opposite extreme, and yet leaders in the community, were the three Kemper brothers, Reuben, Nathan, and Sam.[14] Both extremes of the American population offered a threat, the more respectable elements because they expected the government to meet their needs with greater efficiency, the less respectable hooligans because they thrived on brawls. Both groups had one common grievance against the Spaniards, the fact that they were not Americans. The so-called Spanish yoke provided them with almost none of the benefits of government but neither did it subject them to any significant restraints.

In structure the Spanish government adhered to the principle of rule from above. Over each district ruled a commandant with authority over both military and political matters. He served as commander of the Spanish military force and over the local militia, both so weak as to be scarcely capable of exercising police power over the inhabitants. As civil ruler he appointed the inferior judges, known as alcaldes or syndics, and he himself served as the highest judge and also as the record keeper. He could and did send criminals and rebels against Spanish rule to the dungeons of Morro Castle in Cuba, but more often unruly elements such as the Kemper brothers escaped his grasp. Americans, on occasion, received appointment as officers of the militia, and under the rule of Grand Pre at Baton Rouge the Americans found the commandant highly cooperative and even eager to meet their wishes.

Insofar as American settlers had any real grievance it lay not in oppressive rule but in the almost entire absence of rule of any sort. Herein lay the origin of the movement for independence.

Americans living in the border region of Mississippi and Georgia had a more direct grievance against the Spanish than their friends within West Florida and therefore could be counted on to support any movement which would eliminate the Spanish. The goods they purchased from the outside and the commodities they produced for market must come and go on the rivers which flowed through Florida to the gulf. The Spanish collected customs duties and also reserved the right to prohibit the shipments of arms and ammunition.

In the summer of 1810 settlers in various districts petitioned the new Spanish commandant, Carlos Dehault de Lassus, for permission to hold meetings, and the Spaniard gave his consent because he had neither the funds nor the soldiers to deal with the revolt a refusal would provoke. The meetings struck a popular note and were well attended. A convention at St. John's Plains on July 25 avoided declaring for independence only because of fear of Spanish imprisonment, but they adopted a resolution claiming for themselves full political power subject to the consent of the governor. Not yet ready for an open declaration of independence, they covered their real intent with a grand gesture of voting thanks to De Lassus for permitting them to meet. The *Natchez Weekly Chronicle* promptly assured the members of the convention that "there is not one American heart that does not beat in unison with the people of Florida; and the prayers of seven million freemen are daily offered up to this fountain of all good for the civil and political freedom and universal prosperity of our enlightened neighbors."

At a convention held at Baton Rouge the representatives called for a new system of administering justice and voted in favor of arming the militia. For the first time, a representative of the United States was present as an observer. Through him John Rhea conveyed a message to Governor Holmes that the members favored immediate annexation to the United States and also an inquiry as to whether they could expect support in the event of a Spanish attempt to suppress the revolt. The governor explained that he could not act without instructions.

The insurgents realized that no Spanish official could accept what they had done and that De Lassus had yielded only to gain time. Interception of one of the commandant's communications to Folch confirmed this. The time had passed for turning back. Failure to complete the revolution could only result in many of their number being arrested and confined at Morro Castle. On September 22, another convention ordered the capture of the fort at Baton Rouge. A militia, already organized by a recent immigrant from Kentucky, John Ballinger, marched against the fort at two o'clock in the morning. This military *opéra bouffe* took place in a fort where sections of the stockade lay in ruin and where only twenty-eight Spaniards were on hand. The magazines had only limited supplies, and even these were not available at the time of attack as the officers who had the keys were not on duty. Not a single American suffered injury, but the son of Grand Pre, who had ordered the Spanish soldiers to fire, died in this strange engagement.[15]

The establishment of the independent republic of West Florida followed although the Spanish still held all of West Florida except the immediate area around Baton Rouge. The convention which drew up the frame of government also forwarded a resolution to Washington expressing the hope that the United States would incorporate the new republic. Three requests were made as conditions of annexation: (1) a general pardon to citizens of the new republic who had deserted from the United States army; (2) a loan of $100,000 to be repaid from the sale of public lands; and (3) members of the convention to have their claims to all unoccupied lands confirmed as a payment for the sacrifices they had made.

The offer of annexation occasioned no surprise in Washington. President Madison had been receiving detailed reports on the happenings in West Florida ever since the preceding January. In the weeks prior to the revolt at Baton Rouge he had carefully discussed the details of occupation with both Albert Gallatin and Thomas Jefferson. He confided· that he was worried that Congress, when it reconvened, might well take issue with the constitutionality of annexation by executive act. Gallatin thought there could be no question on that point for Congress had already passed the Mobile Act which assumed that West Florida belonged to the United States, but he expressed concern over how the annexation could be justified to the Spanish.

Madison acted quickly. On October 27 he issued a proclamation taking possession of the territory of West Florida. The rebels had control of only a very small area and the President's act could scarcely be viewed by Spain as anything short of an act of war. He justified his action on the ground that the territory already belonged to the United States, that not to take possession at a time when "confusion and contingencies" threaten it "might be construed into a dereliction of their title or an insensibility to the importance of the stake," that both the United States and Spain might lose the territory if no action were taken, and finally the subversion of Spanish authority and the resulting disorder endangered adjoining territories and facilitated violations of the revenue and commercial laws of the United States. Finally, in one of those characteristic gestures to justice, the President announced that West Florida in the hands of the United States would "not cease to be a subject of fair and friendly negotiations and adjustment."[16]

The Floridians considered the failure to take possession on

the basis of their having conquered the territory a serious mistake and one which failed to express due appreciation of their efforts. Madison's refusal to consent to their land claims disturbed them even more and for a brief time they threatened to resist annexation.

In the period between the revolt at Baton Rouge and the arrival of Madison's proclamation the convention which established the new government embarked on plans for overthrowing Spanish control in the remainder of Florida. A committee of public safety appealed to the people of Mobile and Pensacola to join the newly independent republic and appointed Reuben Kemper and Joseph White as commissioners to bring about the new union. White fell ill and the commission fell wholly to Kemper, a man ill suited for a diplomatic task. He journeyed to Fort Stoddert on the American side of the boundary and proceeded to organize a military force. He had no difficulty in arousing enthusiasm for the cause although he had to disguise his plans due to the opposition of Judge Toulmin who firmly opposed any intervention. A Spanish force captured Kemper's "army" before it reached Mobile. Judge Toulmin placed Kemper under arrest, a most courageous move in view of local enthusiasm for the cause. Rumors of Kemper's plans had caused consternation in Mobile for they fully expected that he would use the occasion as a pretext for looting. Colonel Sterling Dupree, who set up an independent government at Pascagoula, just east of Baton Rouge, plundered the local population, American and Spanish alike.

Actual combat between the forces of Spain and the United States threatened. Governor Folch was as determined to hold Mobile as many Americans were to seize it. A tacit compromise by which the Spaniards permitted American ships to proceed up the river by the fort while the Americans agreed not to attack Mobile, avoided the danger.

Madison's action in taking possession of the larger part of West Florida received the hearty endorsement of practically all of the Republican newspapers and many of the Federalist ones as well. The opposition politicians in Congress more than counterbalanced any praise from the press. In the Senate, Outerbridge Horsey of Delaware saw in the President's move a plot to get the United States into war with Great Britain. The President, he observed, had not consulted that power although she was an ally of Spain and might be called upon to come to her aid in defending the Floridas. Horsey denounced the action of the administration as an act of war against Spain. Madison's argument that West Florida was a part of the Louisiana Purchase, Horsey found spurious. France, he said, had ceded West Florida to England before ceding Louisiana to Spain. Therefore, when Spain retroceded Louisiana to France she could only retrocede Louisiana west of the Mississippi River.[17]

Josiah Quincy of Massachusetts not only denounced that action of the administration but professed to see in the addition of new territory a violation of the compact between the states and an altering of the Constitution. Quincy stressed that it was reducing the older states to a powerless minority. He spoke for the Essex Junto, the close knit oligarchy of Massachusetts merchants who viewed having to share power with the frontiersmen much as they would have viewed having one of their daughters marry a gun-toting Kemper. Quincy portrayed the horror should this expansionist tendency continue for it could only lead to Washington being trampled under by the rude characters who now roamed California and Oregon. In a grand peroration the Massachusetts Congressman warned:

Under the sanction of this rule of conduct, I am compelled to declare it as my deliberate opinion, that, if this bill passes, the bonds of this union are virtually dissolved; that the States which compose it are free from their moral obligations, and that, as it will be the right of all, so it will be the duty of some to prepare definitely for a separation—amicably if they can, violently if they must.[18]

The Speaker of the House ruled that such a statement was out of order but the House then voted on the ruling and upheld Quincy by a narrow margin.

Timothy Pickering, the spokesman for the Essex Junto in the Senate, spent an hour attacking the bill which would have made West Florida, to the Perdido, a part of the Orleans Territory. The speech repeated old arguments and aroused no interest until the senator read a letter written by Charles Maurice Talleyrand, dated December 21, 1804, in which the French foreign minister denied that West Florida had been a part of Louisiana. Senator Smith immediately challenged the right of his colleague to make public a letter which had been communicated to the Senate confidentially. This issue evoked a long debate which ended in a vote of mild censure.[19]

No one expressed the general feeling of the country as well as the new senator from Kentucky, Henry Clay. The quibbling over the claim to West Florida probably did not interest him in the least although he took time to reply to those who questioned it.

Clay boldly rested the case on self interest. The disorder resulting from Spain's inability to maintain its authority and the danger of the territory passing into the hands of another power led Clay to conclude: "We have a right upon eternal principles of self-preservation, to lay hold of it. This principle alone, independent of any title, would warrant our occupation of West Florida."[20] The danger of Great Britain coming to the aid of her ally, Spain, he pushed aside cavalierly with the question, "Is the rod of British power to be forever suspended over our heads?"[21]

Clay's stand on the Florida question had the virtue of frankness. He took the question out of the shadowy realm of legal and moral argument and based it on a nationalistic consideration of self interest. Madison, no less nationalistic than Clay, found it necessary to defend his action on legal grounds. The result impressed no one and served to confirm the opposition in its suspicion that the President was guilty of deceit. Madison somehow convinced himself that West Florida was a part of the Louisiana Purchase but the legal case fell to the ground on the simple fact that Spain had refused to include that province in the retrocession in spite of the pressure exerted by France and France never claimed that it was included.

The real issue lay in the question as to whether West Florida, in the situation which presented itself in 1810, comprised a sufficiently clear threat to the self preservation of the United States to warrant such a bold stroke. West Florida constituted a highly strategic area and in the possession of a stronger power than Spain would have posed a real danger. No immediate danger existed. Moreover, Great Britain, as an ally of Spain and even more as a colonial power in the Caribbean and a trading nation in that part of the world, also had legitimate interests. Madison ignored these, and the nationalistic wing of his party led by Clay did the same. Clearly the United States had committed itself to a nationalism that endorsed unilateral action. That the Federalists, in the absence of any clear and present danger in the Floridas, should have opposed Madison is not surprising. Once again the Republicans had shown themselves reckless in ignoring the nation with which the United States needed so desperately to maintain good relations.

To the distress of the unhappy Federalists the President moved one step further in a special message delivered on January 3, 1811.[22] Faced with the immediate danger of attack from local banditti, Governor Folch had intimated that he would be willing to transfer the Floridas to the United States if he did not receive reinforcements. The President transmitted the offer to Congress and sent along with it a copy of a protest against his action in West Florida filed by the British chargé. He suggested that Congress adopt a resolution stating that the United States could not view any transfer of territory in the New World to a European power with equanimity. Congress approved of his recommendations subject to the proviso that any territory so possessed should still be subject to negotiation.

Fearing that the British would make trouble over the Florida question and never acknowledging that they had a particle of legitimate interest in it, Madison anticipated their protest with stern and undiplomatic warnings a few days after Congress had approved of his recommendations of January 3. The note began with a plaintive defense of American action in West Florida and the steps about to be taken to embrace East Florida. He wrote to William Pinkney:

In this condition of the Spanish Empire, with the antient system of Government expiring, new systems of Rule growing up in her provinces and exposed to events which the vicissitudes of a political and military revolution render incalculable, what more natural, what more conformable to justice, than for the United States in a spirit of friendly moderation to seek security for those indemnities not disowned by Spain herself, but the payment of which has been so long delayed? Should a new Government be established in Spain under any auspices whatsoever and declare itself absolved from the payment of the debts of the old Monarchy, to what source, except a pledge in possession, could the United States recur for remuneration for so many losses which their Citizens have suffered from the effects of the laws and the policy of Spain?[23]

As a diplomatic weapon this carried no more sting than a reading of the 23rd Psalm, but it also revealed a self-righteous and narrow nationalism as irrelevant to the problem of Caribbean control as the scriptural passage.

Madison followed it with a truculent threat that should Great Britain "unhappily yield itself up to such improper desires" as taking the Floridas, the United States would not "hesitate for a moment as to the conduct which they would be inevitably compelled to pursue." Not long before the British chargé in Washington, in a letter to the Secretary of State, had written in protest to Madison's action in West Florida:

Would it not have been worthy of the generosity of a free nation like this, bearing, as it does, a respect for the rights of a gallant people at this moment engaged in a noble struggle for its liberty,— would it not have been an act on the part of this country dictated by the sacred ties of good neighborhood and friendship which exist between it and Spain, to have simply offered its assistance to crush the common enemy of both, rather than to have made such interference the pretext for wresting a province from a friendly Power, and that at the time of her adversity?[24]

Nationalism clothed in moral righteousness and legal argument offered a sufficient shield against the truth of the matter and the President pressed onward.

Governor Folch faced a hopelessly disordered situation created by unruly Americans within his jurisdiction. If he could not obtain aid from his Spanish superiors, then there was less to lose by inviting the United States to use its own troops to restore order. After receiving the approval of Congress of moving into the Floridas, Madison appointed General George Mathews and John McKee, an agent to the Choctaw, to negotiate with Folch. The agents soon learned that Folch had orders to defend his province. In fact, they learned that Folch had not only changed his mind as regards American occupation but that he was furious. When he had made the offer, he had done so because of the danger of the insurgents overrunning the country. Since then he had observed that officials of the United States were cordial to the elements he so much dreaded. He heard representatives of the United States threaten to cooperate with the trouble makers. Worst of all, the United States had incorporated Reubin Kemper and his armed men into the territorial militia. These happenings convinced Spanish officials that the earlier revolt in West Florida had been encouraged and supported by the United States.

Faced by Spanish officials determined to resist, Mathews undertook a campaign to stir up a revolt in East Florida. His activities did not elude the eyes of the new British minister, Augustus Foster, who promptly recited a list of Mathews' doings to Secretary Monroe. Foster followed this information with the highly pertinent question of whether the President would employ armed forces as secretly authorized by Congress if Mathews' activities resulted in a rebellion in East Florida. Foster described the American action as "contrary to every principle of public justice, faith, and national honor."[25]

Monroe had been surprised by the inquiry, but he did not hesitate to reply that the United States could not admit the right of Great Britain to interfere. The United States, Monroe contended, had ample reason to prevent the falling of Florida into the hands of some nation other than Spain. Foster reported that in all probability nothing short of a prospect of war with Great Britain could deter the United States.[26]

Early in September, 1811, Foster confronted Monroe with a report that Mathews was engaged in promoting a rebellion in Florida. To win allies among the inhabitants, said the British minister, Mathews was "using every method of seduction to effect his purpose, offering to each white inhabitant, who would side with him, fifty acres of land, and the guarantee of his religion and property; stipulating, also, that the American Government would pay the debts of the Spanish Government, whether due in pensions or otherwise, . . ." Foster asked Monroe for an explanation "of the alarming steps which Governor Mathews is stated to be taking for subverting Spanish authority."[27] Monroe waited two months to reply and then did not deny Mathews' activities. Instead, he cited American claims against Spain and maintained that the United States looked to Florida for this indemnity. Because of this, said Monroe, "It would be equally unjust and dishonorable in the United States to suffer East Florida to pass into the possession of any other Power."[28]

Even in the midst of the Florida controversy, in November, 1810, the frustrated President had busied himself trying to devise a way to counteract the British in South America. He turned quite naturally to France. As much as he disliked the deceit and effrontery of Napoleon, it was Great Britain with its stranglehold which he really hated, and feeling the hold he was not unduly particular as to where he reached for help. Thus he instructed Armstrong "to bring to the view of the French Government the trade with Spanish and Portuguese America which the British is at this time pushing thro' every avenue which its power and policy can penetrate." This monopoly, Armstrong was to explain, enabled Great Britain to provide the South Americans with all the manufactures and "to maintain a controling (sic) political ascendancy over them" which, in turn, enabled Great Britain to negotiate commercial treaties (he cited the treaty which the British had recently negotiated at Caracas) giving her a privileged position. To prevent such a monopoly France should open her ports to American ships. Thereby, "France and the Nations connected with her would, thro' the medium of American enterprize and navigation, obtain a vent for a large portion of their produce and manufactures which in no other way can find a market in the ports of Spanish and Portuguese America."[29] The vision thus opened up rested on idle opinion rather than hard facts. French manufactures were scarcely likely to replace British manufactures except for certain types of textiles and wines; at least this proved to be the case when the Napoleonic Wars were over.

Madison waited for a period of nine months before Napoleon announced that he was prepared to launch a campaign against the British in South America. On August 20, 1811, the Duke of Bassano summoned Jonathan Russell for an interview for the purpose of explaining the Emperor's policy in relation to South America. This policy was to recognize the independence of every portion which had "the spirit and the physical means to assert it and aid in its achievement." The Emperor had concluded "that the only mode in which this aid could be efficaciously furnished was thro' the concurrence and agency of the U. States." The Spaniards needed arms. To encourage American acceptance of the plan, the Duke explained that of course the Floridas could never sustain themselves and that France wholly approved of their annexation to the United States.[30]

Joel Barlow, the new minister to France, had scarcely become settled in his apartments in Paris when the Duke elaborated on the proposal which had been made to Russell three weeks earlier. The Emperor was prepared to aid the Spanish Americans with arms and ammunition on the condition that they not "connect themselves with England by exclusive privileges of trade." Barlow interpreted this to mean that they must adopt the Continental system. "Secondly," reported Barlow, "the Emperor wishes the United States to establish regular packets between them and France, to run monthly, and he will pay half the expense."[31]

Madison manifested no enthusiasm. He understandably distrusted the government which had failed to make reparations for seizures under the old decrees, which prescribed the kind of goods which American vessels could carry on leaving France, and continued to seize American ships at every opportunity. Moreover, he had come to the conclusion that Napoleon's interest in South America was to retrieve the new republics for his brother Joseph. Madison viewed that project as hopeless. Denied any effective assistance by Napoleon, James Madison could at least take comfort in the fact that Napoleon was far away and unable to exert control over the United States. The British stood at close range, and as Madison saw it, posed a greater threat.

The Florida question, if we seek to weigh it as a factor in bringing about war, defies accurate measurement. By late 1811 it no longer entered into the diplomatic negotiations. No mention of the Florida question appears in the heated exchange between Secretary of State Monroe and Augustus Foster, the British minister, during the first six months of 1812. It is also to be observed that the British ministry did not at any time contemplate action to rescue the Floridas for Spain.[32] Augustus Foster's diplomatic notes possessed a sharpness that had little correlation to the minor importance the British attached to the question. The Florida issue was only one of several points on a circle that finally propelled the United States into declaring war.

Another point on the circle was the question of Canada. The British territory to the north provided the one point of vulnerability. Republicans viewed Canada as the hostage in American hands. The British could not be challenged on the high seas, but Canada could be seized and held until Great Britain acceded to American demands. This was the view that prevailed from the time of the crisis of the Chesapeake Affair down to General Hull's defeat at Detroit in the early days of the war.

Textbooks delight in quoting Henry Clay's statement: "But I must be permitted to conclude by declaring my hope to see, ere long, the *new* United States (if you will allow me the expression) embracing not only the old thirteen States, but the entire country east of the Mississippi, including East Florida, and some of the territories to the north of us also."[33] The occasion for the speech was a Congressional debate late in December, 1810, over the question of West Florida. In a long speech the Senator from Kentucky traced in great detail the question of whether West Florida was a part of the Louisiana Purchase. Clay argued that it was. In reply to Horsey, of Delaware, who charged that Madison used the Florida issue to provoke war with Great Britain, Clay expressed contempt for those who espoused "the pretensions of a foreign nation." In the course of the speech Clay asked, "is the time never to arrive when we manage our affairs without the fear of insulting His Britannic Majesty? Is the rod of British power to be forever suspended over our heads?"[34] Clay gave a high priority, if all of his speeches are considered, to maritime rights, but he accurately reflected in this speech the sense of frustration that Americans developed as they confronted British power on all sides. Nowhere had British power made itself felt so keenly as on the high seas, and her shutting off of the continental markets had contributed in a major way to the economic depression that engulfed Clay's constituents.

In 1811 the developments in the West added another consideration to the question of Canada. Hitherto the interest in Canada had been holding her as a hostage. Now Canada was also viewed as the base from which the British intrigued with the Indians and encouraged them to make war against American frontier settlements. In April 1809, William Henry Harrison, governor of Indiana, secured a 3 million acre cession from the Indians. The Indians were already deeply resentful of the encroachments of Americans. The previous year a leader had stepped forth who promised to halt the advance of the white men. Tecumseh sought to counterbalance the Americans by establishing a confederacy of northern and southern tribes. He and his brother, known as the Prophet, established the headquarters of the confederacy in 1808 at Tippecanoe. When Tecumseh made a trip to the South in 1811, William Henry Harrison set out to destroy Prophetstown. On the way Harrison and his troops were ambushed by the Indians and only escaped after severe losses. The encounter, which became known as the battle of Tippecanoe, created a state of tension in the West.

Up and down the frontier rumors flew of British furnishing the Indians with arms and ammunition and of encouraging them to make war. The reports of British activities that reached Harrison were vague and of a dubious nature, but these were sent off to Washington where Secretary of State Monroe set them before the British Minister in such numbers and with such regularity that the subject of British relations with the Indians in the Northwest dominated the correspondence. Augustus Foster responded with assurances that the British officials in Canada were doing all in their power to discourage the Indians from making war. Monroe gave no credit to British denials. Instead he forwarded new reports of the most flimsy nature indicating that individual Britishers were encouraging the Indians.[35]

Monroe's employment of such reports to substantiate the charge against the British and the fact that these were deemed worthy of publication in government documents lends no great weight to the thesis that the United States went to war to solve the problem of British intrigue with the Indians. War had been largely determined upon before the battle of Tippecanoe in November 1811. James Monroe's emphasis on the Indian question seems rather like the action of a man taking advantage of the situation to embarrass the minister of the country with whom war was already almost a certainty.

The issue was useful to an administration seeking to unify the country in behalf of war. Newspapers throughout the West expressed a genuine fear that the British were enlisting the Indians as allies in a war Americans expected the British to declare. Members of Congress had long spoken of the conquest of Canada, the one soft spot in the British armor. They now ever more frequently expressed the view that Great Britain would present less of a danger if she were deprived of the provinces to the north. Joseph Desha, representative from Kentucky, summed up this feeling on the eve of war. Once Canada had been taken, he said, British intrigue with the Indians would cease and peace would be restored on the frontier. Desha also looked forward to the conquest of the maritime provinces. He hoped to deprive Great Britain of the large naval base in Nova Scotia from which her squadrons had molested American shipping.[36] The question of Canada and the irritation over alleged British intrigue with the Indians in the Northwest contributed in an important measure to the climate of opinion that made war possible.

Canada was another point in that circle that seemed to be closing. Earlier in 1811 Congress debated the renewal of the charter of the national bank. The farmers had long viewed the United States Bank as a monster of the financial interests and they now had the support of many local financial groups who resented the Bank's monopoly of legal tender status for its note issues. Albert Gallatin recommended renewal of the Bank's charter. The Secretary of the Treasury never endorsed the more extreme nationalism of his party colleagues with the result that many members of the party attacked him as a man of foreign birth whose loyalty was open to doubt. His stand on the Bank further antagonized them and a faction led by Samuel Smith, of Maryland, took the lead in bringing about the defeat of the administration measure. The arguments employed by the opponents of the Bank reflected the suspicion with which agrarians so often view urban financial institutions. Burwell exercised a degree of restraint in opposing the Bank, limiting his charges to constitutional grounds, the fact that the Bank was so open to suspicion that to perpetuate it would weaken the Union, and the old familiar argument that it encouraged speculation.[37] It remained for Joseph Desha, of Kentucky, to vent the full feelings of antipathy present on the frontier. Desha saw in the Bank a sinister instrument by which the wealthy of both the United States and Great Britain controlled the nation. The fact that two-thirds of the stock was owned by British citizens gave his argument a nationalistic appeal. He had no doubt that George III owned stock and that the British monarch had conceived the offer of a bonus to the government. To Desha the bonus was nothing but a bribe for buying off opposition. "Banks," he said, "are systems of speculation, calculated to suit the speculating and mercantile class at the expense of the agriculturists—at the expense of those who are the support and sheet anchor of your Government." He proposed that the government confiscate the holdings of British stockholders "to indemnify us in part for the damages we have sustained by British outrages; and, if it becomes necessary, (as I presume it will,) to make use of it in defraying the expenses necessary in the subjugation of the North American provinces, which will have to be resorted to, if you wish to give peace to the land."[38]

The ownership of two-thirds of the Bank's stock by British subjects helped make that nation a symbol of financial oligarchy. The agrarians coupled this to all the other evidence of British power—its control of the seas, its ruination of the European market for American farm produce, its possession of Canada and control of the fur trade in the Northwest, its current success in seizing the markets of South America, and the seeming threat of the British to take over the Floridas. Everywhere Great Britain blocked American enterprise. So it seemed to the agrarians who promptly interpreted British manifestations of power as evidence of a power hungry nation bent on reducing the sovereignty of the United States to an empty symbol. The reaction had its roots in the extreme pride of a recently acquired political independence, in the distrust with which a rural people view urban areas, and a lack of understanding, or perhaps an unwillingness to accept the inevitable relationship between an area still agrarian and producing raw materials and the metropolis which buys its raw material for industrial uses and also employs its capital to finance the operation.

NOTES

1. Arthur P. Whitaker, *The United States and the Independence of Latin America* (Baltimore: Johns Hopkins Press, 1941), pp. 44-47.

2. *Ibid.*, p. 23.

3. *Ibid.*, p. 42.

4. *Diplomatic Correspondence of the United States Concerning the Independence of the Latin-American Nations,* ed. William R. Manning, Vol. I (New York: Oxford University Press, 1925), p. 3.

5. *Ibid.*, pp. 3, 4.

6. Isaac Joslin Cox, *The West Florida Controversy, 1798-1813: A Study in American Diplomacy* (Baltimore: Johns Hopkins Press, 1918), p. 281.

7. *Ibid.*, p. 303.

8. Henry Adams, *History of the United States of America During the First Administration of James Madison* (New York: Charles Scribner's Sons, 1921), I, pp. 38, 39.

9. For a detailed account of the work of these agents and the new consuls see Whitaker, *op. cit.*, p. 79.

10. *Diplomatic Correspondence of the United States Concerning the Independence of the Latin-American Nations,* Vol. I, p. 10.

11. *Ibid.*, p. 6.

12. *Ibid.*

13. *Louisiana under the Rule of Spain, France, and the United States 1785-1807: Social, Economic, and Political Conditions of the Territory represented in the Louisiana Purchase as portrayed in hitherto unpublished contemporary accounts by Paul Allict and various Spanish, French, English, and American Officials,* ed. James Alexander Robertson, Vol. II (Cleveland: The Arthur H. Clark Co., 1911), p. 332.

14. Hodding Carter, *Lower Mississippi, The Rivers of America Series,* ed. Stephen Vincent Benet and Carl Carmer (New York: Farrar & Rinehart Inc., 1942), pp. 140-149.

15. For the developments in West Florida the author has relied largely on the detailed and definitive work of Isaac Joslin Cox, *The West Florida Controversy, 1798-1813: A Study in American Diplomacy.*

16. *Writings of James Madison,* Vol. VIII, pp. 112-114.

17. *Annals of the Congress of the United States, Eleventh Congress, Third Session,* p. 59.

18. *Ibid.*, p. 525.

19. *Ibid.*, p. 83.

20. Henry Clay argued that the United States had a legal claim on West Florida. He rested this contention on the ground that France, in 1762, had made the grants to Great Britain and Spain "at the same in-

stant of time." He concluded that this created ambiguity and that whenever an ambiguity existed in a grant, "the interpretation most favorable to the grantee is to be preferred." The argument is not convincing. See *Annals of Congress, Eleventh Congress, Third Session,* pp. 59-60.

21. *Ibid.,* p. 63.

22. *Writings of James Madison,* Vol. VIII, pp. 130-131.

23. *Diplomatic Correspondence of the United States Concerning the Independence of the Latin-American Nations,* Vol. I, p. 10.

24. Henry Adams, *op. cit.,* Vol. I, p. 315.

25. Augustus Foster to James Monroe, July 2, 1811, *American State Papers: Foreign Relations,* Vol. III, pp. 543-544.

26. Augustus Foster to Lord Wellesley, July 5, 1811, Foreign Office, America II, 5:76 (Public Record Office, London), quoted by Isaac Joslin Cox, "The Border Missions of General George Mathews," *The Mississippi Valley Historical Review,* December, 1925, Vol. XII, p. 318.

27. Augustus Foster to James Monroe, September 5, 1811, *American State Papers: Foreign Relations,* Vol. III, pp. 543-544.

28. James Monroe to Augustus Foster, November 2, 1811, *ibid.,* pp. 544-545.

29. *Diplomatic Correspondence of the United States Concerning the Independence of the Latin-American Nations,* Vol. I, pp. 7-8.

30. *Ibid.,* Vol. II, p. 1371.

31. *Ibid.,* p. 1372.

32. Perkins, *Prologue to War,* p. 275.

33. *Annals of Congress, Eleventh Congress, Third Session,* p. 64.

34. *Ibid.,* p. 63.

35. James Monroe to Augustus Foster, June 10, 1812, *American State Papers,* Vol. III, pp. 464-468.

36. *Annals of Congress, Twelfth Congress, First Session,* p. 490.

37. *Annals of Congress, Eleventh Congress, Third Session,* pp. 580-595.

38. *Ibid.,* pp. 657-658.

The Closing of the Circle

XIV

HISTORIANS interested in causation have conditioned us to think in terms of lists of causes. Although they acknowledge that no single factor can be weighed with any precision and the priority they give varies according to the historian and the time he is writing, they emulate the scientists in seeking to determine what was the decisive factor. Given the number of variables and their intricate relationships, it may be more fruitful to abandon the listing procedure with its implication of assignment of varying degrees of importance for a different concept of causation. Causes may better be viewed as segments of a ring. Impressment, the Florida question, the dispute over alleged British intrigue with the Indians, long time resentment over the dependence of the United States on British credit, and the issue of maritime grievances are all parts of the ring and there is no need of establishing the precise importance of each. Indeed to establish a priority among the causes leads to a kind of mechanistic conception of social causation that is inconsistent with the very nature of society and of human motivation.

By late summer of 1811 Americans were reacting to each of the several causes in a great variety of ways. Only a group of extremist Republicans, the War Hawks, had come to the conclusion that war was necessary. Another large group of Republicans still clung to the hope that Great Britain would yield her Orders in Council. By early autumn that hope had vanished. This significant change had its origin in the Macon Bill No. 2 and Napoleon's adroit maneuver to exploit this law.

Unscrupulous calculation, made bold by a million bayonets, paid scant attention to Madison's plaintive disquisitions on the legal rights of neutrals. Napoleon, playing for the grand prize of dominating Europe, knew that short of defeating the British he could not achieve his goal. Frustrated by the barrier the channel imposed against his regiments, he concluded that there remained only one way to defeat Great Britain. That was to undermine the British economy by depriving her of the markets of Europe. Napoleon knew what sacrifices this would involve for his allies. Thousands of continental merchants must thereby give up their chief means of livelihood, the landed aristocracy, particularly of Russia, must give up the British market which absorbed the produce of their estates, and the commoners must sacrifice the advantages of British textiles, coffee, and other items which could now reach them only in British ships. Undaunted, Napoleon boldly set out to make them conform to his dicta.

His aim of a continent tightly closed against the British had yet to be realized in the spring of 1810. Not that he had failed to strike a blow at the British economy, for there had been times during the past three years when his system had functioned with considerable efficiency. During the last five months of 1807, after the Peace of Tilsit had freed his hands, Napoleon exercised a close surveillance over the system and made the British economy shake under the deficits of merchants, shipowners, and manufacturers. Beginning in 1808 the Continental System failed to keep out British goods. Malta, Gibraltar, Heligoland, Gothenburg and ports in the Baltic and in Holland became entrepôts for British goods. So called contrabanders picked up the goods and took them to the mainland. Where the local authorities refused to shut their eyes to such trade, the contrabanders landed them on beaches at night and the goods found their way to the markets by way of farmers in the vicinity.

The two centers of this trade in 1809 and 1810 were at Malta and Heligoland. The British pushed all trade in the Mediterranean through Malta where they could not only control it but keep the most profitable share of it in British bottoms. Heligoland, the small island in the North Sea, matched the importance of the major European ports. The island, manned by 600 British soldiers, at one time reportedly had a supply of goods valued at 300 to 400 million francs.[1]

The Dutch, heavily dependent on trade, freely ignored the Napoleonic decrees and in this they had the sympathy of Louis Napoleon. The Russians, too, evaded the system with some abandon. Czar Alexander, while having considerable sympathy for the French alliance, confronted hard economic facts. The landed nobility of Russia prospered only to the degree that they could market their surplus abroad. Consequently Alexander closed his eyes to violations of the promises he had made to Napoleon at Tilsit and which he had repeated on several occasions thereafter.

Napoleon, not one to soften in the face of challenges to his system, undertook new measures in 1810 designed to make it effective. While removing his troops from many of the German states, he established a military cordon along the shores of the North Sea and the Baltic Sea, maintaining control of such key cities as Danzig and Hamburg. Faced with the unwillingness of his brother Louis to enforce the system in Holland he incorporated that country into his empire. Sweden, to whom he had restored Pomerania, received warning that if she continued to permit contraband traffic in that area, she would be deprived of the territory. In brief, in the winter and spring of 1810, while Congress entertained itself with speeches on the obnoxious aristocratic tendencies of a navy and debated the dangers to states rights in strengthening the army, Napoleon prepared for a stern enforcement of his Continental System.

Napoleon's measures presented no empty threat for the British economy, which, far more than any other of its day, rested on a highly complex financial and commercial system. Unless her own manufactures and the raw materials of her colonies could be marketed, the value of the pound sterling would decline and her economy would collapse. The products of her colonies marketed on the continent provided the funds for the colonies to buy British manufactures just as American purchases in England were financed by remittances from the continent. By 1810 the pound had declined in value from 25 francs to 17.[2] Well might Napoleon attack the problem of enforcing the Continental System with vigor.

The United States presented a major problem to Napoleon. In the first place, Americans outnumbered all other contrabanders. When word of Jefferson's Embargo reached Europe, many American captains decided to remain and engage in illegal trade. To do this it was necessary for them to comply with the Orders in Council and carry British cargoes. British authorities readily granted licenses for this trade. By 1810 the licenses averaged 1800 a month. When American vessels docked at a port under Napoleon's control they were subject to seizure if the customs officials found that they had yielded to British controls—Napoleon preferred to say "if they have denationalized themselves." Customs officials outside of France frequently closed their eyes and made no real effort to pry into the secrets which American captains did their best to maintain. As we shall see Napoleon regarded these Americans as tools of the British, and he treated them accordingly.[3]

Secondly, he would be greatly aided in undermining the economic system of the British if he could induce the United States to cut off trade with England for the American market played so important a role in the British economy that this alone was close to an adequate substitute for the loss of the continental market. Therefore Napoleon constantly sought to embroil the United States with the British—eventually he succeeded.

Napoleon decided on bold measures. Not one to be bothered by petty scruples, in April 1810 he ordered his agents in the

Hanse towns and the officials in Prussia and Denmark to admit American vessels and then seized them. Thus he would be able to relieve some of his own financial burden by the sale of the goods while putting an end to remittances to England with which Americans paid for British manufactures. Denmark and Prussia begged to be excused on the ground that many of the American ships were bona fide neutrals, but Napoleon dismissed this as fantasy. On word that numerous convoys were approaching Prussia under the American flag, he ordered: "Let the American ships enter your ports! Seize them afterward. You shall deliver the cargoes to me, and I will take them in part payment of the Prussian war debt."[4]

Napoleon justified the seizures as reprisal for the Non-Intercourse Act which provided for seizure of French ships entering American ports in violation of that law. In the words of his foreign minister "His Majesty felt bound to order reprisals on American vessels, not only in his territory, but likewise in the countries which are under his influence. In the ports of Holland, of Spain, of Italy, and of Naples, American vessels have been seized, because the Americans have seized French vessels."[5] To these words of explanation he added an admonition. Either the United States must take sides against Great Britain or "become again, as before the Revolution, the subjects of England." Their present course, wrote Cadore, "renders them more dependent than Jamaica, which, at least, has its Assembly of Representatives and its privileges."[6]

Such distortion did not go unchallenged. Minister Armstrong stated the facts. The Non-Intercourse law had not resulted in any seizures of French vessels. The United States had informed France of the law before it was applied in contrast to the French who gave no warning. Napoleon's protest against the law was only recent; When he had been informed of it the previous June he had not protested. As to the French admonition that a nation has a duty to protect its sovereign rights, Armstrong replied that the United States certainly did have a duty to resent the outrages of France, and he reminded Cadore that there were not less than 100 American ships in French possession or in possession of her allies.[7]

On March 23 Napoleon formalized his policy of seizures in a decree issued from Rambouillet. Not until two months later did this decree appear in an official publication and Cadore had not informed Armstrong. The decree ordered the seizure and sale of all American vessels which had entered the ports of the Empire, or of its dependencies, since the previous May. Armstrong informed Secretary of State Smith that four commissioners had been sent to Amsterdam with orders to take possession of American property and that in France, ships which had been released, were now being seized again.[8] At the close of May, Madison confided to Jefferson: "The late confiscations by Bonaparte comprise robbery, theft, and breach of trust, and exceed in turpitude any of his enormities not wasting human blood."[9]

Before word of the Rambouillet decree reached Washington, the Macon Bill No. 2 had become law, and in a letter of June 5 President Madison explained the law to Armstrong and the opportunity it gave France. Alert to the dismaying reports of French seizures of American ships, Madison warned that he would not give effect to the law unless the seizures came to an end and restoration of seized property took place. "The only ground short of a preliminary restoration of the property, on which the contemplated arrangement can be made," the President wrote, "will be an understanding that the confiscation is reversible, and that it will become immediately the subject of discussion, with a reasonable prospect of justice to our injured citizens."[10]

Madison thus left the door ajar to invoking the law prior to a settlement of the question of French seizures. Napoleon abhorred the new American law for it opened the way to trade between Great Britain and the United States. Thereby the British could keep their economy going indefinitely even though he should effectively close the continent. The way to avoid this calamity would be to accept the offer held out by the Macon Bill, revoke the decrees, and thereby bring into effect the American Non-Intercourse law as regards Great Britain.

On August 5 the Duke of Cadore wrote to General Armstrong of Napoleon's decision. A more impudent communication from a chief of state is difficult to imagine. The Emperor had reviewed relations with America. He had expressed his approval of Jefferson's Embargo for, while it was prejudicial to France, it had not been offensive to her honor. The Embargo had caused France to lose her colonies of Martinique, Guadaloupe, and Cayenne, but His Majesty was quite willing to overlook this. The Non-Intercourse law had been both injurious and insulting making necessary French measures of retaliation. Now that the Americans had corrected their error His Majesty had revoked the Berlin and Milan decrees.[11]

This left the Madison administration with a great many questions. General Armstrong, about to leave his post in Paris, made a series of pointed inquiries of the Duke of Cadore. Had the Rambouillet decree been recalled? What was the present scope of regulation of American ships under the license system? Would Americans whose ships and property had been seized be remunerated? Armstrong suggested that the invoking of non-intercourse with England would depend on the answers given to these questions.[12]

The answers could scarcely have assured the Madison administration that France had in good faith entered upon a new system. The decree of Rambouillet had been cancelled. In reply to the question of restrictions on American ships entering or leaving French ports, Cadore replied "that American vessels, loaded with merchandise, the growth of the American provinces, will be received without difficulty in the ports of France, provided they have not suffered their flag to lose its national character, by submitting to the acts of the British Council. . . ." Of course, this seemed to abolish the edicts without yielding the policy, for the edicts had only barred ships which had complied with the British restrictions. As to the restoration of merchandise already seized, Cadore held that "it having been confiscated as a measure of reprisal, the principles of reprisal must be the law in that affair," a very unassuring reply.[13]

On November 2 President Madison issued a proclamation announcing the repeal of the Berlin and Milan decrees and that, if Great Britain did not rescind her Orders in Council, the Non-Intercourse law would be invoked three months hence. In forwarding a copy of the proclamation to the American legation in Paris Secretary of State Smith stated that it had been issued on the assumption that France would restore sequestered property. In short, full of doubts about the good faith of France, the Madison administration reserved the right to withhold the proclamation due February 2 if Great Britain had not withdrawn her Orders in Council.

Fearful of being duped the United States kept close watch to see if the French proposed to follow up their promises. In December Secretary of State Smith addressed a series of inquiries to General Turreau. The replies did not promise the slightest change in French policy. Rather, as Robert Smith concluded, it seemed the two policies were identical except that whereas formerly American ships had been excluded now American products were barred. After listing the products which France would not admit, the Secretary of State observed that they had constituted the great mass of exports from the United States to France and that "no practical good, worthy of notice, has resulted to the United States from the revocation of the Berlin and Milan decrees."[14] Turreau replied that his statements rested on decrees issued prior to the Duke of Cadore's letter of August 5 and that there would unquestionably be a change.

Jonathan Russell, Chargé d'Affaires at Paris, gave only the most discouraging reports from Paris during the early weeks of December. He waited for the President's proclamation, felt certain it was aboard the frigate *Essex* but that ship had been held in quarantine for the want of a bill of health. Russell told Cadore that he considered this strange for there was little danger of disease in the winter season and there had been no reports of affliction in the port from which the *Essex* had sailed.[15] Russell also reported that the *New Orleans Packet* had been seized at Bordeau.

The developments in late December failed to clarify the situation. The release of the *New Orleans Packet* on December 17th aroused new hope, but on Christmas day the French minister of justice instructed the Council of Prizes that while the Berlin and Milan decrees were suspended, the vessels which had been seized should remain in sequestration, "the rights of the proprietors being reserved for them until the 2nd of February next." At that time sequestered ships were to be released.[16]

On January 15 the President announced that all trade with Great Britain would be prohibited as of February 2. Because the Macon Bill was not precise in specifying who was to determine whether Great Britain had revoked the orders, and this would result in long delays while courts made the decision, additional legislation was required. The Madison administration wished Congress to enact a new law to give the President the power to determine whether the British had revoked the orders.

Not until February 2, 1811 did debate get underway. Supporters of the administration argued that President Madison could not question the good faith of the French, that diplomatic courtesy made it necessary for him to accept the revocation of the decrees at face value. They admitted that French depredations had not ceased, but they also held that enough time had not elapsed from the date of Napoleon's receiving the information of the proclamation of November 2, 1810 to warrant any conclusion that the decrees had not been revoked. Eppes delivered a lengthy speech analyzing the diplomatic correspondence aiming to show that President Madison had pressed the French with the greatest of energy, seeking the removal of all grievances. To question further would have been to close the door to relief from the depredations suffered in the past.[17]

The opposition conducted a campaign that portrayed Napoleon as the unscrupulous dictator, the master of deceit, the oppressor of the smaller nations, whose mad ambition would certainly override any promises made to the United States. Federalists cited the most recent news from France, the holding of the *Essex* and the sequestration of the *New Orleans Packet*. They pounded vigorously on the fact that Napoleon's order to the Court of Prizes called for sequestration of American ships until February 2. Congressman Daniel Blaisdell of New Hampshire expressed fear that the United States "after having been insulted, robbed, and deceived," was about to throw itself "into the embraces of that monster, at whose perfidy and corruption Lucifer blushes and Hell itself stands astonished." The United States had no more than a promise and, in the light of Napoleon's record no one could have any confidence in him. James Milnor, of Pennsylvania, asked: "But, sir, do these people really believe that property of our citizens will be given up after the second of February, and in consequence of the measure we are now about to adopt? When did that voracious monster ever disgorge the plunder he had once received into his insatiable maw?"[18]

John Randolph's motion to repeal the Macon law surprised no one for the Virginia Quid was invariably in the opposition.[19] The action of William Burwell, a long time supporter of the administration, in opposing the breaking off of commercial intercourse with Great Britain, marked a new turn. After reiterating his argument that the British market alone could not meet the needs of the agriculturalists, Burwell philosophically observed that American property "could not exist under such a system of rapine as had been pursued." The defender of the planters swung over to a position which many a Federalist had maintained: "We must wait for some change in Europe in which we cannot be instrumental, to enable us to act; until which it would not be proper to take any step in relation to either of the belligerents."[20]

Burwell's shift must have given comfort to the Federalists, but they gloomily observed that few votes would be changed by the merits of arguments. Recognizing that they did not have the votes, they resorted to the tactics of proposing amendments, consuming time by reiterating their arguments and moving adjournment. The Republicans finally pressed home their advantage in numbers. After an all night session of February 26, the clerk noted: "The House adjourned after a most desultory and fatiguing session of eighteen hours, the last four of which a quorum was not present, nor could other members be induced to attend."[21] The following day the House passed a truncated version of the original Eppes bill. It made the President the final authority as to the revocation of both Orders in Council and decrees, provided that American owned ships leaving Great Britain before February 2 were not to be seized and barred the entry of British ships and goods. The Senate, engaged in heated debate over the Bank bill, did not act until March 1. The bill passed both houses with large majorities, 20 to 7 in the Senate and 65 to 36 in the House of Representatives.

The prohibition against the entry of both British ships and goods served the purposes of Napoleon for it closed the one big gap in his Continental System. And this time British goods would be effectively excluded. A smuggle proof net was to be drawn that would do away with the evasions that had made a shambles of earlier trade restrictions. One of the features of the new law provided that customs officials, members of the armed forces, and informers should share the proceeds from the sale of goods that had been seized. Before long British merchants would testify that the American market was effectively closed.

Both British and American positions on the question of neutral rights soon crystallized. The United States made repeal of the Non-Importation Act prohibiting the importation of British goods contingent upon the repeal of the Orders in Council restricting trade with the continent and the revocation of the order of blockade issued in May, 1806. The British held out some promise of relinquishing the Orders in Council but at the same time made it clear that they could not yield their principles on blockades.[22] A few days prior to William Pinkney's final departure from London at the close of February, 1811, Lord Wellesley, the British foreign minister, wrote: "It is, perhaps, unnecessary to repeat the desire of this Government to relinquish the Orders in Council, whenever that measure can be adopted without involving the necessity of surrendering the most important and valuable maritime rights and interests of the United Kingdom."[23]

In the spring of 1811 the British held 27 American ships pending a ruling by the Court of Admiralty on the legality of the orders. The ships were valued at $257,300 and their cargoes at $571,000. On May 30 Sir William Scott rendered his ruling on the orders. They were, he said, legal only as a measure of retaliation against the French edicts. If those edicts had been repealed, then the orders would no longer be valid. He then declared that a final decision would be postponed so that claimants might have the opportunity to provide any evidence in support of the opinion that the edicts had been repealed.[24] On June 25 Scott announced that no such evidence had been supplied. As regards the letter of the Duc de Cadore, Scott termed that to be "nothing more than a conditional revocation: it contains an alternative proposed, either that Great Britain shall not only revoke her Orders in Council, but likewise renounce her principles of blockade— principles founded upon the ancient and established law of nations; or that America shall cause her neutral rights to be respected; in other words, that she shall join France in a compulsive confederation against this country."

The bellows of Napoleon's foreign office put new life into the smoldering embers of the dispute between the United States and Great Britain. The Orders in Council had been justified by the British as a measure of retaliation against the French decrees. In repealing them conditionally France provided the United States with a weapon to use against the British. The United States seized it with eagerness. The British did not recognize the change that had taken place in the United States and therefore remained casual in their consideration of American demands for repeal of the Orders in Council.[25]

Augustus Foster's letters to James Monroe gave no reason for hope that the Orders in Council would be repealed. Instead British determination to adhere to the orders appeared firmer than ever. Foster added a new requirement to the conditions already stated as necessary for repeal. In a letter to Monroe dated July 26, 1811, he explained that not until France admitted British goods carried on neutral ships would Great Britain consider Napoleon's Berlin and Milan decrees revoked.[26] James Monroe waited to reply until October 1 and then called Foster's new point "a pretension" on which it "is almost impossible to reason."[27] The British position snuffed out the last bit of hope of a repeal of the orders.

This was the position that the American nationalists felt compelled to contest. From the summer of 1811 the American leaders acted and spoke as men caught in a *cul de sac*. That the British would not yield had become clear, and that the United States could not accept the British dicta became a conviction. William Pinkney left Great Britain because he felt that there was nothing left to negotiate. Secretary of State James Monroe wrote to Jonathan Russell in London in November: "The Orders in Council are considered as war on our commerce, and to continue until the Continental market is opened to British products, which may not be pending the present war in Europe." "The United States," said this highly sensitive nationalist, "cannot allow Great Britain to regulate their trade, nor can they be content with a trade to Great Britain only, whose markets are already surcharged with their productions." In a final summation of the administration's view of the situation Monroe wrote: "The United States are, therefore, reduced to the dilemma either of abandoning their commerce, or of resorting to other means more likely to obtain a respect for their rights. Between these alternatives, there can be little cause for hesitation."[28]

Nor did the situation change during the winter of 1811-1812. Jonathan Russell attended Parliament on February 28 to listen to the debates on the Orders in Council as they related to the problem of relations with the United States.

To Russell the debates proved "the inflexible determination of the present Ministry to persevere in the Orders in Council without modification or relaxation." In fact the British leaders had said that a reexamination of relations with the United States could only result in "reproaching her in a manner to increase the actual irritation, and to do away with what Lord Bathurst stated to be the feeble hopes of preventing war."[29] Russell closed on a doleful note: "I no longer entertain a hope that we can honorably avoid war."

James Madison did not find it easy to give up his hope for reaching an agreement with the British. He had led the way to instituting non-importation of British goods with some confidence that economic coercion would bring peace. In June, 1811, he had written to Jefferson that no word had been received since the non-importation had gone into effect. After weighing the situation he had said that the administration "must remain somewhat in the dark till we have more on the subject. . . ."[30] He had based his slim hope on the belief that Napoleon would revise his policies when he learned of the Non-Importation Act.

In the summer of 1811 Madison finally had to face the fact that Napoleon had not changed his policies and that Great Britain was not prepared to yield any ground. The decision by the admiralty court in June, the *Little Belt* episode in June, and the firmness of Augustus Foster in his conference with the Secretary of State, swept away his last bit of hope. He concluded that Great Britain would make no concessions unless France admitted British goods. "The question to be decided therefore by Congress, according to present appearances simply is," he wrote, "whether all the trade to which the orders are and shall be applied, is to be abandoned, or the hostile operation of them be hostilely resisted." Summing up the attitude at home for John Quincy Adams, now in Europe, the President wrote that he expected war although he thought "the execution of it will be put off till the close of the session approaches."[31]

The position of James Madison was shared by many Americans. On November 19, 1811 the Maryland Senate passed resolutions recommending the use of force if Great Britain persisted in violating American rights on the high seas.[32] In December the Ohio legislature passed a resolution denouncing British practices on the sea and promising full support of a war.

Congress assembled on November 4, 1811 in response to an early call from President Madison. The President summoned them ahead of the regular date for meeting so that they might give prompt consideration to "the posture of our foreign affairs." In his message Madison pointed to the fact that Great Britain had put the Orders in Council "into more rigorous execution." He recited the wrongs inflicted by the British and emphasized especially the insistence of Great Britain on admission of her own goods into enemy ports before she would revise her policy. "With this evidence of hostile inflexibility, in trampling on rights which no independent nation can relinquish," said Madison, "Congress will feel the duty of putting the United States into an armor and an attitude demanded by the crisis, and corresponding with the national spirit and expectations."[33] Then he called for specific defense measures.

The nation moved down the road toward war. Since 1806 Madison had adamantly insisted on resisting British measures. His policy had led to what Henry Lee had aptly described as "half war and half peace."[34]

"Half war and half peace" is a precarious situation not easily maintained. War may seem preferable. And, indeed, war soon did appear to be the lesser evil. On January 25, 1812 the Virginia General Assembly passed a series of resolutions condemning Great Britain. One of them revealed the psychological strain. It read: "Resolved as the opinion of this Assembly, that however highly we value the blessings of peace, and however we may deprecate the evils of war, the period has now arrived when peace *as we now have it,* is disgraceful, and war honorable."

The winter and spring brought forth pledges of support.

On February 20, 1812 a Republican meeting at Bennington, Vermont, promised that Great Britain, when war came, would find the Federalists "notwithstanding their noon day caballing, and midnight intrigues, to be but as a dew-drop on the locks of our American Hercules, which he can shake from him at pleasure." From Virginia Jefferson reported "everybody in this quarter expects the declaration of war as soon as the season will permit the entrance of militia into Canada & altho' peace may be their personal interest and wish, they would I think, disapprove of its longer continuance under the wrongs inflicted and unredressed by England."

From Clarksburg, Virginia the President's old friend, J. G. Jackson, at the close of March wrote: "War alone can furnish a remedy for this deplorable malady (the Federalist dissension) of the body politic, & a chastisement for insufferable insults daily heaped upon us by the enemy." "My voice is for war," wrote Jackson, "& I could willingly add my arm too if we engage in it vigorously."[35]

On April 3 Madison sadly reported that the Percival administration in London would continue in office and "that they prefer war with us, to a repeal of their orders in council." "We have nothing left therefore," he observed, "but to make ready for it."[36]

With war impending the President had to consider the safety of the merchant fleet and seek to bring it home before hostilities commenced. He recommended an embargo of sixty days. Congress extended it to ninety days. Madison explained to Jefferson that the change had been made to meet the wishes of those "who wished to make it a negociating instead of a war measure, of those who wished to put off the day of war as long as possible, if ultimately to be met & of those whose mercantile constituents had ships abroad, which would be favored in their chance of getting safely home."[37]

James Madison, deeply aware of the sharp divisions among the people on the question of peace or war, had hoped that unity might be achieved if France should cease restricting trade, stop seizing American ships, and restore commercial relations to normal. Of course, France did not oblige him. Joel Barlow, sent to persuade the French government of the importance of removing all obstacles to regular commercial intercourse, was lampooned by Henry Adams for his mad chase after Napoleon in the illusory hope that the Emperor would grant his requests. To picture the conscientious emissary as a Don Quixote is to do him less than justice. He had few if any illusions concerning Napoleon and correctly discerned that Napoleon's only interest was to involve the United States in war. On April 22 he wrote to Madison expressing regret at his failure and bemoaning the fact that it meant war with Great Britain. "Perhaps the horror I have for that war is scarcely felt by any other of my countrymen," he wrote. "It arises from a cause that I do not like to explain on paper," the nationalistic poet observed. Then he summed up the reasons for his deep regret: "It may be perceived in a view of the critical state of England, the present posture of this continent & the moral character of its master."[38]

Madison had come to despise Napoleon too. In a letter to Jefferson he confided that there was something to be said for declaring war against both nations. Jefferson dismissed the idea as Quixotic. It would not quiet the opposition, it would create greater problems in fighting the war, and "insulate us in general negociations for peace, making all the parties our opposers." Perhaps Jefferson perceived in the President's offhand suggestion a proposal that the President was considering seriously. He knew Madison well and may have concluded that his successor's desire always to appear fair and just would lead him into a trap. If so, it explains the quite unusual tone of his reply. The letter was a stern warning that denounced the idea as

a solecism worthy of Don Quixote only, that of a choice to fight two enemies at a time, rather than to take them by succession and the only motive for all this is a sublimated impartiality at which the world will laugh, and our own people will turn upon us in mass as soon as it is explained to them, as it will be by the very persons who now are laying that snare.[39]

Those opposed to war made frenzied attempts to halt the march of events. Early in June Congress received a great many petitions. A group of citizens in Philadelphia and Delaware counties in Pennsylvania stated that "the United States are not impelled to war against Great Britain."[40] Several petitions from Northampton county in the same state likewise opposed war.[41] A memorial from New York expressed the view that Great Britain would soon repeal the Orders in Council and that no action should be taken. Among the 58 signers were John Jacob Astor, two presidents of banks, three presidents of insurance companies, and thirteen directors of banks.[42] On June 12 a memorial signed by Charles Carroll, of Carrollton, and a considerable number of citizens in Arundel county in Maryland came before Congress.[43] On the same day James Lloyd, member of the Senate, presented a memorial from the House of Representatives of Massachusetts deprecating war.[44]

The protests had no effect. James Madison had sent his war message to Congress on June 2. Two days later the House of Representatives voted 79 to 49 in favor of war. Thirty-nine of the seventy-nine votes for war came from the states from Maryland to Georgia. Of the votes for war 13 were cast by representatives from Virginia, 4 from North Carolina, 10 from South Carolina, 1 from Georgia, and 6 from Maryland. Pennsylvania representatives cast 15 votes for war. The remaining affirmative votes came from a widely scattered area including New England. All of the members from the western states voted for war.

The final vote in the Senate took place on June 17. Those opposed to war had admitted that the nation had a just grievance, but they stressed the lack of preparedness. Dire warnings of the British capture of American ships and coastal cities and probable failure of the campaign against Canada failed to have any effect. Of the 19 votes for war, 3 came from New England, 4 from the middle states, 3 from the western states, and 8 from the states from Maryland to Georgia.

In a private letter to a friend James Madison explained his decision to go to war. He wrote: "The conduct of the nation against whom this resort has been proclaimed left no choice but between that & the greater evil of a surrender of our sovereignty on the Element, on which all nations whose agriculture & commerce are so closely allied, have an essential interest." He attributed the British restrictions on American commerce to the British desire to protect her own unlawful commerce with enemy controlled territory from American competition.[45]

To a nation so dependent on foreign commerce as the United States this political tenet was much more than a theoretical statement of the principle of sovereignty. The war in Europe had resulted in the abrogation of the normal rights of neutrals and the closing of markets.

Farmers in the South and West blamed their economic plight on the shutting off of markets by the British. South Carolina suffered from a serious drop in cotton prices. A contemporary observer estimated that to come out ahead a cotton farmer must receive 20 cents per pound. In February, 1810 the price had fallen to 14 cents and the following year it dropped to 8 cents. Cotton was the most important product of South Carolina. The depression in that state explains in large part why its representatives in Congress strongly supported war.[46] Farmers who raised tobacco likewise suffered from a fall in prices. In March, 1812 Madison's agent in Liverpool informed him: "I have not been able to do any thing satisfactory with the tobacco you were so good as to consign me in 1810. It is all on hand."[47] As early as 1809 George Campbell of Tennessee, speaking in Congress, had said, concerning the effect of British restrictions,

Tobacco will find no market; cotton a temporary market only—for, although Great Britain will receive it, yet, as we have more on hand than she will immediately want, or can make use of, and as we cannot go to France, and our trade with the Continent will undoubtedly be interrupted by Great Britain, she has nothing to do but wait a few days, weeks, or months, and buy it at her own price.[48]

In April, 1811, the editor of the *Lexington Reporter* charged that the chief factor in bringing about a decline in the prices of tobacco and cotton was the closing of the continental markets by Great Britain.[49] Samuel McKee of Kentucky had the economic situation in mind when he called for the use of force in combatting British restrictions. He asked his colleagues in Congress, "How long shall we live at this poor dying rate, before this non-importation law will effect the repeal of the Orders in Council?"[50]

In December, 1811, John C. Calhoun countered the criticisms of John Randolph who charged the advocates of war with base motives. Calhoun explained, what was true, that the people of the South and West attributed the low prices on produce to the acts of the belligerents and not to the Embargo and Non-Intercourse acts. Calhoun summed it up:

they see in the low price of the produce, the hand of foreign injustice; they know well, without the market to the Continent, the deep and steady current of supply will glut that of Great Britain; they are not prepared for the colonial state to which again that Power is endeavoring to reduce us.[51]

The causes for the decline in agricultural prices were many and the decline continued after the close of the Napoleonic wars. But what is important is that so many contemporaries attributed their difficulties to the British.[52]

It is one of the ironies of history that at the very time the American farmers lost all faith in the efficacy of economic coercion that policy was on the verge of success. In April and May of 1812 the Committee of the Whole House of Commons heard the testimony of more than 100 British manufacturers and merchants describe how the loss of the American market had rendered thousands unemployed and had reduced the laboring class to the first soup kitchens in modern history.[53]

Birmingham presented a scene of acute distress. Every manufacturer was overloaded with stock. Should the prevailing conditions exist twelve months longer, predicted a prominent banker and entrepreneur in the iron and nail trade, it would result in "convulsions too dreadful for my apprehension." Asked for the cause, Mr. Atwood, the banker, testified:

Certainly in a great degree to the cessation of intercourse with the United States of America, very far in the greatest degree; but in other respects to the stoppage of all Continental intercourse; but that not so large an amount as the intercourse of the United States; when I say that the manufactures of Birmingham exported to the United States of America amount to about £800,000 or a million per annum, I wish to observe that they are almost entirely composed of labour, there is no great expense or scarcely any in the raw material, and therefore that £800,000 or one million is now lost to the labouring mechanics.

The nail industry in the vicinity of Birmingham was described by Thomas Potts, Birmingham merchant, as "extremely depressed." Potts testified that during the American Embargo of 1808 there had been considerable smuggling but now it was impossible. James Ryland, a plater of coach harness and saddlery furniture, said he had exported from two-thirds to three-fourths of his wares to the United States and that since the closing of that market he had "piled up a stock two or three times as large as it ever was." Manufacturers of buttons, candlesticks, locks, ceramics, jewelry, carpets, and textiles repeated the doleful story of large stocks on hand, losses, and unemployment. And most of them explained that if the Orders in Council were revoked they could fill orders for the United States at once, orders placed on the condition that those Orders in Council be revoked.

Manufacturers from Sheffield placed equal stress on the importance of the American market and how all difficulties would be removed if that market were opened again. Time and again they stated that the American market had absorbed from one-third to two-thirds of what they produced. Woolen manufacturers from Lancashire repeated the same story. John Grundy had employed 600 in good times. Half of his production had been sold in the United States. He stated that he had £7,000 in orders ready for America when the Orders in Council were repealed. John Wood of Bolton described the unemployment and distress in his community. There workers were living on oatmeal and potatoes, and now they had only short rations of these. A trustee of the Cloth Hall at Leeds testified that two-thirds of the woolens manufactured there went to American markets.

One of the most tragic stories involved Spitalfields. John Honeyman, a manufacturer of silks, said one-half of the men were unemployed. So great was the distress that the Quakers had established a soup kitchen for the relief of the poor.

Equally disturbing to the British were the reports of manufactures having started in the United States since that country had prohibited British imports. Several noted the progress Americans had made in the manufacture of nails. One witness submitted statistics on the number of new cotton mills within thirty miles of Providence, Rhode Island. These totalled 68 in number and had more than 47,000 spindles in operation.

Those witnesses engaged in shipping continued to support the Orders in Council in spite of the disaster the orders brought to the manufacturing districts. They described their business as prosperous and predicted a decline should the orders be revoked. The Orders in Council, making American ships subject to seizure, raised insurance rates so as to give British shipping a competitive advantage in trade with the continent. The license system, by raising the costs to Americans, had the same effect. The merchants predicted severe losses if the orders were repealed. They foresaw American ships going to France, taking on continental manufactures, and then disposing of them in Spain, Portugal, and Brazil, and eliminating British merchants from the trade with these countries. Merchants testified that great gains had been made in the Mediterranean trade due to British controls. This trade was centered at Malta. Americans were permitted to carry goods from Malta to France, Italy, and the Levant, but all goods going to Malta had to come in British bottoms.

The license system gave the British control of trade with France. Napoleon had pursued a similar license system in trade with England, and this trade had increased sharply in the last fifteen months. If licenses were abolished, merchants believed that Americans would take over the trade and with disastrous results. French manufactures would find their way to former British markets. More serious than the effect on British manufactures would be the effect on the British West Indies. Americans would provide France with raw materials from the Spanish and French West Indies.

The testimony of these merchants offered proof of Madison's charges that under the pretext of military necessity, Great Britain had established a system of controls that made the seas a part of the empire. The testimony of the manufacturers likewise offers proof that James Madison's contention that Great Britain needed the United States as much as the United States needed Great Britain was based on solid economic ground.

In May, while the hearings were still in progress, the political opposition to the ministry in Parliament launched a vigorous attack on the Orders in Council. Alexander Baring and Henry Brougham now had the advantage of the overwhelming testimony of the manufacturers to support their case. The ministry reminded them that the Orders in Council were included in the royal prerogative and therefore not subject to the control of Parliament.[54] But stubborn adherence to the prerogative was impossible in view of the disaster that prevailed in the manufacturing districts.

On June 16 Lord Castlereagh announced that the ministry would make a proposition to the United States agreeing to "suspend" the orders on two conditions. The United States must suspend the Non-Intercourse Act and must seek "to prevail on Buonaparte to restore the rules of commerce to their ancient customary limits." This did not satisfy the critics of the orders.[55] They demanded that repeal not be subject to the United States seeking to change the policy of Napoleon. At this point in the debate George Canning, the *bête noir* of the Madison administration, arose and called for immediate revocation. In his speech Canning said that the Orders in

Council had been necessary. He explained that political, and not economic, considerations had been their justification.[56]

On June 23 the Order in Council of January 7, 1807, and the Order in Council of April 26, 1809, were officially revoked.[57] Jonathan Russell wrote at once to Secretary of State James Monroe telling the good news. It came too late to avoid war, but it represented a recognition on the part of Great Britain that the United States was too important to her economically to permit war over minor issues. Throughout the nineteenth century mutual awareness of the economic interdependence of the two countries was to make possible the settlement of thorny disputes and the preservation of peace.

NOTES

1. For an interesting description of Heligoland see M. Adolphe Thiers, *History of the Consulate and the Empire,* translated by O. Forbes Campbell and H. W. Herbert (Philadelphia: Claxton, Remsen, and Heffelfinger, 1879), Vol. III, p. 356.

2. *Ibid.,* p. 357.

3. James Madison complained repeatedly of the American shippers undermining the position of the United States by subjecting themselves to British regulations and protection. The shipowners received direct encouragement from the British government. Madison referred to the British invitation in these words: "A more disorganizing and dishonorable experiment is perhaps not to be found in the annals of modern transactions." In the eyes of Madison the British were offering an inducement to Americans to violate American laws. See James Madison to William Pinkney, July 18, 1808, *The Writings of James Madison,* VIII, p. 34.

4. Thiers, XII, 50, quoted by Henry Adams, *History of the United States of America During the First Administration of James Madison* (New York: Charles Scribner's Sons, 1921), Vol. I, p. 226.

5. *Annals of Congress, Eleventh Congress, Third Session,* Appendix "Relations with France," p. 1222.

6. *Ibid.*

7. *Ibid.,* p. 1225.

8. *Ibid.,* p. 1230.

9. *The Writings of James Madison,* VIII, p. 102.

10. *Annals of Congress, Eleventh Congress, Third Session,* Appendix "Relations with France," p. 1231.

11. *Ibid.,* p. 1235.

12. *Ibid.,* p. 1239.

13. *Ibid.,* p. 1240.

14. *Ibid.,* p. 1268.

15. *Ibid.*, p. 1246.
16. *Ibid.*, p. 1250.
17. *Annals of Congress, Eleventh Congress, Third Session*, pp. 938-946.
18. *Ibid.*, p. 1003.
19. *Ibid.*, p. 865.
20. *Ibid.*, p. 874.
21. *Ibid.*, p. 1062.
22. Wellesley to Pinkney, December 29, 1810, *Annals of Congress, Twelfth Congress, First Session*, pp. 1721-1723.
23. Wellesley to Pinkney, February 23, 1811, *Annals of Congress, Twelfth Congress, First Session*, p. 1737.
24. *Ibid.*, p. 1742.
25. Perkins, *Prologue to War*, p. 275.
26. Augustus Foster to James Monroe, July 26, 1811, *American State Papers*, Vol. III, p. 443.
27. James Monroe to Augustus Foster, October 1, 1811, *ibid.*, p. 445.
28. Monroe to Russell, November 27, 1811, *Annals of Congress, Twelfth Congress, First Session*, p. 1756.
29. Russell to Monroe, March 4, 1812, *Annals of Congress, Twelfth Congress, First Session*, p. 1763.
30. Madison to Jefferson, June 7, 1811, Madison Papers.
31. Madison to J. Q. Adams, November 15, 1811, Madison Papers.
32. The resolutions passed by state legislatures and by meetings of Republicans cited are to be found in the Madison Papers. The President transmitted many of them to Congress and they were printed in the *Annals of Congress*.
33. *Annals of Congress, Twelfth Congress, First Session*, pp. 11-13.
34. Henry Lee to Madison, August 19, 1811, Madison Papers.
35. J. G. Jackson to Madison, March 30, 1812, Madison Papers.
36. Madison to Jefferson, April 3, 1812, Madison Papers.
37. *Ibid.*, April 24, 1812, Madison Papers.
38. Joel Barlow to Madison, April 22, 1812, Madison Papers.
On May 2, 1812, Barlow wrote to the President: "You will have perceived that the pole star from which I have all along graduated my compass was to remove the cause of war with England. The object of this government being directly contrary, you will easily discern at least one of the causes of the delays they have practiced not only in completing the arrangements I had prepared, but in answering official letters on pressing subjects, in giving up ships which they really meant to give up, in explaining themselves distincly (sic) on any point that should bear upon our relations with England, & finally in the studied omission of the United States on the occasion of the Duke's report of the 10th of March, of which I took notice in my letter to the Secy. of State of the 15th of that month." Madison Papers.
39. Jefferson to Madison, May 30, 1812, Madison Papers.
40. *Annals of Congress, Twelfth Congress, First Session*, p. 1482.
41. *Ibid.*
42. *Ibid.*, p. 255.
43. *Ibid.*, p. 262.

44. *Ibid.*, p. 259.

45. Madison to B. Ludlow, July 25, 1812, Madison Papers.

46. The situation in South Carolina is ably discussed by Margaret Kinard Latimer, "South Carolina—A Protagonist of the War of 1812," *American Historical Review*, LXI (July, 1956), pp. 914-929.

47. James Maury to Madison, March 20, 1812, Madison Papers.

48. *Annals of Congress, Tenth Congress, Second Session*, pp. 1481-1482.

49. An excellent article dealing with the fall in agricultural prices and the coming of the war is that of George Rogers Taylor, "Agrarian Discontent in the Mississippi Valley Preceding the War of 1812," *Journal of Political Economy*, XXXIX (1931), p. 500.

50. *Annals of Congress, Twelfth Congress, First Session*, p. 508.

51. *Ibid.*, p. 482.

52. Taylor, *op. cit.*, Vol. XXXIX, pp. 471-505.
See also Reginald Horsman, "Western War Aims, 1811-1812," *Indiana Magazine of History*, LIII (March, 1957), pp. 1-18.

53. The account of the effects of the 1811 embargo on England is based on the testimony given before the House of Commons by manufacturers and merchants. The author used the microcard copies of the minutes of the hearings. The transcript is a most illuminating source for students interested in the conditions of English manufacturing and the status of labor as well as the workings of the Continental System and the British Orders in Council. Because the documents lack pagination, further footnote citations would have little or no value. See *House of Commons Minutes of Evidence Taken at the Bar of the House, upon taking into Consideration the Petition of Several Merchants, Manufacturers, and others, of the City of London, interested in the Trade with the United States of America: and also, the Petition of several Merchants and Manufacturers of Manchester who are extremely concerned in the Trade to the United States of North America respecting the Orders in Council.*

54. Cobbets, *Parliamentary Debates*, Vol. XXIII, p. 537.

55. *Ibid.*, p. 542.

56. *Ibid.*, p. 547.

57. *Ibid.*, p. 716.

Postscript

XV

T HE UNITED STATES signed the Treaty of Ghent in 1815 bringing an end to the war. The treaty said not a word about impressment, the American definition of neutral rights on the high seas, nor did it annex any territory. Insofar as the settlement provided for any of the American aims stated at the beginning of the conflict, the achievement was most modest. British merchants lost their privileged position in the Northwest. This was not a trivial gain, for it marked the end of a British design to create a buffer state, but measured against the list of aims proclaimed at the outbreak of war, it can scarcely be viewed as a great military and diplomatic victory.

This modest gain does not suffice to explain why the country, scarcely with a dissenting voice, looked back upon the war as justified and upon its results without any sense of disillusionment. In the immediate post-war years the public gloried in the exploits of the navy and Andrew Jackson's victory at New Orleans. The commissioners who negotiated the Treaty of Ghent suffered no political retribution because they had failed to achieve stated goals. Rather, they emerged as heroes, and John Quincy Adams, Henry Clay, and Albert Gallatin went on to positions of prominence.

The public's glorification of the war may at first glance appear as nothing more than an effusion of patriotic sentiment glossing over the failure to achieve the stated war aims, but this hasty judgment is checked when it becomes clear that sober and hard-headed statesmen in private letters judged that the war was well worth while. They did not magnify the naval and military victories of the war. John Quincy Adams resented the glorification of the rather minor military achievements and stated frankly that the United States had not won the war; at best, he said, the struggle ended in a tie. Albert Gallatin did not deceive himself as to the realities; he, too, had helped make peace in circumstances that indelibly impressed upon his mind the harsh realities of American failures in the war. Yet both men viewed the results of the war as a net gain.

The gains were of two kinds. European nations now accepted the previously untried experiment of a republic governed by the principles of a free society as an established and permanent institution capable of pulling itself together for defense of its interests. In July, 1817, Gallatin, then in Paris, wrote to Jefferson: "At no period has America stood on higher ground abroad than now, and every one who represents her may feel a just pride in the contrast between her situation and that of all other countries, and in the feeling of her perfect independence from all foreign powers."[1] In part this respect was based on the prosperity of the United States and its great resources, but the public was likewise impressed by the ability of the United States in the recent war to stand up to Great Britain.

It was not, however, the respect that the United States had won abroad but the respect that Americans had gained for themselves that impressed most observers as the greater gain. The extreme political factionalism that had rent Americans ever since 1789 had posed the danger that they would be unable to unite for their own defense against threats from foreign powers. The British had been misled by this factionalism into feeling that Americans were incapable of pulling together to resist her.

This new confidence among Americans flowed from a conviction that the pre-war years, and especially the struggle itself, had taught them that more conservative political and economic policies were necessary if basic republican principles were not to lead to political anarchy and wild-flying factionalism productive of great evil. The Federalists largely disappeared as an effective political party, but no less a Republican than James Madison enunciated Federalist principles in his message to Congress in 1815. The marked change in the outlook of the Republicans led Albert Gallatin to write to Matthew Lyon on May 7, 1816:

. . . The war has been productive of evil and good, but I think the good preponderates. Independent of the loss of lives and of the losses in property by individuals, the war has laid the foundation of permanent taxes and military establishments which Republicans had deemed unfavorable to the happiness and free institutions of the country. But under our former system we were becoming too selfish, too much attached exclusively to the acquisition of wealth, above all, too much confined in our political feelings of local and State objects. The war has renewed and reinstated the national feelings and character which the Revolution had given, and which were daily lessened.[2]

Gallatin's observations are confirmed by the legislation Congress enacted, the creation of the second national bank, the first steps toward the system of protective tariffs, and the first modest Federal support of internal improvements.

Thomas Jefferson saw in the changes taking place the betrayal of republican principles. He interpreted the controversy stirred up over slavery at the time of the Missouri Compromise as a clever ruse on the part of the old Anglomen whereby they would be able to foist on the country their long frustrated plans for legislation favorable to conservative northern merchants.[3] Jefferson's disappointment is understandable, but the shift that took place was less a betrayal of his principles than it was an adjustment of those principles to fit the bitter lessons that war had taught concerning the importance of a sound currency, improved means of transportation, the fostering of domestic manufacturing, and a more adequate system of defense.

The shift that Jefferson regretted did not touch the traditional approach to foreign policy. Indeed any significant change in the popular attitude toward foreign affairs was to be postponed for more than a century. Franklin Roosevelt telling his son Elliott on the desert of North Africa that American boys would not be dying on the islands of the Pacific tonight were it not for the evil imperialism of the western European powers is a reminder of how long old attitudes persisted.[4]

The self-conscious image of two worlds, one aristocratic, dominated by courts and special privilege and given to arbitrary intrigue in foreign affairs, the other republican, virtuous, and open to reason, characterized the early national period. This image constituted the fiber of American nationalism, and a tougher textured fiber could not be found. It was a nationalism that derived its strength from idealism. Americans prided themselves on being the model republican society that the rest of the world would emulate. Others were held in bondage by the privileged classes, but America was the land of opportunity where demonstrated individual worth rather than birth was the test of a man. This concept, prominent during the Revolution, continued to flourish and made it easy to look upon every issue that arose with foreign nations as a moral question.

That American of Americans, John Quincy Adams, pointed his finger at what he considered the fundamental difference between Europe and America. Although he wrote these words in 1823 and in reference to recognition of the Latin American republics, they accord with his sentiments and the sentiments of most of his countrymen prior to 1812:

The policy of all the European nations towards South America has been founded upon selfish principles of interest, incongruously combined with erroneous principles of government. Since the restoration of the Bourbons, the European alliance of emperors and kings has assumed as the foundation of human society the doctrine of unalienable *allegiance*. Our doctrine is founded upon the principle of unalienable *right*. The European allies, therefore, have viewed the *cause* of the South Americans as rebellion against their lawful sovereign. We have considered it as the assertion of natural right.[5]

Whether one examines the writings of Jefferson, Madison, or John Quincy Adams, one finds repeatedly a symbol of America and another of Europe. One is always seen as monopolistic, as subordinating rights to the interests of those in power, as intriguing against liberty. The other is individualistic, relies on the exertions of individuals, seeks privileges, rebels against authoritarianism, and relies on the faith that the liberation of individual energies in a free society will contribute most effectively to national power.

This moralism did not inhibit a hard-headed pragmatic approach to foreign policy. The founding fathers made the best of both worlds, appeal to justice and energetic defense of national interest. Alexander Hamilton stood alone in frankly basing foreign policy on national self-interest. Thomas Jefferson and James Madison were no less energetic in supporting national interests, but they clothed their demands in terms of moral justification. This was not a devious employment of rhetoric but a sincere expression of their honestly held views.

Like the later arguments in behalf of manifest destiny, Wilson's Fourteen Points, and Franklin Roosevelt's war for the Four Freedoms, the founding fathers' rhetoric was a force in itself. Rather than a mere cloak for achievement of national goals, the ideology was a dynamic force, a propellant perhaps quite as strong as land hunger, trade, profits, or national pride. The nationalistic idealism provided a mystique that made successful negotiations unlikely. This is not to say the failures were wholly the product of American attitudes. Neither the British nor the French were free of their own particular brands of nationalist feeling, and both pursued policies that allowed little leeway for a diplomatic antagonist short of submission.

The diplomacy of the founding fathers was not, of course,

wholly a product of psychological forces. Economic interests conditioned policy to a great degree. The need for credit and the dependence upon foreign markets wrecked the felt preference for non-entanglement. Land hunger undergirded the continental expansionism that contributed to conflicts with the European powers.

Probably equally influential in shaping foreign policy, and especially the day to day determination of positions to be taken, was political party warfare. James Madison's arguments against the Jay Treaty outran the really objectionable provisions. The intensity of feeling they betray can only be understood in terms of the controversy with the Federalists. The Federalist hostility to France in 1797 and 1798 was not wholly a response to French abuses and threats although these were grievous. By this time the Federalists believed that their Republican rivals were ready to accept French aid in overthrow of the government. When they turned against France, they were at the same time turning upon their domestic political opponents.

This party rivalry explains a part of the extremism after 1807, and the Republican adherence to the policy expressed in the Embargo, Non-Intercourse and Macon acts. The Federalists did not lack solid arguments in their opposition to Republican foreign policy in the years 1807 to 1812, but the documents show that Federalist seeking of party advantage was a factor of importance. The extremism of the ultra Federalists in their hatred of the Jeffersonians explains in large part their pro-British feelings.

The fact that party politics engendered emotions making foreign negotiations difficult should not obscure the fact of the seriousness of the problem. The Napoleonic Wars in Europe brought serious injury to the American economic system. Both belligerents contributed to the injury. Today as a great power the United States has manifested hostility to new nations who contravene the American view of the cold war. Great Britain and France took a similar attitude toward the new republic that placed its own interests above the interests that guided them as belligerents. For the United States there was no solution except the restoration of peace in Europe, if one means by a solution access to the markets of Europe. British policy was blamed, but French seizures suggest that had British policy been different, the Americans would still have suffered seriously.

The United States could not isolate itself economically from the effects of the Napoleonic War. No one wanted war at least until the autumn of 1811, but few were willing to accept the consequences of the European struggle. To accept it without manifesting a sense of injury, even if only by the making of angry gestures that could have little effect, was to be guilty of submission.

This study is an attempt to shed light on the foreign policies of the founding fathers. Although its original aim was no more than that, the predicament of the fathers may suggest to some their own predicament, a generous spirit so distorted by nationalism as to lead to a dangerous unilateralism in foreign affairs.

NOTES

1. Henry Adams, *The Life of Albert Gallatin* (New York: Peter Smith, 1943), p. 565.

2. *Ibid.*, p. 560.

3. *The Writings of Albert Gallatin*, ed. Henry Adams (Philadelphia: J. B. Lippincott and Co., 1879), Vol. II, p. 178.

4. Elliott Roosevelt, *As He Saw It* (New York: Duell, Sloan and Pearce, 1946), pp. 115-116.

5. *Memoirs of John Quincy Adams*, ed. C. F. Adams (Philadelphia: J. B. Lippincott and Co., 1875), p. 452.

Index

Adams, Henry, 95, 290

Adams, John: quoted, 2, 15, 18, 38; on ties to Great Britain, 14; foreign relations, 20; on pursuit of commercial treaties, 31; Dana's visit to Russia, 32-33; British and Northwest, 60-61; rhetoric of French revolution, 125-126; on the French, 126-127; and development of parties, 127; opinion of Monroe, 28; policies and recommendations of, 128-129; analysis of French policy, 130; on McHenry's appointments, 138; weighs message to Congress, 138-139; appointment of Murray, 139-140; instructions to, 140-141; new treaty presented to Congress, 141; mentioned, 17

Adams, John Quincy: in Russia, 33; quoted, 117, 136; on freedom of seas, 119; and Talleyrand's intent, 133; on Republican opposition, 135; evaluation of Jefferson, 147-148; on Parson's pro-British leanings, 237; on glorification of war, 301; difference between U.S. and Europe, 303-304; mentioned, 2

Adet, Pierre: actions as minister to U.S., 124-125

Agrarians: interest in foreign relations, 7-8; views on Jay Treaty, 111

Alien and Sedition Acts, 137

Allen, Ethan: mentioned, 61

Alliance, treaty of: provisions of, 24, abrogated, 141

Ames, Fisher: charges against Madison's programs, 100-101; mentioned, 85

Anderson, William: on Macon law, 241

Armstrong, John: succeeds Livingston in Paris, 160; instructions re: Latin America, 250-251; reply to Cadore, 278-279

Articles of Confederation: drafting of, 20-21; foreign affairs and, 46-47; opponents of centralization, 47-48; postwar reconstruction, 48-49; arguments for replacement of, 50 ff.

Bacon, Ezekiel, 203

Ballinger, John: and militia at Baton Rouge, 257

Index

Index